M000024537

Lesbian Postmodern

Between Men ~ Between Women

Lesbian and Gay Studies

Lillian Faderman and Larry Gross, editors

Between Men~Between Women
Lesbian and Gay Studies

Lillian Faderman and Larry Gross, editors

The Lesbian Postmodern

Edited by
Laura Doan

Columbia University Press
New York

Columbia University Press

New York   Chichester, West Sussex

Copyright © 1994 Columbia University Press
All rights reserved

Library of Congress Cataloging-in-Publication Data

The lesbian postmodern/edited by Laura Doan
    p.   cm.—(Between men-between women)
        Includes bibliographical references.
        ISBN 0–231–08410–2. –ISBN 0–231–08411–0 (pbk.)
        1. Lesbians' writings, American—Criticism.
    2. Lesbians—Intellectual life. 3. Lesbians in literature.
    I. Doan, Laura. II. Series.
    PS 153.L46N48   1994
    810.8'09206643–dc20   93–6235
                                                CIP

Printed in the United States of America

c 10 9 8 7 6 5 4 3 2 1
p 10 9 8 7 6 5 4 3 2 1

Contents

Preface

Disagreement abounds (even among the contributors to this volume) over what constitutes a "lesbian" and what is understood by the term *postmodern*. Consequently, our point of embarkation in imagining something called the lesbian postmodern promises to unsettle, rather than settle, a complex array of questions. The willingness to risk whatever might arise from the conflation of two such highly contested terms as *lesbian* and *postmodern* (whether tentative speculations, destabilizing contradictions, or inconclusive conclusions) is, in part, what this project is about. One immediate result is this departure from a conventional introduction, that space where the editor does the trick with the round peg and square hole by proclaiming the magical cohesion of remarkably diverse approaches taken by individual essayists. It is essential, every editor learns, to smooth over the disjunctions among the essays and impress the as yet unconvinced reader of the project's coherence. But it is unlikely that the articulation of any single unified formulation or construction of a lesbian postmodern will emerge. So, how might we proceed and, more important, what expectations might we dangle before the reader? In entering this new and unpredictable terrain, we can at least express confidence that the configuration of something called the lesbian postmodern will enable us to pose and address questions, both provocative and critical, about the interventions of categories of sexual identity and difference into postmodern culture.

Few of the contributors, however, enact this intervention without hesitation, discomfort, or even skepticism; so much is at stake in theorizing these two concepts—lesbian and postmodern—in relation to one another. Our project tests limits (of epistemology, of identity, of subjectivity, of disciplinarity) and problematizes and undermines polarities (such as political efficacy and theoretical formulation, or essentialism and constructivism, or modernism and postmodernism, or margin and center). *The Lesbian Postmodern*, on the one hand, traces how some lesbian cultural theory and production, in foregrounding a politics of difference and marginality, critiques patriarchal and heterosexual hegemony through a variety of postmodern strategies and techniques. As such, the volume represents an attempt to demand the recognition of lesbian visibility in the postmodern terrain vis-à-vis cultural production. On the other hand, some essays note how a postmodern aesthetic, with its valorization of difference, sexual plurality, and gender blurring/blending and, in some cases, an obsession with self-reflexivity, ambivalence, contradiction, subversion, and the parodic assists lesbian cultural production.

In the introduction, Robyn Wiegman provides an initial "mapping" of the lesbian postmodern; like several of the essays that follow, this survey of the problems and issues raised by the phrase undoes itself as readily as it constructs something else. In part I, "Theorizing the Lesbian Postmodern," essayists scrutinize the shifting definitions of the very terms of the project and work toward exposing the radical potentialities, as well as the limitations and dangers, forced and engendered by that conceptual territory. In part II, "Textual and Performative Strategies," contributors turn to literary and visual representation to discern how, if contemporary lesbian writers and artists plunder postmodernist strategies just as postmodernist culture plunders the lesbian, a lesbian postmodern might enable an interventionist or transformative politics. Throughout the introduction and this two-section format, essayists probe a complicated network of interrelated questions and issues—race, ethnicity, class, postcolonialism, commodification, and "popular culture"—overturning the discrete separation of disciplinarity, expanding the cultural canon, and transgressing boundaries and borders.

Mediation between the positions of feminist and postmodern theorists has been scant. Feminist resistance to postmodernism is well documented, as several essays will point out; in short, some feminists are concerned about the perceived loss or collapse of political agency. This seems akin to burying one's head in the sand for, as this anthology will demonstrate, the postmodern is already offering lesbian theorists, writers, and artists multiple strategies of resistance and thus invites a reading of the "lesbian" as a powerful destabilizing agent of political culture and discourse. Lesbian feminists should remain circumspect and critical about the possibilities, implications, and dangers of postmodernism (such positions are represented here), but lesbian theory cannot ignore its presence. What can be gained, except to short-circuit theoretical possibilities, from the refusal to move beyond the sorts of rigid polarities (lesbianism is political and postmodernism is not; lesbianism is sexual and postmodernism is not; lesbianism is about identity and postmodernism is not) that have thus far dominated contemporary debates? Postmodern lesbian cultural production calls for, indeed demands, a postmodern lesbian cultural theory. The essays in this volume explore a realm as yet untouched in literary and cultural criticism and gender theory: no one has posited the existence of a specifically lesbian postmodern—an analysis of the convergence of postmodernism and feminism is barely under way. This project is therefore timely, perhaps urgent; it breaks new ground, just as postmodernism allows its cultural producers to break old rules.

Contributors

Terry Brown is Director of Women's Studies and Assistant Professor of English at the University of Wisconsin—River Falls. She is currently writing a book with John Nguyet Erni on tourism, the sex industry, and AIDS in Thailand.

Sagri Dhairyam recently completed her dissertation at the University of Illinois at Champaign-Urbana and is currently working on a study of lesbian poets that explores the connections between race, sexuality, and literary status. Her essay on Audre Lorde appeared in a recent issue of *Feminist Studies* and an article on Brian de Palma's films is forthcoming in the *New Orleans Review*.

Laura Doan is Associate Professor of English at the State University of New York at Geneseo. In addition to editing *Old Maids to Radical Spinsters: Unmarried Women in the Twentieth-Century Novel* (University of Illinois Press, 1991), she has published articles on feminist criticism and contemporary British fiction and culture in a number of journals, including *Genders*, *American Literary History*, *Minnesota Review*, *Works and Days*, and *Mosaic*.

Cathy Griggers teaches feminist cultural studies, gender studies, and media theory in the Literary and Cultural Theory Program at Carnegie Mellon University. She has published articles on the cinema, popular culture, film theory, and gay and lesbian studies in journals such as *differences*, *Semiotica*, and *Postmodern Culture*, and in anthologies such as *Theory Goes to the Movies* and *Fear of a Queer Planet*. She is coproducer of two pedagogical videos, *Discourse/Intercourse* and *Hirohito's Funeral*.

Elizabeth Grosz teaches critical theory at Monash University, Victoria, Australia. She is the author of *Sexual Subversions: Three French Feminists* (Allen and Unwin, 1989), *Jacques Lacan: A Feminist Introduction* (Routledge, 1990), and *Volatile Bodies: Toward a Corporeal Feminism* (Indiana University Press, 1994).

Judith Halberstam is Assistant Professor of English in the Department of Literature at the University of California, San Diego. She is currently completing a book on gothic monstrosity from the nineteenth century to the present. She is also planning a book-length study of representations of female masculinity. Halberstam writes a column on queer culture for *On Our Backs*.

Dana A. Heller is Assistant Professor of American literature and literary theory in the Department of English at Old Dominion University. She is the author of *The Feminization of Quest-Romance: Radical Departures* (University of Texas Press, 1990). She is currently working on a study of family romance in contemporary American literature.

Colleen Lamos is Assistant Professor of English at Rice University. The author of articles on James Joyce, Georges Bataille, and lesbian theory, she is currently completing a book manuscript, "Going Astray: Gender and Sexual Errancy in Modern Literature."

Emma Pérez, a tejana, is Assistant Professor at the University of Texas, El Paso in Chicana/o Studies where she teaches Chicana/o history and theory. Her publications include "Sexuality and Discourse: Notes from a Chicana Survivor," in *Chicana Lesbians*; excerpts from her novel "Gulf Dreams" in *Chicana Lesbians* and *An Intimate Wilderness*; and "She Has Served Others in More Intimate Ways: The Domestic Service Reform in Yucatán," in *Aztlán*. She is writing a social history of Mexican-American women in Houston from 1900 to 1940.

Judith Raiskin is Assistant Professor of Women's Studies at the University of California, Santa Barbara, where she teaches courses on postcolonial literature, feminist theory, and the construction of sexuality. Her book on postcolonial women writers from South Africa and the Caribbean is being published by the University of Minnesota Press.

Erica Rand is a dyke activist and cultural critic and Assistant Professor in art history at Bates College. She has previously published articles in *Genders, Art Journal, Afterimage,* and *Eighteenth-Century Studies* and is currently doing further work on Barbie's queer accessories.

Judith Roof teaches literature, film, and feminist critical studies at the University of Delaware. She is co-editor of *Feminism and Psychoanalysis* and author of *A Lure of Knowledge: Lesbian Sexuality and Theory* and essays on feminist theory, modern drama, psychoanalysis, law, and lesbian studies.

Jean Walton is Assistant Professor of Contemporary Critical Theory in the English Department at the University of Rhode Island. Her nearly completed book (*No Gender Where None Intended*) explores extortion, impotence, and male subjectivity in the post/modern writing of Samuel Beckett.

Robyn Wiegman is Assistant Professor of Women's Studies and English at Indiana University. Her essays on feminist theory and American cultural studies have appeared in *American Literary History, Cultural Critique,* and the *Journal of the History of Sexuality,* and in a variety of anthologies, including *Unspeakable Images* and *Screening the Male.* She is coeditor with Judith Roof of the forthcoming *Who Can Speak? Authority and Critical Identity* and with Diane Elam of *Feminism Beside Itself.* Her book-length study, *Economics of Visibility: Race and Gender in U.S. Culture,* is forthcoming from Duke University Press.

The Lesbian Postmodern

Between Men **Between Women**

Lesbian and Gay Studies

Lillian Faderman and Larry Gross, editors

1 Introduction: Mapping the Lesbian Postmodern

Robyn Wiegman

It is no longer clear that feminist theory ought to try to settle the questions of primary identity in order to get on with the task of politics. Instead, we ought to ask, what political possibilities are the consequence of a radical critique of the categories of identity?
—Judith Butler, *Gender Trouble*

Operating as points of systemic failure, configurations of lesbian sexuality often reflect the complex incongruities that occur when the logic or philosophy of a system becomes self-contradictory, visibly fails to account for something, or cannot complete itself.
—Judith Roof, *A Lure of Knowledge*

Those familiar with contemporary debates about the meaning of the postmodern will no doubt recognize the plagiaristic gesture that frames my discussion, where Andreas Huyssen's often-cited "Mapping the Postmodern" is interrupted, one might say, by the entrance of the lesbian into (and onto) the postmodern's critical scene. This lesbian interruption is decidedly artificial, not because the lesbian's relation to the postmodern is in any sense inauthentic but rather because there is not, as yet, a constituted object of inquiry known as "the lesbian postmodern." Its invention for the purposes of this anthology marks for me a temporal association between two potentially liminal figurations: that of lesbian sexuality as the undermining moment in heterosexual representational regimes on the one hand, and the reassessment of feminism's identity politics in light of postmodern critiques of Enlightenment philosophies on the other. In this context—in this ironic wedding of seemingly subversive sexuality to the body of postmodern theory—the act of plagiarism that incites this essay not only foregrounds the appropriative commodity production underlying current academic discourse (where both the lesbian and the postmodern are consumable topics) but it also prevents "the lesbian postmodern" from revealing itself as something either autonomous or wholly new. Instead, the lesbian postmodern can be recognized as simultaneously intervening in critical debates that have, up to now, seemed almost completely ignorant of the implications of the sexual while performing its own contrivance—indeed its own fetishization— of the lesbian and the postmodern as they have been constituted as critical currency by contemporary academe.

As a contributor to the anthology, my relation to the commodification of the lesbian and the postmodern is unambiguously complicit, even if I plan to argue that through this conjunction, through this incipient terminological marriage, some of the founding assumptions of contemporary feminist theory can be challenged and, at least potentially, displaced. If I were willing to turn to modernist ground, I might rationalize this complicity by asserting my intention to retrieve or restore the lesbian to her rightful cultural and critical visibility, a project of reclamation through which the figure of the lesbian could be named, defined, and owned by a so-called lesbian herself. But can my claims for the lesbian as lesbian, for what "I" am or am supposed to be, deter in any way the commodifying moment through which the lesbian appears, bound here to one of the most egregiously overused and misconstrued theoretical terms circulating in Western academic discussion? Rather than freeing myself from the commodity aesthetic, wouldn't my claim to know the lesbian simply confirm my position as her most masterful consumer, a commodity myself now mastered by the image I take myself to be?

Because the lesbian has become a category of speculation and intrigue, operating (at times distinctly, at others obliquely) under the sexy appellation "queer theory,"[1] my complicity with the commodifying gesture of the contemporary academy cannot be overlooked simply because I can identify or be identified with any of the various registers in which the lesbian has come to exist. While I could claim to be, as lesbians often have done, the referent for the representational figure of the lesbian, her "real," "material" being, an embodied oracle, my participation in her commodification—in the alienation and abstraction of myself as commodity—would not thereby be relieved. There is no innocent way to wear the category, no categorical innocence. As Judith Butler has helped me to see, to "be" a lesbian—in the academy, in this anthology, in the bar, or in the grocery store—is a seductive, subjectively necessary, but disturbingly territorial and regulatory regime. "To install myself within the terms of an identity category would be to turn against the sexuality that the category purports to describe," she writes, "and this might be true for any identity category which seeks to control the very eroticism that it claims to describe and authorize, much less 'liberate'" (*Inside/Out*, 14).

In her Foucauldian-inflected interpretation of the way lesbian identity functions to define and limit activities that exceed the normative heterosexual script, Butler recasts the now familiar equation between lesbian identity and sexual liberation, suggesting that it is precisely through such an equation that the colonization of lesbian sexuality is achieved. In this way, she posits an understanding of the identity formation of the lesbian that is deeply contrary to the primary assumptions of the contemporary women's community where the lesbian (along with her lesbianism) functions as the centrical force of collective engagement, the definitive framework for affirming sociopolitical sameness. This is perhaps most pointedly witnessed in the burgeoning popular culture that accompanies the lesbian's collective movement through the public sphere. Music, clothing, vacation cruises, festivals, artwork, publishing—in all these areas, lesbian identity functions as the means for defining the specificities of both production and consumption. While this relation—of lesbian-made, -sold, and -owned materials—approximates in the 1990s a tamed separatism, it is more than disturbing that the commodification of the lesbian as a category of identity is often what passes, inside and outside the lesbian community, for evidence of political progress. At a recent women's music festival, for instance, the growth of the merchant area—in terms of both the number of products available and their diversity—was lauded by one performer as a sign of growing lesbian political power. But if political power means a cultural visibility framed by the commodity aesthetic, what kind of position of power—and empowerment—are we claiming? Can we unproblematically herald the consolidation of

the lesbian as a category of being when this being is increasingly signified by our saturation in commodity production, both countercul-
tural and, to a limited but growing extent, "mainstream" as well?[2]
Must we, in other words, embrace a liberation contingent on producing, marketing, and then vampiristically consuming "us"?

These questions do not presuppose that the deployment of the lesbian as market commodity at women's music festivals or elsewhere is
only a matter of capitalist enterprise, nor do they intend to invoke a
purer "self" awaiting discovery beneath the layers of contemporary
commodification. To question the reduction of the political to the
dimensions of cultural consumption is not to dismiss out of hand the
implications of "women's culture" as a marginal site of production, a
countermemory, a place for the consolidation of alternative practices
and discourses. But marginality alone is no guarantee of political
effectiveness and transgression, and the movement within lesbian
communities toward increasingly cultural forms of collective identity
engagement has the effect of depoliticizing sexual differences and at
the same time homogenizing their production. For in demarcating the
lesbian as both the beginning and the end of sexual differences, her
constitution ends up *negating* difference at a variety of psychological
and sociosymbolic levels. As Butler (via Foucault) would say, the very
mechanism that makes possible the lesbian's emergence in public
space as a categorical being—the constitution of her being as lesbian—thus works to contain her most radical possibilities. Such containment is clearly, and quite importantly, more than academic,
though its articulation within the academic realm raises issues specific to the production of power and knowledge there.

But where and whether the lesbian is fashioned by "us" or for "us"
or even in high disregard of "us," her fashioning is complicated,
indeed contradicted, by the context of commodification in which
"she" and "we" are embedded—a context so thick that politically we
can no longer afford to be naive about it. Given the growing ability of
the lesbian to initiate and partake of the construction and commodification of her identity, I hope it is not an insignificant political gesture to have begun by foregrounding my own hesitation at contributing to the lesbian's proliferation as critical currency. And yet, though
the issue of commodification propels this rather belabored introduction, establishing the consumptive context of identity formation that
characterizes the representational regimes of the contemporary academy as well as popular U.S. culture,[3] we have little alternative action

but to participate. After all, the commodification of the lesbian of which I write is a yes/no option extended to us; it is not a check we deposit by choosing to sign our name on the back. *That* signature will always precede us.

For this reason, we cannot presume to take up the question of the political—and cannot adequately address the political—by attempting to wend our way back to that now mythic moment prior to commodity production. Nor can we comfort ourselves with the assurance that commodity production by us and for us transforms the signature, "the lesbian," into any adequate naming of us. Perhaps even the quest to be adequately named, to posit meaning and being in relation to the identity and seeming fullness of the name, is inadequate as the primary condition framing the political for us. The negotiation of our critical currency demands instead the transformation of political engagement from the utopic project of being (or ascribing being to the) lesbian to another kind of engagement, something quite different, quite potentially other. Such an other engagement cannot be telegraphed in advance, at least not without engendering the kinds of exclusions that have marked the lesbian's construction that I have criticized above. It is precisely the risk and possibility encountered here—beyond the pre-ordained meanings of the political that modern epistemologies so rigorously settle—that provokes me to join the collective project of elaborating this yet-to-be-known entity, *The Lesbian Postmodern*.

Mapping the Territory

If I have now succeeded, at least provisionally, in undermining the sanctity and security of the lesbian as a category of being, it remains to be seen how I understand the postmodern and exactly what the project of mapping its imbrication with the lesbian would mean. For while contemporary theoretical discussion has increasingly foregrounded questions of the postmodern, its articulation is in no way settled. Is it an aesthetic? A style? A historical period? A referent for commodity culture? A philosophy of history? A historical philosophy? And what are the political implications of positing the postmodern in any of the above ways and of connecting it to the figure of the lesbian? What, in other words, can the lesbian—as a politics, discourse, identity of bodies, subjectivity, and sexual practice—mean and be within the critical context of the postmodern?

Reframing the plagiaristic gesture of my essay's title by working out its debt, I want to initiate an exploration of these questions by turning to Andreas Huyssen's elaborate project of drawing "a large-scale map of the postmodern which surveys several territories . . . on which the various postmodern artistic and critical practices . . . find their aesthetic and political place" ("Mapping the Postmodern," 236). Like others who have set out to define and characterize the postmodern, Huyssen opens his discussion by asserting that a change "in sensibility, practices, and discourse formations" in contemporary western societies "distinguishes a postmodern set of assumptions, experiences, and propositions from that of a preceding period" (234). While not willing to claim an entire paradigm shift for western cultural practices, Huyssen nonetheless suggests that we accept the postmodern as a "historical condition" (235), a conceptualization that for most of us recalls, on the surface, Lyotard's *The Postmodern Condition*. But unlike Lyotard, who focuses on questions of epistemology, representation, and the failure of metanarrativity (such as modernity or its antithetical twin Marxism) to legitimate the production of knowledges, Huyssen begins by locating the postmodern in the artistic revolt against modernism found in post–World War II innovations in architecture, literature, and the visual arts. As such, Huyssen's framing of the postmodern as a historical condition carries very little of the problematic of history that underlies Lyotard's discussion; instead, it relies on ordering events and concepts under a rubric of mapping and sequential time.[4]

This difference—between history as a recounting of a sequence of events and history as the problematic of temporality and sequentiality—has crucial implications for thinking the postmodern as well as for articulating the relationship between the lesbian and a political project no longer unequivocally committed to modernist categories of social identity. But even as I say this, I recognize the need for a fuller account of Huyssen's map, for a demonstration, in particular, of the way the rhetorical imbrication of time and location draw out for him the figure of "the other," and how such a drawing out disturbingly reconvenes the hierarchies of social categories that a postmodern politics most needs to disassemble. It is through a certain understanding of history, in other words, that the very contours of Huyssen's map begin to take shape—contours that, for me, ultimately bring into question not simply the ideological investment underlying map making but also the possibility, as well as political desirability, of mapping the postmodern itself.

In focusing on artistic practices and the critical discourses that analyze them, Huyssen challenges interpretations of postmodernism that view it simply as an antipolitics of style, as the end of artistic critique. Instead, he sees in the postmodern the possibilities of a critical art, but one that no longer adheres to the "domesticated" (242) version of modernism set in place in the 1950s—a domestication through which modernism entered "the liberal-conservative consensus of the times" (243) via institutionalization and canon formation. In responding to this domestication, the postmodernism of the 1960s, "in the form of happenings, pop vernacular, psychedelic art, acid rock, alternative and street theater" sought to reclaim modernism's earlier adversarial aesthetic. To trace modernism's lost critical edge, Huyssen turns to architecture where, in the wake of World War I and the Russian Revolution, Europe's rebuilding was cast as a "new Enlightenment" (239). But beneath the demand for a "rational design for a rational society" (239), Huyssen laments, was "a utopian fervor which ultimately made it veer back into . . . the myth of modernization" (239). Modernist housing projects, for instance, "rather than standing as harbingers of the new life . . . became symbols of alienation and dehumanization, a fate they shared with the assembly line, that other agent of the new that had been greeted with exuberant enthusiasm in the 1920s by Leninists and Fordists alike" (239).

While one may want to argue with Huyssen's specific account of twentieth century architecture, his broader point is to demonstrate that by midcentury, modernism could no longer articulate its critique of modernity but had become complicit with it. As in other artistic fields, most notably literature and painting, the post–World War II period witnessed—with its anticommunist fervor engendering both censorship and a misplaced cultural protectionism—the consolidation of modernism as "high culture," an institutionalized art of canons and museums. In this context, the postmodern revolt against modernism "sprang precisely from the success of modernism, from the fact that . . . [it] had been perverted into a form of affirmative culture" (243). It is on this form of modernism, torn away from its resistance to modernization, that Huyssen's engagement with the postmodern is based.

But why read the consolidation of modernism with modernization as the productive means for postmodernism's emergence? For Huyssen, such a reading makes possible an understanding of the postmodern as relational, as a condition whose various meanings are to be found only in upending the now familiar debate: does postmodernism represent a historical continuity or radical rupture with modernism?[5] The either/or figuration of this debate, according to Huyssen, obviates the complex interplay between modernism and its incomplete successor, the postmodern. "Modernism as that from which postmodernism is breaking away remains inscribed into the very word with which we describe our distance from modernism" (236). As such, postmodernism "represents a new type of crisis of that modernist culture itself" (268). In the context of late capitalism, this crisis figures for Huyssen in the relationship between art and society, where the modernist privilege ascribed to the art object as agent and embodiment of social change can no longer be assured under the twin pressures of institutionalization and commodity production. In the postmodern, he sees the opportunity to rearticulate modernist artistic practices by appealing to a whole range of their exclusion, including most centrally that of mass culture, the degraded other to high modernist art. Here, at the level of the popular, "the promise of a 'postwhite,' 'postmale,' 'posthumanist,' world" (246) can be both nourished and actively forged.

As this last statement might suggest, Huyssen grounds the proto-utopian hopes of postmodernism in a reclamation of the popular that ties it to the figure of "the other," s/he who can subvert, through the perspective of marginalization, both the high/low cultural split articulated in the dominant realm and that realm's representational (political as well as artistic) homogeneity. The turn to the creative and critical productions of "women and minority artists" (250) thus maps their "recuperation of buried and mutilated traditions, their emphasis on exploring forms of gender- and race-based subjectivity . . . and their refusal to be limited to standard canonizations" (250) as a primary contribution to the postmodern critique of high modernism. His nod to the recent public skirmishes around curricular reform in the United States, now known as Western civilization versus multiculturalism, becomes a specific example of the postmodern's threat "to the stability and sanctity of canon and tradition" (251). In this way, the political dimensions of the postmodern are quite directly harnessed to the centrality of difference, which, at the level of the popular, can interrupt the rigidity of modern art's high cultural sphere and the homogeneity of its canonical formulations as the privileged productions of those both white and male.

In reading "the erosion of the triple dogma modernism/modernity/avantgarde . . . [as] contextually related to the emergence of the problematic of 'otherness' " (269), Huyssen brings into the orbit of postmodern definition the political movements of the 1960s and 1970s. While he is not alone in ascribing to the postmodern the increasingly visible cultural coordinates of gender, race, and class,[6] and while this definition links the aesthetic to a broader cultural sphere, I want to linger over the trajectory he charts from modernism's "domestication" to postmodernism's radical popular culturalization. Not only does this simply seem to reverse modernism's own terms—upholding the degraded popular as the means for a politically progressive critique—but it curiously mobilizes a vocabulary entrenched in sexual difference to claim the possibilities of "postmale" transcendence. For what else does "domestication" entail if not an incipient feminization of that more serious, more definitively radical and disruptive modernism found on Huyssen's map before the Second World War?[7] If the institutionalization that Huyssen laments is coterminous with domestication, what are we to make of the articulation of cultural power underlying the implied split between public and private, where domestication signals the force field in which hegemonic repression and recuperation seems to exist most strongly? How, in other words, can the emergence of "women and minority artists"—the traditional agents of the domestic—undo the domestication of modernism that underwrites its complicity with modernity?

Huyssen doesn't answer these questions, primarily because the gendered language of the domestication of which he writes is rendered transparently. It is, as well, a decidedly minor moment in his narrativization of the postmodern, a convenient bridge for moving from the constellation of cold war politics to the social movements of the 1960s and the artistic practices they spawned. But it is a curious bridge, this hailing of the figure of "the other" as both precondition and framework for mapping the postmodern's radical definition. Doesn't such a version of postmodernism repeat the modernist compulsion to appropriation, "domesticating" the domestic, to use Huyssen's terms? If, as Huyssen claims, "feminist criticism has so far [in 1984] largely stayed away from the postmodernism debate" (250)—an observation that extends to the critical concerns of discourses of race in the early eighties as well—what does it mean to marshal "women and minorities" as central figures of the postmodern? This last question is not meant to imply that the postmodern must legitimate its relation to "women and minorities" by demonstrating a vested interest in the postmodern by feminist and "minority" discourses. One can recognize a disjunction between the critical concerns of "women and minorities" and their significance (as producers of alternative practices and discourses) to conversations about postmodernism. And yet in the way Huyssen sees "women and minorities" as the difference that posts the modern, there is an implied reliance on the other *as other* for the politics of the post-modern to be achieved.

In surveying the "territories" of the postmodern, then, in deciphering where "the various postmodern artistic and critical practices could find their aesthetic and political place" (236), the map Huyssen draws becomes the negative scene for modernism's instruction, an unwitting accomplice to modernism's own canonical terms. This is the case even though Huyssen posits the sign of "the other" as emerging culturally to signify autonomously, through "self-assertion . . . into public consciousness" (247). But in the decade that has nearly passed since this mapping was drawn, our awareness of the overlay of popular culture with the internationalizing conquest of commodity production makes autonomy and self-assertion—particularly in its counterhegemonic formation—a more contradictory terrain. As Huyssen himself would agree, the complexities of the status of "the other" in an economy contingent on producing and marketing difference require a level of deeper suspicion in contextualizing the "self-assertion" ascribed to the new-found representational visibility of women and so-called minorities. Might it not be more politically productive, in fact, for "the other" to be let loose from her modernist appointment with the finalities of an "aesthetic and political place"—relieved, that is, from perpetual attendance to modernism's conceptual, subjective, and artistic lack?

These comments are quite obviously intended to call us back to my opening discussion of that other, seemingly absent other, the lesbian, whose invisibility on Huyssen's map as an outlaw of her own (drawn out from the closet of universal "woman") may be mistaken by some as a definitive problem of the postmodern that only a return to the modern can reshape.[8] But as my discussion of the lesbian's commodified presence within the women's cultural scene begins to indicate, it is along the modernist axis of self-assertion and visibility that both a lesbian consumer market and a marketed commodity repeatedly named *lesbian* has been achieved. To nostalgically applaud the lesbian's insertion into commodity production as the fuller grasping of modernism's denouement is to conveniently forget modernity's political investment in categorical identities as well as the disciplinary function they have served only too well.

Undoing the Map

In the context of a conversation about "the other" and our need to wholly reconceptualize this understanding of cultural differences, the shift in the previous sentence from modernism to modernity is no minor transposition. It signals the double registers in which the question of the postmodern has been approached: as implicated in the history of art and aesthetics on the one hand and in that of social theory on the other. On Huyssen's map, with its articulation of the historical bound to a sequential unfolding of artistic practices, the other is featured as the radical difference through which postmodernist aesthetics most effectively transcends the limitations of modernism, especially its tie to modernization. But this does not yet say much about the question of cultural differences within the framework of postmodern social theory, or about what difference history itself might make were we to think it differently. It is precisely the possibility of this different thinking that deterritorializes the historical familiarity of Huyssen's strategy of the map, revealing the map to be informative but inadequate to the political dimensions and possibilities of the postmodern, especially as we begin to approach the constellation called here the lesbian postmodern.

This is not meant to be a dismissal of Huyssen in the name of a more radical or transgressive politics. I'm not particularly interested in joining the fashionable theoretical competition to carve out for my own analysis a place of immutable political transcendence, as though the issue of the political within the postmodern must continue to be staged as a contest of correct metanarrativity. As Huyssen quite rightly notes, too much of the modern/postmodern debate has already been reduced to "Mirror, mirror on the wall, who is the least conservative [or most radical] of us all?" (254). Instead, I want to call into question the conceptual framework of the map: its metaphoric and symbolic emphasis on fixity and location and its determined and determinating move of setting the postmodern (along with our own configuration of the lesbian) in "place."

While my preceding reading of Huyssen's essay establishes its overarching concern with artistic practices and their historical periodization, it is significant that he raises the issue of postmodernism's articulations as—and indictments of—theories of the social as well. This he does in his discussion of Habermas's well-known defense of modernity, in which postmodernism is depicted as part of the neoconservative backlash since the decades following the sixties. But in placing the philosophical conversation that concerns the politics of postmodernism in this way—as a historical fact coincident with Habermas's 1980 Adorno-prize lecture—it becomes clear that any rethinking of the historical (or the philosophical for that matter) remains in a very real sense outside of Huyssen's chronological view. Because the map requires the consistency of incremental time to define and determine location, the philosophical debate about modernity and postmodernity—about the possibilities and problems of the Enlightenment's tie to rationalism, Man, and the knowing human subject—must be confined to a specific temporal conjunction, namely, the 1980s. While a limited understanding of the material might welcome this contextualization of the emergence of discussions of the postmodern, such an emergence does not in itself locate the postmodern, even if it does cite one of its contemporary signatures. Ironically, such a citing most pointedly betrays the impulse toward incremental time and historical location as aligned not with the postmodern but with the modern itself.

In saying this, I am, of course, relying on a more Lyotardian understanding of the postmodern where, as he says, "postmodernity is not a new age" ("Re-Writing," 8), is not the sequential successor to modernity, "is not modernism at its end but in the nascent state, and this state is constant" (*Condition*, 79). Postmodernity, then, as Diane Elam glosses, "is a rewriting of modernity, which has already been active *within* modernity for a long time" (*Romancing the Postmodern*, 15). From this angle, Huyssen's reading of postmodernism as the history of artistic practices and/or critical discourses citing its name, traced by decade in a developmental periodicity, maintains the repressions on which modernity itself is based: both the complexity of temporality and the impossibility of legitimizing historical knowledge as a progressive narrative of origin and descent. While for Huyssen, the *post* in *postmodern* marks the sequential difference between a "then" and "now," setting the relationship between events into place, for Lyotard the *post* undoes the epistemology of historical sequence, marking the excess of accountability that modernity excises from its historicizing frame.[9] Given this kind of difference, it is no surprise that through Lyotard, Huyssen's map of the postmodern fails its postmodern use.

For a number of feminists who have approached the question of the postmodern, it is this circumvention of historical metanarrativity that defers any kind of positive embrace of the postmodern, especially as

Lyotard's challenge to overarching narratives of history has been directed toward both Enlightenment and Marxian accounts of social being. Linda J. Nicholson and Nancy Fraser, for instance, worry that Lyotard's posting of modernist history moves political practice (as well as its legitimation and theorization) to the level of the local, thereby disabling "critique of broad-based relations of dominance and subordination along lines like gender, race, and class" ("Social Criticism Without Philosophy," 23). In response, they call for a postmodern feminism that eschews the foundationalism of Western philosophies while attending "to large political problems" (34), a feminism that is "pragmatic and fallibilistic . . . using multiple categories when appropriate and forswearing the metaphysical comfort of a single feminist method or feminist epistemology. In short, this theory would look more like a tapestry composed of threads of many different hues than one woven in a single color" (35). This image of a tapestry is an arresting choice for the figuration of a postmodern feminism, not simply because of its unabashed pluralism but also because it emerges after the authors assure us that "there is nothing self-contradictory in the idea of a postmodern theory" (34). But wouldn't there be something politically useful for feminism in interpreting postmodernism as the nascent state of modernity, as precisely the embodiment and encodement of contradiction—as, in fact, the refusal to jettison contradiction in favor of modernity's quest for totality and coherence, for a singular and romantic tapestry, unified regardless of its many colored threads?

In this regard, one can imagine a feminism not only immensely aware of its self-contradiction, but committed to explorations of the contradictions of "self" through which the modern social subject is called into being. I am not suggesting here that feminism can marshal the postmodern by simply claiming—instead of repressing—contradiction even though much contemporary theory, feminist and nonfeminist alike, often reduces the postmodern to a facile embrace of contradiction, multiplicity, and flux. As Diane Elam discusses and as Judith Roof notes in this volume, the knowledge of contradiction, inserted in the place of modernity's knowing subject of history, simply reverses the terms by which Enlightenment thought functions. Now we know that we can't possibly know, and in this we master the category of knowledge, overcoming its indeterminacy and instability. To move from the perceived coherence of the rational subject to one formed in contradiction and conflict does not in itself mark the postmodern. Nor can we rely on the fact of our awareness of feminism's deeply contradictory relation to modernity and patriarchy as the precondition for political transformation, as if the intellectual grasp we attain leads to liberation. This, too, is modernity claiming us. As such, one can only agree with Nancy Hartsock's assessment in her essay, "Foucault on Power" that, "for those of us who want to understand the world systematically in order to change it, postmodern theories at their best give little guidance" (159). But to counter her negative inflection, I'd have to add that the failure of postmodern theories to guide us to systematicity and the illusion of knowledge as liberating power is, indeed, quite rightly so—the very point at which modernity undoes itself by revealing its excess, the postmodern.

Hartsock's lament, echoed in a more nuanced way by Fraser and Nicholson, is a lament for the lost or (as she seems to feel) stolen map, for the teleological narrative of liberation, that epistemological relationship to the world that guarantees transcendence. But the postmodern doesn't provide the crystal ball that can lead us to the utopic "home" in the eye of the storm. It refuses, in fact, the impulse to forecast, forcing us instead to exist in the contradictions of a present that can never be entirely full to us either. For me, this is not nihilism or despair, not the end (or the beginning) of feminism. Nothing that dramatic or epochal. But it is something quite radically different from feminism's role as inquisitor and equalizer of modernity's gender biases. To reference feminism's role in modernity does not mean, however, that we must rush to discard such a role altogether (as though we could), recasting ourselves in the clothes of a postmodern new; such a move merely ups modernity's own ante by pretending that the postmodern succeeds the modern, that it has the teleological ability to birth itself anew. The postmodern doesn't transcend the modern; it rereads the modern, not from beyond, but from within.

Given this, what do we make of the often-leveled feminist criticism that the postmodern renders the contemporary significance of coordinates of gender, race, and class indeterminable at the level of broadscale social organization and institutionalization? If, as we have seen with Huyssen, modernism's lack can be serviced by "women and minorities," what happens to categories of difference under the rubric of post/modernity once the forward thrust of Enlightenment narrativity has been challenged for its illusory epistemology and revealed as quite exceedingly Eurocentric and male? What I find most interesting when Fraser and Nicholson, to continue that example, cite the postmodern as making impossible a "critique of broad-based relations of dominance and subordination along lines like gender, race, and class" (23) is the way they tacitly assume that the categories of gender, race, and class are *fully adequate* to the task of defining and critiquing relations of domination. I would want to counter this assumption, especially in the context of contemporary feminist theory, whose energy has been turning increasingly to the elisions, exclusions, and amputations that the categorical litany of differences unwittingly produces.[10] For even as the multiplication of categories beyond the singularity of gender has made possible a rethinking of the complexities of women's varied social positioning, their conceptualization as discrete categories works precisely by cordoning off and hence limiting the potential excessibility of difference.

To play the game of categories, then, as Fraser and Nicholson seem to insist we must, is to wager the political for a conceptual framework that apprehends differences—their multiple, oversaturated, and contradictory formations—as parallel universes, separate and ultimately total in their knowability. While much recent feminist work, including my own,[11] tries to rethink the relationship between categories, to trace their contaminations and overdeterminations, it is not at all certain that the deep disparities between genders, races, and classes can be understood and/or ameliorated only within the conceptual field of gender, race, and class. After all, to speak of race is not to speak of or against racism, and we could well say the same of gender and sexism, sexuality and heterosexism, and class and classism. It might be the case, in fact, that the circulation of these categories in critical discourses functions quite often to short-circuit the interrogation of differences as well as the possibilities of the political itself. To lament the map, to dream the tapestry: these overtures to the political seal the fate of a future that has already been.

Encountering the Lesbian

When the modernist desire for mapping meets the feminist territories of gender, race, and class, it is difficult to ascertain why the lesbian at first sight is nowhere to be seen. Perhaps she is hiding within gender, waiting to emerge as its mythic transcendence. Perhaps she is off to the side, assessing (and despairing over) her hardly optional options: a lifestyle, an orientation, some sexless difference that busts up the trinity without varying its routine. If she appears outright, wearing boots and flashing her whips and nipple clips, she is debated according to contemporary sex-correct definitions. If she shows up in her party dress, she risks being dismissed as too overtly unqueer. So much is at stake, it seems, in her practice and practical definitions; so much rests on categorical fashion.

If the language above reconvenes on one level the modernist mythology of a fully conscious and directed subjective position—of a lesbian agent powering the representational field—it also quite overtly delineates modernity's inherent limitation, that point at which the trajectory of a progressively liberating and seemingly self-naming subject encounters subjection, the by-product of identity's disciplinary function. The policing of the lesbian, so often understood and resisted in relation to the judicial-military structure, comes home here to roost, providing the means for negotiating a "middle" ground of difference that can appeal to (as well as help to determine) both those inside and outside the group. As the context in which the modern subject can simultaneously be defined and contained—convinced that is, through the apparatus of her subjection, in the onward march to collective liberation—"the lesbian" (like other categories within identity politics) inhabits the very epistemology of unconflicted temporality marking modernist history that I have been critiquing.

So what is the lesbian postmodern? The language itself constrains, acting too much like a category, too much like a name. And yet, this is precisely the contradiction embodied by the phrase, transforming what in some sense should be an action, an activity into a static, protogeneric formulation. But as I hope to have suggested, there can be no map of the lesbian postmodern, no setting her definition in place. She can be located only in excess of these modernist traits—somewhere between and beyond categorical crisis and the logic of a system that visibly fails. As my paraphrasing of the Butler and Roof quotes preceding this essay entails, the lesbian postmodern marks a different kind of encounter, one that necessarily abandons the dream of symmetry and equivalence, moving away from the epistemology of identities, rights, and reason that would guarantee the less than liberatory achievement of (an always bourgeois) cultural legitimacy. Quite rightly, or so it seems to me, the lesbian postmodern slips and shifts Monique Wittig's decidedly modernist proclamation: not just that the lesbian is "not a woman" but the lesbian is not—cannot continue to be—"the lesbian" either.

Notes

1. *Queer theory* is a term coined, it seems, by Teresa de Lauretis. In her introduction to the special issue of *differences* called "Queer Theory: Lesbian and Gay Sexualities," she traces the way the conceptual framework for discussing lesbian and gay sexualities has shifted in the twentieth century from an early emphasis on "homosexual" to a gender undifferentiated "gay," to the present specificity of lesbian and gay. But, as she remarks, this specificity, which purports to recognize differences, most often elides them in "the contexts in which the phrase is used, that is to say, differences are implied in [the phrase] but then simply taken for granted and even covered over by the word 'and' " (v–vi). The turn toward the word *queer* is intended to displace this displacement of difference, to mark a mutual eccentricity that takes the problems of "differences between and within lesbians, and between and within gay men, in relation to race and its attendant differences of class or ethnic culture, generational, geographical, and socio-political location" (viii) as central. While I certainly agree with the political imperative of such a project, it seems to me that the deployment of *queer* so far, as Judith Mayne remarked at the 1992 Console-ing Passions Conference, actually neutralizes differences.

2. See Clark, "Commodity Lesbianism," for a discussion of the way popular advertising in the United States is increasingly fixing on lesbian coded images.

3. On this, I am referring to the more inclusivist representational economy that now governs various media, an economy in which the targeting of new consumer markets entails attention to those figures once wholly excluded from dominant representations, such as African-Americans and gays and lesbians.

4. The idea of the map recurs throughout a variety of often conflicting postmodern theoretical discussions, from Jean Baudrillard's *Simulations* to Fredric Jameson's "Cognitive Mapping." In *Simulations*, Baudrillard begins his discussion with the Borges tale in which cartographers draw a map so detailed it covers the territory it sets out to represent. Baudrillard criticizes the "cartographer's mad project of an ideal coextensivity between the map and the territory" (3), asserting instead that we can no longer privilege the idea of a referential real. "The territory no longer precedes the map," he claims, "nor survives it. . . . It is the map that precedes the territory . . . the map that engenders the territory . . . the territory whose shreds are slowly rotting across the map" (2). In thus denouncing the possibilities of totalizable theories based on the premise of the map—of the ability to render knowable incommensurabilities through the arrangement and assemblage of detail—Baudrillard casts doubt on the epistemological assumptions of modernity.

Jameson, on the other hand, deploys the concept and image of the map as a purposeful reclamation of totalizing analysis, a post-Marxian insistence on both the possibility and necessity of understanding culture in global terms. By dividing the history of cultural organization into three distinct and discontinuous stages of "capitalist space" ("Cognitive Mapping," 348), Jameson conceives of the map, its cognitive apprehension, as encompassing the very future of socialist politics. Here, the ability to map the space of multinationalist capitalist arrangements has the potential to turn back the alienation and fragmentation wrought by capitalism's global expansion. Such a mapping is, for Jameson, aesthetic, though he is quite clear in stating that he has no definitive conception of what such an aesthetic socialist practice might bring.

As will be clear in my ensuing conversation, my commitment to the question of political transformation ultimately thinks the relationship between liberation and map making in ways incompatible with both Jameson and Baudrillard. But because of space limitations—and because of the terms set forth by my engagement with Huyssen's mapping of the postmodern—neither Baudrillard nor Jameson are addressed with the attention they deserve.

5. One might notice that in this regard Huyssen is in agreement with Lyotard.

6. See, for instance, Hutcheon, *The Politics of Postmodernism* and Owens, "The Discourse of Others."

7. This is an interesting reversal of the more popular association of the postmodern with the feminine, as the subversion of modernity's emphasis on unicity and the gendered universalism of man.

8. While critical of Enlightenment exclusions, Hartsock, for instance, rejects the postmodern in order to claim the Enlightenment values of autonomy, natural rights, and human transcendence, arguing that "we need to sort out who we really are . . . to develop an account of the world which treats our perspective not as subjugated or disruptive knowledges, but as primary and constitutive of a different world" ("Foucault on Power," 171). While recognizing the "false 'we' " (171) deployed throughout her essay, Hartsock nonetheless tends to group categories of otherness together under the rubric of the dominated in strict opposition to the "ruling class, race, and gender" (172). But, significantly, her categorical others are devoid of sexuality as difference, an omission that enables her to position Foucault as the "white boy" (166) who "writes from the perspective of the dominator" (165). In reclaiming the teleology of human liberation at work in modernity by trying to work out its elisions, Hartsock repeats its categorical logic. Given the structure of her argument, one wonders what it might mean if she could read Foucault's text as gay.

9. For a more developed and nuanced discussion of temporality and sequentiality in terms of the postmodern, see Elam, *Romancing the Postmodern*.

10. I am thinking here in particular of the work of Hortense Spillers with its implicit insistence that categories don't simply overlap but so thoroughly saturate one another that gender (to take her prime example) rarely refers to the same constellation. Differences in racial positioning must therefore be understood to produce quite different (feminine) genders. See also Berlant in "National Brands/National Body," who takes Spillers' point and develops it in a discussion of commodity culture.

11. My forthcoming study, *Economies of Visibility: Race and Gender in U.S. Culture*, evinces my own grappling with categories of difference, focusing in particular on the way the discourse of sexual difference has been used to repeatedly reframe white racial supremacies. For those who may mistake my criticisms here

as a dismissal of categories altogether, I can only reassert my central concern: we are investing too heavily in analyses based on "gender, race, and class (and/or sexuality)" as *the only means*—the only valid political territory—for thinking differences in order to eliminate hierarchies.

Works Cited

Baudrillard, Jean. *Simulations*. Translated by Paul Foss, Paul Patton, and Philip Beitchman. New York: Semiotext(e), 1983.

Berlant, Lauren. "National Brands/National Body: *Imitation of Life*." In Hortense Spillers, ed., *Comparative American Identities: Race, Sex, and Nationality in the Modern Text*, pp. 110–40. London and New York: Routledge, 1991.

Butler, Judith. *Gender Trouble: Feminism and the Subversion of Identity*. London and New York: Routledge, 1990.

——. "Imitation and Gender Subordination." In Diana Fuss, ed., *Inside/Out: Lesbian Theories, Gay Theories*, pp. 13–31. London and New York: Routledge, 1991.

Clark, Danae. "Commodity Lesbianism." *Camera Obscura* 25–26 (January/May 1991): 181–201.

de Lauretis, Teresa. "Queer Theory: Lesbian and Gay Sexualities: An Introduction." *differences* 3 (Summer 1991): iii–xviii.

Elam, Diane. *Romancing the Postmodern*. London and New York: Routledge, 1992.

Fraser, Nancy, and Linda J. Nicholson. "Social Criticism Without Philosophy: An Encounter between Feminism and Postmodernism." In Linda J. Nicholson, ed., *Feminism/Postmodernism*, pp. 19–38. London and New York: Routledge, 1990.

Hartsock, Nancy. "Foucault on Power: A Theory for Women?" In Linda J. Nicholson, ed., *Feminism/ Postmodernism*, pp. 157–75. London and New York: Routledge, 1990.

Hutcheon, Linda. *The Politics of Postmodernism*. London and New York: Routledge, 1989.

Huyssen, Andreas. "Mapping the Postmodern." In Linda J. Nicholson, ed., *Feminism/Postmodernism*, pp. 234–77. London and New York: Routledge, 1990.

Jameson, Fredric. "Cognitive Mapping." In Cary Nelson and Lawrence Grossberg, eds., *Marxism and the Interpretation of Culture*, pp. 347–57. Urbana and Chicago: University of Illinois Press, 1988.

Lyotard, Jean-François. *The Postmodern Condition: A Report on Knowledge*. Translated by Geoff Bennington and Brian Massumi. Minneapolis: University of Minnesota Press, 1984.

——. "Re-writing Modernity." *SubStance* 16 (1987): 3–9.

Owens, Craig. "The Discourse of Others." In Hal Foster, ed., *The Anti-Aesthetic*, pp. 65–90. Port Townsend, Wash.: Bay Press, 1984.

Roof, Judith. *A Lure of Knowledge: Lesbian Sexuality and Theory*. New York:

Columbia University Press, 1991.

Spillers, Hortense. "Mama's Baby, Papa's Maybe: An American Grammar Book." *diacritics* 17 (Summer 1987): 65–81.

Wiegman, Robyn. *Economics of Visibility: Race and Gender in U.S. Culture.* Durham, N.C.: Duke University Press, 1994.

Wittig, Monique. "One is Not Born a Woman." In *The Straight Mind and Other Essays*, pp. 9–20. Boston: Beacon Press, 1992.

Part One

Theorizing the
Lesbian Postmodern

2　Racing the Lesbian, Dodging White Critics

Sagri Dhairyam

To assemble this essay for a collection on the lesbian postmodern has proved a peculiarly fraught endeavor, particularly as the essay has undergone a tortuous process of revision and rethinking since the editor first laid eyes on it—since, indeed, I articulated a lesbian self over the complex resistance of a colored body. I do not directly evoke the motley of postmodernism but do battle with it by indirection in an attempt to subvert its manifestations for my contest against critical self-negotiation. Always already futile, the battle is rigged by the complicitous authority of my name as academic that has long provided me with a means to arbitrate my outness as a lesbian. I stumbled across my attraction to women through the intricate worlds of an educated, upper-class, Catholic-Hindu, third-world, Indian woman before I consciously came to name myself a lesbian and occupy the luxury of the name's attendant roles. That conscious, critical act of naming, variously empowering as it has been, could not but curtail my mobility in discourses once readily available. Indeed, my self-conscious empowerment of a lesbian self entails less conscious collusions in first-world privilege and colonizing difference from other colored women whose bodies suffer less visible because less academically articulated oppression—although it is arguably the more threatening for that. Inasmuch as my role as academic facilitated my transition to named lesbianism, it disquiets me: the developmental telos of my journey from not-lesbian to lesbian is simultaneously an ironic journey from Indian and silent otherness to Western and articulated subjectivity. The journey traces a means to cultural privilege in order to know my body and its desires, a move that perforce shapes the lesbian body that I come to know.

So the turgid intellectualism of these speculations minimizes the risks of speaking a lesbian body in professional space as they underwrite my stake in disciplinary, and in this case academic, power. Important as it is to asseverate that identity is overdetermined by culture and history, this emphasis ultimately underwrites the notion of identity as a conscious strategy borne by the right critical thought. Polarized around essentialist and constructionist perspectives, the binarism of these critical debates seems variously, yet consistently, to devalorize the former. Rather than argue for the value of either position, however, my intervention suggests that it is the polarized structure of the debate itself that proves invaluable to academics vested in carving spaces for their professional signatures through publication and institutional tenure. Indeed, the disciplinary constraints that shape our academic institutional voices force a premium on self-conscious, critical negotiation that perforce relegates the affective immediacies of the body to the shadows.

Yet, even as we acknowledge that the cultural boundaries defining straightness are suspect acts that keep an implicit lesbianism at bay and define the parameters for its manifestations, we gloss over our internalized fantasy of the lesbian who plays herself through our bodies, a fantasy not only sexed queerly but raced white. "Queer theory" comes increasingly to be reckoned with as critical discourse, but concomitantly writes a queer whiteness over raced queerness; it domesticates race in its elaboration of sexual difference. In order to confront the dual implications of an other who is always already internal to straight as well as to white subjectivity, I raise the problematic of racial difference through the lens of lesbian identity. This is not to subsume race into sexuality or to render their oppressions homologous, but rather to force whiteness to confront its investments in heterosexuality, masculinity, and literacy. In so doing, indeed, I hope to write the differentials of power at stake for queer women of color.

The very ability to "pass" as educated, as white, as heterosexual, even if one chooses not to do so, is to exert a certain purchase in power. The different modes of passing available to a woman, even if refused, define her identity through unchosen mobilities in discursive systems. Indeed, I argue that rather than the self-consciously critical, political choice that defines identity, it is precisely the discourses that we cannot foresee—discourses that impel our resistance but frame our complicity—that produce us as active lesbian selves. Not a telos of developing critical consciousness, then, but our very collusions, often unconscious, in dominant discourses force our resistant identities. Michel Foucault emphasizes as much in a conversation with Gilles Deleuze when he remarks that

> The intellectual's role is no longer to place himself "somewhat ahead and to the side" in order to express the stifled truth of the collectivity; rather, it is to struggle against the forms of power that transform him into its object and instrument in the sphere of "knowledge," "truth," "consciousness," and "discourse." . . . It is not to "awaken consciousness" that we struggle . . . but to sap power, to take power. ("Intellectuals and Power," 207–8)

In his suspicion of the contemporary intellectual's will to legislate right thinking, Foucault admits, even as he undermines it, his complicity in theoretical discourses. Intellectual identity, so long invisible to itself, is made all too visible in its complicities with colonializing structures of power.

Working through his insights, Judith Butler, in an influential essay that theorizes lesbian/gay sexuality, suggests that "the very professionalization of gayness requires a certain performance and production of a 'self' which is the constituted effect of a discourse that nevertheless claims to 'represent' that self as a prior truth" ("Imitation," 18). Her argument follows through on the Foucauldian premises of her earlier *Gender Trouble*, which situated any identity as the product of the very discourses seeking to legislate it. In these terms, lesbian/gay identity is effected by the dominant heterosexual matrix that it contests. Yet, though all identities are performative, some of them, such as compulsory heterosexuality, have gained the status of unquestioned truths, naturalized in the cultural imagination through their lengthy histories. Only the risks that alternative gender configurations run in their negotiations with history highlight these truths as "regulatory fictions" legislating difference (*Gender*, 141). Read thus, Butler's argument intimates that any sustained performance of identity through sociohistorical contexts is a reification of performance into essence. In this context, it is surely significant that for Butler the most effective political performances that denaturalize these congealed truths are parodic acts of gay identity, for parody places the performative aspects of identity in italics and thereby effectively denies itself any lasting force.

Parodies satirize belief and affective identification; they are, indeed, performances that draw attention to their own performative character, their momentariness. Butler underlines that parody does not ask to succeed; rather it proliferates in different subversions at any time. In *Gender Trouble*, her turn to parody as a means to subvert the usual resort to ontological foundationalism has drawn fire from readers Aware of the problematic valences of her move, in her later reflections on "drag" as simultaneously parodic and performative disruption of the heterosexual regime Butler seeks to problematize the easy recuperation of parody as subversion. Suggesting that the notion of a proper gender cannot but manifest itself in the ways it is improperly performed, Butler positions gender itself as always already in drag, a fakery of what it wants to be. In so doing, she underlines that drag is not dependent on a volitional subject who decides to dress up in different genders or sexualities; rather, it is an effect, a subject-position produced through the very discourse it imitates and contests ("Imitation"). Despite the promise of her speculations, however, successful drag remains an act that perforce exposes the failure of its performance and thus undermines the notion of identity as such.

Through the later "Imitation and Gender Insubordination" Butler contends that identities are compelled to repeat themselves precisely because of their inability to fulfill their desire to be. In arguing that the psychic subject is "constituted internally by differentially gendered Others and is, therefore, never, as a gender, self-identical" (27), her essay follows through on the Lacanian inflections of *Gender Trouble*. The self that is produced through separation attempts to incorporate an "Other" to allay its loss. Thus, "the disruption of the Other at the heart of the self is the very condition of that self's possibility" (27). Yet, if stressed another way, the very impossibility of "being" a gender initiates a belief in gender: the lack that structures gender identity provides the imperative for that identity. Identity is precisely what it cannot be—the very differences that striate lesbian identity frame an imperative to affirm lesbianism. Butler concedes as much but asks that the dynamics of this psychic identification lead us to adjudicate "subversive" repetitions and so guard against any "truths" that lesbian identity may seek to define.

Not surprisingly, this instability manifests itself most disruptively in sexuality where to locate eroticism is to lose it; thus, the unconscious, defined as "the excess that enables and contests every performance" (28–29), leads Butler to work sexuality against identity. But this is also to mark sexuality as the utopic site of disruptive excess where drag is compelled to perform as drag, in a move not uncommon to poststructuralist theory or to modernist literature. An effective politics of identity enacts itself through sexualized, because parodic, disruption of normative identity practices.

Seduced as I am by Butler's performative subject-as-effect that is always already complicit in the discourses it contests (a move disarmingly evocative of Foucault's remarks to Deleuze), I distrust the appeal of her central figure of drag as subversive identity practice. Drag as critical trope mocks its own desire to be and inevitably reveals itself as fakery. Is it not, thus, also a trope for self-reflexivity even if not volitionally assumed by a critical subject? In the double bind of Butler's argument, are we who are in necessary drag able to perceive the necessity apart from the drag, or do these produce each other? If so, are we not inextricable from our drag? How then do we produce the continuous interrogation of origin to disrupt the metaphysical lodgings of foundationalism? Not unless, I would argue, our various other identities collude more directly in the system we wish to subvert. Thus Butler, as white and academic philosopher-theorist who is produced by the very discourses of academia, may tell us about stone-butches and powerful femmes and, indeed, produce a discourse of drag that feeds back into the authority of a critical intellectualism capable of provoking yet legislating what is dangerous in philosophical thought.

Ironically, even as she acknowledges the affective imperative for belief in identity precisely because identity is constituted from lack, Butler erases the urgency of that imperative in her evocation of drag as utopic site of excess. More disturbing, in privileging the parodic aspects of sexuality through drag, she implies that, unlike sexuality, other identities of race or class have more at stake in foundationalist identity politics and are therefore less able to mobilize subversive drag. Identities that cannot sustain themselves through history triumph in her formulations because of the very differences that tear them apart against the "regulatory fictions" of essence that are sustained over time. But to safeguard the openness of the signifier in an anxiety for a future of radical democracy is also to overwrite the all-too-material forces of a present that would erase dissident identity. More problematic, it implies that such safekeeping of the signifier is in the hands of discerning critic-philosophers who may evaluate and analyze performances of identity even as they decide which ones work most subversively. Finally, the critic-philosopher's own performance as product-of-systems-of-power is rendered invisible as the intellect evaluates sexuality and the body.

Butler's influential *Gender Trouble* appeared in bookstores in late 1989 and has in the last three years gained the status of canonical text that brought into academic visibility the field of "queer theory," a field that, in turn, was fast legitimated by a rush of books on lesbian and gay literature and theory. The 1992 PMLA directory confirms institutional ratification of the field with an advertisement, "announcing the first in the field . . . *GLQ: A Journal of Lesbian and Gay Studies.*" The emergence of *GLQ* comes as no surprise when journals such as *differences* and *Discourse* have brought out special issues on "queer theory" and lesbian and gay studies,[1] and course offerings in universities echo the emphasis as well. That the recent academic efflorescence of queer theory makes a spectrum of sexualized bodies increasingly visible is not to be denied; yet the very bodies visible in academia are also produced by academic discourse as subject-effects of the professional discourses that empower their subjectivity, as Butler herself suggests.

In particular, the rubric of queer theory, which couples sexuality and theory and collapses lesbian and gay sexualities, tends to effect a slippage of body into mind: the monstrously feminized body's sensual evocations of smell, fluid, and hidden vaginal spaces with which the name lesbian resonates are cleansed, desexualized into a "queerness" where the body yields to intellect, and a spectrum of sexualities again denies the lesbian center stage. Inasmuch as "queerness" outs lesbian and gay identity, it also closets them; even as academic discourse denaturalizes the discourses of sexual pleasure, it legislates new privacies. To take a representative example, Eve Kosofsky Sedgwick's admirable sketch of the paradoxes of "outing" and its figurations of the closet suggests the binarisms at work in an epistemology structured by heterosexuality. In so doing, however, it erases the mobilities of racial "outing" that work through an intersecting epistemic regime of racism. In contrasting the processes of homophobia and racism, Sedgwick remarks that "racism . . . is based on a stigma that is visible in all but exceptional cases" (*Epistemology of the Closet*, 75). Inasmuch as work on sexuality, such as Sedgwick's own, insistently draws attention to sexuality as process, produced by discursive sites of power, it erases the ways in which racist discourses work through the cultural imaginary continuously to produce the all-too-visible stigmata of race that may be taken for granted and thus overlooked.

As the controversy on lifting the ban on gays and lesbians in the military continues, jokes and cartoons flourish; many of them work along the tested lines of contrasting/comparing the entrance of blacks into the military with that of lesbians and gays as the former now appears to be the lesser evil. We "at least know who the blacks are" unlike the queers whose threat becomes their very ability to "pass" for straight. As in Sedgwick's logic, queers constitute the greater threat because they are endemic to the heterosexual structure; the boundaries that define straightness can never be quite sure they are adequately placed. In contrast, the boundaries that police racial difference continue to be securely entrenched in the physical markers of racial traits. That uncontested visibility of racial difference, incessantly inscribed on the colored body, ironically erases the cultural politics that maintain a dominant white culture in the United States. As Michael Omi and Howard Winant so effectively point out in *Racial Formation in the United States*: "The meaning of race is defined and contested throughout society, in both collective action and personal practice. In the process, racial categories themselves are formed, transformed, destroyed, and reformed . . . [in a] process by which social, economic, and political forces determine the content and importance of racial categories, and by which they are in turn shaped by racial meanings" (288).

In a telling instance, Omi and Winant recount that "passing" acquires different weight in various American cultures; where certain "black" individuals may "pass" as "white" in the United States, they would not "pass" as "black" in many Latin American countries. Situated thus, the sign of blackness shifts in value in different cultures, and, more significant, that shift in value reassigns the physical markers for race. That blacks who "pass" as white in the United States cannot "pass" as black in Latin America suggests that when whiteness is the privileged category, the burden of race is borne by the nonwhites who may need to prove whiteness but can take their blackness for granted. The racial diversity of Latin America, in contrast, distributes the burden of proof in a proliferation of racial categories; blackness in that context would demand particular markers of race for itself—for example, that one is not Chicana or Indian. The oft-evoked contrast between the visibility of race and the invisibility of queer sexuality, then, hierarchizes queer sexuality over race by ignoring the cultural terrorism that maintains race as a stable category to contain its manifestations. Thus, the raced body continues to face discrimination and physical threat and is often deprived of space to exert self-critical maneuvers.

On another level, as Tomás Almaguer details in his article on Chicano gay identity, the emergence of a modern gay sensibility has everything to do with "cultural and structural factors which differentiate the experiences of the white and non-white population in the U.S." ("Chicano Men," 86). An affirmatory homosexual identity, in its very resistance, underlines the sanctions of both race and class that enabled its emergence. Indeed, the articulatory processes of lesbian/gay identity are situated in an all too familiar dialectic that pits the speaking queer subject against the silent, closeted native. As postcolonial critiques of the structures of Western epistemology emphasize, the fraught relation between the other and the same maintains a native object who is indispensable to the knowing and desiring subject authorizing the quests for historical knowledge. Homi Bhabha, for instance, speculates on a racial imaginary organized around the phallus that predicates itself on the ethnic other as lack. In a similar move, radical feminist Luce Irigaray uncovers the structuring phallogocentrism of Western discourse where the only spaces for women to speak themselves are in the interstices between discourses that signify them as impossible other, as lack.[2] In displaying the organizing logocentrism of Western discourses on race and women, both Bhabha and Irigaray empower specific critiques of particular discourses within Western thought. This is not to render the processes of othering the native homologous to those of othering the lesbian or the woman; rather, I suggest that Bhabha's and Irigaray's speculations italicize the articulatory processes of discursive power and the latter's production of different sites for subjectivity. Musing on similar dynamics, Gayatri Spivak argues that the blind spot between the tactics of local, shifting hegemonies of power (for example, the emergence of queers in academic discourse) and the overarching logocentrism of Western discourses needs repeatedly to be contested ("Word").

Indicating that the cultural apparatus of the West foregrounds and institutionalizes the Eurocentrism of theory, postcolonialist thinker Vivek Dhareshwar explores overlapping concerns. To his way of thinking, only the systematic interrogation of alternative modes of knowledge that are informed both by political vision and an awareness of epistemic/cultural privileges may displace theory's institutionalized constraints. In fact, Dhareshwar's focus on the Eurocentric institution of theory distinguishes it from "ethico-political movements which demand a rearticulation of ethico-political questions of identity and representation" ("The Predicament of Theory," 235).[3] The distinction, however, is not as clean or self-evident as he claims: the institution of theory comprises often conflicted discourses of poststructuralist negotiations with epistemology, language, disciplinary power, and socioeconomic relations, which, though influential in varied academic disciplines—such as literature, history, and anthropology—hardly constitute a monolithic or consolidating ideology. Nonetheless, his observations help to expose the places from which theory operates—more specifically, the professional corridors of universities in the United States where the liberal facade of academia ironically insulates the critic from immediate activist engagement.

Yet, in this context, it becomes crucially ironic that postcolonialist theory itself has gained such a purchase in academic thought; Spivak ranks high in the American academy as do Bhabha, Dhareshwar, and other Asian postcolonial critics, who, even as we fulminate against the elitism of theory, are simultaneously engaged in proving that we can do it as well as the West. I am not denying the usefulness of critical engagement within academic boundaries, but I wish to underline that the micropolitics of racial discrimination put professional Asian Indians like myself at risk differently from academics of other races. Yet, in the disciplined spaces within academia, the knowing critic may separate the discursivities of context and displace the risk of essence, but, in so doing, she legitimates, interestingly enough, a knowledge that remains Eurocentric in the binarism of its epistemic structures where critical engagement cannot but separate itself from the material violences of quotidian maneuvers.

Though academic analyses locate identity as a contingent filiation of discourses and help to destabilize a regime of heterosexual same-

ness, in the process, these analyses run the danger of erasing the experiential and affective realities of alternative sexualities and/or raced
communities, which must constantly struggle not only to affirm their
pleasures but to describe their terrors. Rendering experiential realities
into discursive constructs available for objective analyses finds only
too ready justification in the history of Western intellectual thought,
where the despised territory of the body marks itself as feminine and
native. Women are relegated to the domestic sphere of the house to
which their sexuality is confined, and colored peoples have historically been treated as pets, allowed responsibility only under the benevo-
lent colonial aegis of the white supervisor. Insofar as constructionist
theorizing dislodges sexuality as a prediscursive and essentialist given,
the persistent carnality of sexual practice renders the intellectual focus
on discursive contextuality equally problematic.

As in Spivak's warning about critical negotiations with racial or
subaltern identity,

> One cannot forget that the knowledge venture of imperialism,
> which was absolutely spectacular . . . was, in its inception, Euro-
> centric cross-culturalism. . . . [I]f one establishes an interdisciplinary
> space which does not engage with the most important arena (a
> silent, unemphatic arena) of warring power in the disciplines them-
> selves, where the people who don't publish much, who don't teach
> very well, engage day after day, as with distribution requirements,
> let us say, if one doesn't budge them, *but proliferates interdiscipli-
> nary, anti-essentialist programs, in fact one provides an alibi, once
> again, for the ruthless operation of neo-colonialist knowledge.*
> ("Word," 135; emphasis mine)

Her admonition makes evident the gap between the interdisciplinary
space of abstract theoretical speculations and the politics of particular
disciplinary requirements that renders "the ruthless operation of neocolonialist knowledge" possible. For minority programs dependent on
academic beneficence, intertextual negotiation ensures their continued
existence. Native American studies', black studies', and women's
studies' programs, among others, necessarily offer interdisciplinary
curricula through different departments for certification or for degree
requirements; yet, such interdisciplinary negotiation also affirms the
realities of the identities at stake in these programs. That one is a
woman, black, and/or native American may well provide justification
for lobbying support or for enrollment. Situated thus, intertextual

thinking is exactly a means to assert identity through difference. In contrast, abstract critical analyses that fulminate against essentialist strictures, ironically enough, operate through the security of established, and funded, departments, such as the humanities, English, modern languages, philosophy, and so forth. Their antiessentialist negotiations, I would add, legitimate the place of the academy in the dominant culture, providing as they do for the role of the critic who continues as cultural arbiter while remaining authoritatively unmarked as white, educated, and often, though by no means always, male.

Dominant cultural discourses ally "whiteness" with "masculinity." If histories of gender asymmetry bleed white women of power, these women are, nevertheless, masculinized in their cultural privileges over black and colored women. Since the inception of feminism, black feminists have insisted that the asymmetry structuring their relations to white women allows for insidious discourses of patronage and condescension that are endemic to the hierarchies of institutional power. It is surely significant, then, that "the race for theory" that Barbara Christian details ("Race"), is a race already won by default through masculinized white privilege, a privilege that allows its members the energy required for the race. Black and colored women compete in a spectrum of other races even to be allowed through the gateposts of theory. In running a gamut of cultural contests for privilege, sexual and racial, colored lesbians necessarily reread the silence of the mute bodies that enable both feminism and, now, queer theory to affirm their legitimated and professional spaces in academia. In the process, these theories' repeated corroboration of the native as other in Western discourse becomes evident.[4] The muted object who must be discovered to be known, the native occupies the dumb center in historical narratives of gender and sexuality.

Italicizing feminism's investment in academic and professional privilege, Margaret Ferguson, in a caveat to papers delivered at a conference, intimates that the self-aggrandizing elitism of theoria necessarily striates feminist counterknowledges, particularly through white, educated women's investments in professional discourses in universities. In implicit agreement with many of Spivak's misgivings, she advises that the papers are, despite their originality of thought,

> problematically marked by their respective institutional positions
> and psychic investments therein—by what we might therefore term

professional ideologies. . . . A question that is very hard for a literary critic to answer performatively—in practice—though she may well say yes to it in theory . . . is, *"Are feminist strategies of reading written and visual texts transferable to such things as social and political institutions [among them, I would add, our own universities]?"* ("Commentary," 42–43; emphasis mine)

Ferguson underscores the double edge of "institutional positions and psychic investments therein" that makes feminist subjectivity in academia possible. Whereas she goes on to delineate a split between theory and performance for feminist critics, I return to Foucault's acknowledgment of systemic forms of power that "transform [the intellectual] into its object and instrument in the sphere of 'knowledge,' 'truth,' 'consciousness,' and 'discourse,' " with which I began this essay ("Intellectuals and Power," 207). Seen through Foucault's perspective, the split Ferguson makes visible proves to be an indication of the ways in which feminist and queer theories collude in and transfer institutional power in "the sphere of 'knowledge' [and] 'consciousness.' " The point, then, is not to ponder if these theories are transferable into material practice but to question the ways in which such "transference" of theory transforms and co-opts its objects of knowledge. Such theoretical co-optation may initiate change, but in that very process it domesticates its manifestations. Ultimately, the distinction between theory and practice works to cover up the means by which theoretical discourse acts as an agent of systemic power by distancing theory from the material violences of everyday life. To contest the ease of the distinction is to make apparent theory's collusions in disciplinary privilege that locate us as critics and intellectuals not only through publication and tenure but through the quiddities of behavior and speech, decorous markers of race and class.

To undermine the valorization of intellectual worth is also to contest disciplinary norms that naturalize such positioning and that are themselves implicated in the perpetuation of the positions of subject/knower and object to be known. Necessary to movements for political change precisely because of the activity of criticism, the role of the critic as the interpreter par excellence depends upon the high cultural affiliations of the activity of "reading" or interpretation. The critic deciphers cultural meanings, teaching others not as qualified as herself. In Antonio Gramsci's concept of the organic intellectual, which has influenced so much recent thinking on popular culture, for example, the function of the intellectual is justified even outside the parameters of "high" theory as the product of processes that follow upon the formation of new classes and specializations. Repositioned along Gramscian lines, the charges of elitism that are leveled so frequently at poststructuralist writing extend to indict a spectrum of authoritative readers who are variously positioned as authorities. Feminist lesbians like Adrienne Rich, for example, often see themselves in the position of teachers who are not even necessarily defined by their academic functions. Rich herself, though sensitive to the paradoxes of teaching, an activity shaped and legitimated by the patriarchal institution of the university and its hierarchies, nevertheless repeatedly justifies the need for intellectuals who open up avenues to those less informed.

The value of literature (though a literature shaped by alternative canons) and of the literary critic (although one open to the demands of marginalized others) is intrinsic to Rich's notion of the intellectual. As in her essay on "Teaching Language in Open Admissions," Rich denigrates, by implication, the activities of reading and writing outside the spectrum of the literary as well as their political efficacy:

> What fascinates and gives hope in a time of slashed budgets, enlarging class size, and national depression is the possibility that many of these young men and women may be gaining the kind of critical perspective on their lives and the skill to bear witness that they have never before had in our country's history. At the bedrock of my thinking about this is the sense that *language is power, and that, as Simone Weil says, those who suffer from injustice most are least able to articulate their suffering; and that the silent majority, if released into language, would not be content with a perpetuation of the conditions which have betrayed them.* (67; emphasis mine)

I quote at some length because Rich's proclamations on language as power suggestively conflate language with literary language: the silent majority's suffering is tellingly connected to their inability to mobilize language, that is, language of a certain literate kind. In the slippage from language at large to literary skill, Rich justifies the need for intellectuals, such as herself, who can help oppressed young men and women to gain "the kind of critical perspective on their lives and the skill to bear witness that they have never before had." Again the stress on critical perspective testifies to the power of a certain kind of "reading" that is entrenched in the discipline of the literary. Once we are able to articulate ourselves critically, we are able to deal with "slashed budgets, enlarging class size, and national depression."

In contrast, for Margaret Ferguson the activities of reading and writing, and the norms of literacy, position themselves in the United States as constructed discourses or counters in very material games of socioeconomic and cultural power and often as colonizers' weapons. The micropolitics of slashed education budgets have to do with who is taught and where such teaching takes place. As Ferguson provocatively sets up her question and answer, "What do practices of reading and writing taught and tested in North American schools have to do with illiteracy and the poverty that accompanies it in Central America? An answer to that question . . . [would call attention] to the ways in which competing *ideologies* of literacy are central to the vexed socio-economic relations between the First and Third World" ("Commentary," 38). These "competing ideologies of literacy" intersect with and shape the subject positions available to women and men of color. Thus, even within the frame of academic discourse, the debate carried on in an issue of *New Literary History,* a journal entrenched in the literary discipline, attests to the ways in which positions of theoretical and critical proficiency allow black male critics Henry Louis Gates, Jr., and Houston A. Baker, Jr., to "pass" in whiteface in contrast to Joyce A. Joyce who occupies a position as the "other of the other"— the woman to a black man's articulateness and the black to white feminists' considerate patronage.

If power is entangled with resistance, as theoretical cliché stipulates, there are no clean subject positions for resistant identities outside disciplinary formations or outside the contaminations of Western epistemology. Neither are local movements for ethicopolitical change outside the traps of power: involved as they are in rearticulating identity, these movements for change are caught in the necessity for an authority that celebrates its own naming. Wresting subject positions for themselves, such movements cannot but exclude the uninitiated or the nonbelievers. If Butler laments the necessity for exclusion or forcible appropriation as tactics playing into an ontological foundationalism, her anxiety assumes a utopic dimension in its concern for an/other future that annuls the exigencies of the present.

Iterated performances of alternative identity channel discursive power differently in seizing spaces for selfhood and the demands of different bodies; with each reiteration, they render manifest hitherto invisible, because uncontested, reifications of essence. In forcing their lived realities into the dominant imaginary, alternative identities necessarily produce new margins of silence. Yet those margins, revealed as such, begin their bid for the center; thus, the exclusionary complicities in systemic power lead to resistance and change. Even, for example, as lesbian identity becomes barely visible, women of color who are lesbians contest its structures of determination as do S/M lesbians, as, in fact, did lesbianism with feminism. Indeed, the very belief in affective and experiential reality that constitutes selfhood inevitably acknowledges the social and cultural contexts that position or impel their emergent identities. For instance, Simon Watney, in his attempts to tackle this paradox, plays on the associations of the terms *homosexual* and *gay*—where the homosexual is the material result of repressed and othered desire, and the gay man celebrates a utopian collectivity:

> Historically, "the homosexual" has been incited to think of his core essence as a perverse negative of heterosexuality, which is taken as the norm right across the major discursive fields of sociology, anthropology, psychiatry, medicine, jurisprudence, politics, education and psychoanalysis. The gay man, on the contrary, affirms his sexuality in a category which is fundamentally socio-political, and implies no intrinsic common factor with other gay men beyond the workings of power on the entire range of homosexual desire in all its variant forms, which are unified only in their collective affirmations of value and validity. (*Policing Desire*, 27)

In Watney's use, the term *gay* as the name for positive communal identification depends upon it being "fundamentally socio-political [which] implies no common factor with other gay men beyond the workings of power . . . in all its variant forms." His blatantly constructionist emphasis on the "fundamentally socio-political" locates the realities of named gayness within material discourse and counterpoints Butler's delineation of identities as produced by the very discourses that they seek to counter. Yet Watney pushes the emphasis to the point where it becomes utopian. The logic of his argument indicates that the critical "I" that analyzes gayness has ultimately no authoritative place from where to delineate the histories that bring gay identity into being. Instead, the "I's" own self-participation in a "collective affirmation of value and validity" initiates, at the moment of its utterance, an authority contingent upon its own acceptance into communal discourses. The critical intellect is thus necessarily implicated in the exclusions that gay identity compels in the very act of naming itself gay—a recognition Butler fights to resist in self-consciously maneuvering "drag" as a category of subversive parody that escapes such exclusionary blindness. However, inasmuch as she seeks to disrupt the exclusions that her lesbianness enacts, the contexts that make her identity available through academic publications and political rallies overwrite the self-reflexivity of the differences she foregrounds. Overdetermined as her lesbianism is by the other selves that produce Judith Butler, it must, nevertheless, participate in a communal "I" to exist at all. "The fundamentally socio-political" frames the necessary interaction between identities and privileges—racial, communal, and institutional among others—that contrive the conditions for the emergence of queer theory. Identified as lesbian or gay, the critical intellect that scrutinizes those identities is complicit in their production.

Watney's distinction between the homosexual and the gay proposes that where the gay inevitably has to recognize his experiential and affective realities in the practice of his carnal desires, the homosexual becomes a taxonomic category for an academic enquiry that positions itself outside such necessary acknowledgment. Of course, the distinction is slippery and the gay overlaps with the homosexual in its valences, especially as gay identity bleeds into queer theory, but Watney's labels prove useful in revealing the dimensions of a gayness that is inextricable from its perverse pleasures. The distinction italicizes a gayness that is always already in excess of its contexts in its celebration of "homosexual desire in all its variant forms," in the specific moments of the body's sexuality. The homosexual may be depicted through academic histories but the gay escapes their analyses. Fundamentally sociopolitical as it is, gayness is a celebration of an identity that through the very contingency of its manifestations questions the authority of the subject that deconstructs it; it refuses to play "other" in epistemic games of history and anthropology. Watney's sketch plays into Butler's delineation of a utopian sexuality whose excess disrupts its co-optation into foundationalist logic, but for Watney, in contrast to Butler, the excess of gay identity performs its sexuality through its *unavoidable exclusions.*

The paradoxes constitutive of acts of will/naming that construct identity, such as Watney's, modify Butler's call, useful as it is, for a politicized theory of performative identity. The performative not only acknowledges our inescapable collusions in systems of discursive

power that produce us as subjects, but italicizes the affective and experiential realities that destabilize the objectivities of history and context. In the genealogy of theoretical reflections on the performative, J.
L. Austin's influential speculations argued that performative speech
acts, in contrast to the constative, initiate a new reality through their
very utterance. Austin used the notorious example of the act of marriage when the words "I do" instate a wedded reality or social contract. Of course, for such acts to be effective, the social contexts in
which they are spoken, as he recognized, must legitimate their performance. In a valuable rethinking of Austin's performative, however,
Derrida emphasizes that speech acts, both constative and performative, are infinitely iterable, and as a result their contexts can never be
taken for granted nor depended upon. In Derrida's negotiations, the
performative act positions itself as a discursive text whose meanings
can never be fixed for posterity ("Signature"). As such, even the act of
marriage is not a contract that has remained stable through history;
the "I do" spoken today initiates a different reality from marriages in
other centuries, different cultures, or even from one wedded couple to
the other. Nevertheless, iterable and unstable as its "meaning" is, the
performative speech act reshapes the sociohistorical contexts that
usher it into being. Even the act of marriage, for example, authorizes
a new tax status for the wedded and legitimated couple in today's
state. Butler, of course, draws upon a needed Foucauldian dimension
that extends Derrida's emphasis on the iterability of speech acts to
foreground the systemic power of discursive formations that situate
the performative as an act of both complicity and resistance.

Implicated in the micropolitics of power in a capitalist democracy,
the speech act that initiates wedded reality wields, without question,
the vested authority of both state and church. As Jean-François
Lyotard underlines in his rewriting of the performative from Austin
and John Searle,

> [the performative speech act's] effect upon the referent coincides
> with its enunciation. . . . [It] is not subject to discussion or verifica-
> tion on the part of the addressee, who is immediately placed within
> the new context created by the utterance. *As for the sender, he [sic]
> must be invested with the authority to make such a statement.* (*The
> Postmodern Condition*, 9–10; emphasis mine)[5]

The authority that enables the performative to restructure reality is a
voiced authority of language; at the same time it is an authority that

is material and participates in vectors of power and repression through disciplinary formations. Paradoxically, however, the act of voicing identity colludes in disciplinary power to divert that power— wresting the authority to speak one's name cannot but use that power to define other areas of silence in turn. Movements for lesbian identity, for black lesbian identity, for Native American gay identity, for S/M lesbians, for third world women's rights, among others, invoke a spectrum of such overlapping yet conflicted speech acts indicative of the predicaments of resistance and power. Yet, the dominant discourses that impose the exclusionary boundaries propelling these names into being, ironically enough, cannot afford to recognize the margins that enforce their own dominance. Even the dominant matrix of compulsory heterosexuality, for example, continually has to maintain the parameters for straightness. In these contexts, we cannot rest assured that the proper names that assert selfhood for marginalized communities will continue to be heard. To say that we are black lesbians or colored lesbians is to assert continuously that these names exist and that they define an identity; yet, their repeated acts of self-utterance place them constantly and variously at risk in the sociopolitical contexts making their emergence possible. In the paradoxes that constitute their realities, only the reiterated performances of named selfhood through shifting contexts enable the boundaries that make their identities/subjectivities visible—much as the word *lesbian* itself became a social reality and a name for sociosexual identity.[6]

To put it another way, I suggest that the performative has its place in the gap between intention and effect or between mind and body. The performative speech act evolves from the encounter between language and body; in Shoshana Felman's evocative phrase, it becomes an act "of the speaking body" as each contaminates the other (*The Literary Speech Act*, 94).[7] Locating the performative as the body that speaks is also to write speech as of the body; in so doing we resist the slide from body to language to literacy to literature, and so, indeed, to theory, which relentlessly returns the critical intellect to pride of place. Rather, the speech act voices itself through the signifier of the obstinate body that straddles the parameters of dominant discourses, both complicit in and resistant to them. It often thereby risks mutilation, forcible coercion, and death. Particularly when gayness is metonymically conflated with AIDS and disease, to be gay is perforce to mobilize the risks of the body as signifier. Indeed, this has historically been the case for racial or even religious dissidence.

When skin color and physical traits italicize the continued threats that racial identity runs without any concomitant imperative for self-conscious positionality, the performative act of identity voices itself through the body. The visible stigma of race is endlessly produced through discourses that effect the boundaries for white culture. The marked, raced body is repeatedly discovered and re-enacted through a matrix of imperiled whiteness for which any taint of color—black, brown, red, or yellow—signifies biological and genetic as well cultural contamination. To reflect on racial identity through sexuality, as I have done in this essay, is not to subsume the one into the other; rather, it is to highlight the color of the body as both all-too-material difference and as fantasy. Indeed, to examine race through sexual identity is to force whiteness to confront its bloodless, because invisible, body that sucks race dry.

Only when whiteness, masculinity, and education still enjoy the discursive privilege of "passing" as invisible can the intellect be sanctioned without any need to reflect on the colonizing fantasies of its physically threatening body. As I alleged early on, to enjoy the ability to "pass" is to enjoy a purchase in power; I extend this logic to assert that the ability "to pass" as invisible even while executing power is the mark of ultimate security in the world we live in. Hardly a matter of critical self-negotiation, identities that are both raced and sexed enact affectively embodied realities that are necessarily purblind to the extent of the risks they run, the exclusions they perpetrate—in order to continue to exist at all.

The essay is for Madhu Dubey whose unremitting sensitivity to the nuances of race impelled my refigurations of lesbian identity.

Notes

1. See Teresa de Lauretis, ed., *Queer Theory: Lesbian and Gay Sexualities*, special issue of *differences* 3(2) (1991); Cheryl Kader and Thomas Piontek, eds., *Essays in Lesbian and Gay Studies*, special issue of *Discourse* 15(1) (1992).

2. See Homi Bhabha and Luce Irigaray, *This Sex*; for useful commentary, see Modleski, *Feminism*, 119–20, on the hitherto untheorized connection between Irigaray and Bhabha.

3. For commentary on the ethnocentrism of Western academic practice and the difficulty of theorizing spaces for subaltern subjectivities, see Young's valuable

study that focuses on the work of postcolonial thinkers Said, Bhabha, and Spivak.

4. Bruce Robbins's argument about professionals, particularly in academic discourse, indicates that to operate within the institution is willy-nilly to forsake oppositionality, to become a professional. Yet he suggests that emerging professions attest to changes in cultural and institutional discourses. He indicates that "[the] push from below [does not] result in a diminishment of 'publicness' but rather (as new groups pushed their way into decision-making positions) a diminished white, male *share* in public discourse" ("Oppositional Professionals," 18). His corroboration, of course, rests on "the exemplary authority of feminism," which has forced its way into the academy over the past two decades. Robbins's argument, however, makes a metanarrative of feminism, which becomes "a good guy" that is incontestably exemplary—perhaps understandable from a politically conscious, white, educated male's perspective, but hardly so from the perspectives of minorities silenced and made other by professional feminists.

5. Lyotard is interested in language games and their effects and uses the performative as one among different types of language games. Derrida, however, argues that the notion of the performative has to account for the graphematic structure of language that invokes infinite contexts; the performative, in his rereading, can never be conscious of its intention, nor can any intention ever govern its effect; rather, structured into any performative speech act is its iterability, the possibility of its citation in different contexts, and, incumbent on this, its constant possibility of failure. See Derrida, "Signature"; also see Austin, *How to Do Things with Words*, 4–12. For an overview of Austin's notion of the performative in contemporary literary discourse, see Arac, *Critical Genealogies*, 106–7, 112.

6. For studies on lesbian identity, see Faderman and Krieger; for an etymology of the name *lesbian* and the ways in which it has come to connote identity, see Stimpson, *Where the Meanings Are*, 97–98.

7. Felman uses the encounter between psychoanalysis and literature to emphasize that it is the misfire of the performative that is precisely its value. She takes up Derrida's rewriting of Austin to expand on insights only hinted at by Derrida; see *The Literary Speech Act*.

Works Cited

Almaguer, Tomás. "Chicano Men: A Cartography of Homosexual Identity and Behavior." *differences* 3(2) (1991): 75–100.

Arac, Jonathan. *Critical Genealogies: Historical Situations for Postmodern Literary Studies*. New York: Columbia University Press, 1989.

Austin, J. L. *How to Do Things with Words*. 2d ed. Edited by J. O. Urmson and Marina Sbisà. Cambridge, Mass.: Harvard University Press, 1962.

Baker, Houston A., Jr. "In Dubious Battle." *New Literary History* 18(2) (1987): 363–69.

Bhabha, Homi K. "The Other Question—The Stereotype and Colonial Discourse." *Screen* 24(6) (1983): 24–31.

Butler, Judith. *Gender Trouble: Feminism and the Subversion of Identity*. New York: Routledge, 1990.

——. "Imitation and Gender Insubordination." In Diana Fuss, ed., *Inside/Out: Lesbian Theories, Gay Theories*, pp. 13–31. New York: Routledge, 1991.

Christian, Barbara. "The Race for Theory." *Cultural Critique* 6 (1987): 50–63.

Derrida, Jacques. "Signature Event Context." In *Margins of Philosophy*, pp. 307–30. Translated by Alan Bass. Chicago: University of Chicago Press, 1982.

Dhareshwar, Vivek. "The Predicament of Theory." In Martin Kreiswirth and Mark A. Cheetham, eds., *Theory between Disciplines: Authority/Vision/Politics*, pp. 231–50. Ann Arbor: University of Michigan Press, 1990.

Faderman, Lilian. *Surpassing the Love of Men: Romantic Friendship and Love Between Women from the Renaissance to the Present*. New York: Morrow, 1981.

Felman, Shoshana. *The Literary Speech Act*. Translated by Catherine Porter. Ithaca: Cornell University Press, 1983.

Ferguson, Margaret W. "Commentary: Postponing Politics." In Elizabeth Weed, ed., *Coming to Terms: Feminism, Theory, Politics*, pp. 34–46. New York: Routledge, 1989.

Foucault, Michel. "Intellectuals and Power: A Conversation between Michel Foucault and Gilles Deleuze." In Donald F. Bouchard, ed., *Language, Counter-Memory, Practice: Selected Essays and Interviews*, pp. 205–17. Ithaca: Cornell University Press, 1977.

Gates, Henry Louis, Jr. "'What's Love Got To Do with It?': Critical Theory, Integrity, and the Black Idiom." *New Literary History* 18(2) (1987): 363–69.

Gramsci, Antonio. "The Intellectuals." In *Selections from the Prison Notebooks of Antonio Gramsci*, pp. 5–23. Edited and translated by Quentin Hoare and Geoffrey Nowell Smith. New York: International Publishers, 1971.

Irigaray, Luce. *This Sex Which Is Not One*. Translated by Carolyn Porter and Carolyn Burke. Ithaca: Cornell University Press, 1977.

Joyce, Joyce Ann. "The Black Canon: Reconstructing Black American Literary Criticism." *New Literary History* 18(2) (1987): 335–44.

——. "'Who the Cap Fit': Unconsciousness and Unconscionableness in the Criticism of Houston A. Baker, Jr., and Henry Louis Gates, Jr." *New Literary History* 18(2) (1987): 371–84.

Krieger, Susan. "Lesbian Identity and Community: Recent Social Science Literature." In Estelle B. Freedman et al., eds., *The Lesbian Issue: Essays from SIGNS*, pp. 223–40. Chicago: University of Chicago Press, 1985.

Lyotard, Jean-François. *The Postmodern Condition: A Report on Knowledge*. Translated by Geoff Bennington and Brian Massumi. Minneapolis: University of Minnesota Press, 1984.

Modleski, Tania. *Feminism without Women: Culture and Criticism in a "Postfeminist Age."* New York: Routledge, 1991.

Omi, Michael, and Howard Winant. *Racial Formation in the United States: From the 1960s to the 1980s*. New York: Routledge, 1986.

Rich, Adrienne. "Teaching Language in Open Admissions." In *On Lies, Secrets, and Silence: Selected Prose, 1966–1978*, pp. 51–68. New York: Norton, 1979.

Robbins, Bruce. "Oppositional Professionals: Theory and the Narratives of Professionalization." In *Consequences of Theory: Selected Papers from the English Institute, 1987–88*. New Series, no. 14, pp. 1–21. Baltimore: Johns Hopkins University Press, 1991.

Said, Edward W. *Orientalism*. New York: Pantheon, 1978.

Searle, John R. *Speech Acts: An Essay in the Philosophy of Language*. Cambridge: Cambridge University Press, 1969.

Sedgwick, Eve Kosofsky. *Epistemology of the Closet*. Berkeley: University of California Press, 1990.

Spivak, Gayatri Chakravorty. "In a Word: *Interview*." *differences* 1 (1989): 124–55.

Stimpson, Catherine. *Where the Meanings Are: Feminism and Cultural Spaces*. New York: Routledge, 1989.

Watney, Simon. *Policing Desire: Pornography, AIDS, and the Media*. 2d ed. Minneapolis: University of Minnesota Press, 1989.

Young, Robert. *White Mythologies: Writing History and the West*. London: Routledge, 1990.

3   Lesbians and Lyotard: Legitimation and the Politics of the Name

Judith Roof

When I was invited to submit an essay to this collection, my response was to disagree with the collection's premise. I am not only critical of the idea of any essential link between ways of life or identities defined by sexual orientation and a set of diverging philosophies about the condition of knowledge, consumer culture, and aesthetic practices but am also suspicious of any superficial stylistic connection that pretends that the alliance is deeper. When I responded that I disagreed with the idea of the lesbian as constituting anything in and of itself, the editor replied that such a statement was itself postmodern. But, of course, I didn't know whether it was postmodern because it was a position taken by a lesbian, a view held by someone in the nineties, or whether the objection was not necessarily postmodern at all but instead grounded in a more psychoanalytically based approach to identity and sexuality.

Because somehow the link is in the air (as postmodernism in a ghostly and insubstantial form is currently ubiquitous), it is useful to consider what drives the connection between lesbian and postmodern and what is gained and lost therefrom. I suspect, and will argue, that the name postmodern provides a legitimating metanarrative for a lesbian identity politics. Joining the lesbian and the postmodern positions—the lesbian in the desirable place of flux, challenge, and apparent radicality—by augmenting a sexual and/or political category with characteristics of the postmodern's own cultural critique is an essentially conservative ploy. At the same time such a connection borrows the postmodern's own legitimating metanarrative of contemporary "correctness" both to authorize and to empower a lesbian epistemology. And at the heart of the association is a continued insistence on identity, which, despite its postmodern inflection, still organizes lesbian critical practice.

Guilt by Association

The emergence of activist gay and lesbian groups and the naming of the postmodern occur at about the same time. Del Martin, Phyllis Lyon, and others founded the Daughters of Bilitis in the autumn of 1955, a year after Arnold Toynbee first used the term *postmodern*. The DOB began as a social alternative to exploitative gay bars and was conceived as a "*safe* place" with an encoded name. Its members soon embarked on the more public endeavors of education and the "fight for understanding of the homophile minority."[1] A participant in the postwar shift toward a recognition of American society's non-homogeneous elements, the DOB formed on the heels of the primarily male Mattachine Society that promoted the idea of homosexuals as a distinct minority. The foundation of such groups signaled the advent of a visibly eccentric plurality in America; their new visibility was as much a symptom of a shift in the social mindset as the reactionary House Committee on Un-American Activities whose paranoia was the resistant other side to the sense that "something else" was indeed there.

Conveying the impression of a movement toward a lack of consensus and the recognition of parts that do not fit, the term *postmodern* also organized within its rubric what otherwise seemed to have no center; it became the locus of that which is not quite the same as the modern or anything else. Affecting the "status of knowledge," as Jean-François Lyotard suggests in *The Postmodern Condition*, the postmodern condition involves the rejection of legitimating metanarratives that form the basis for deciding what is true. The loss of such metanarratives and the concomitant skepticism about the possibility of a totalizing vision results in the multiplication of truths and categories. Understandings of the postmodern are widely diverse, ranging from Ihab Hassan's outline of a divergent literary aesthetic to Jean Baudrillard's analysis of the disjunction of image and referent to Fredric Jameson's analysis of the impact of late capitalism to John McGowan's idea of the postmodern as "a distinct shift in the way that humanistic intellectuals . . . view the relation of their cultural work to society at large."[2] The act of naming the postmodern identifies and defines these diverse truths, aesthetic practices, and conditions of knowledge, linking them to theories of economic, social, or epistemological causation.

Emerging from the same historical conditions, representing the divergent and the unrepresentable (or that which attempts to represent it), the lesbian and the postmodern appear to be analogous, if not related phenomena. Their connection is further nourished by the haunting similarity of at least some of their cultural configurations.[3] By the mid-eighties some critics (and not usually the same some) see the lesbian and the postmodern as categories that challenge centered logic and identity, the lesbian confronting heterosexuality and gender, the postmodern questioning subjectivity, knowledge, and truth. But this perception of shared attributes is mainly retrospective, the product of an analogical historicism; only the organizing aegis of a poststructuralist mindset allows a vision of the similarity of the two loci of apparent aberration. Different phenomena brought together in the suggestion of a shared context, the lesbian and the postmodern are less an equation than a very contemporary comparison generated finally not by any postmodern intellectual practice but rather by a very traditional drive for identity, certainty, and legitimation.

What's in a Name?

"Daughters of Bilitis" was a strategically encoded name; it rendered a subcultural presence imitatively official by evoking the idea of a female "fraternal" society keyed into a cryptic reference to Pierre Louys's lesbian work *Bilitis*. In the fifties the purpose of a group so named was to normalize lesbian existence within a quasi-visible community. By establishing an accessible circle of real lesbians, its founders hoped that the myths of sexual pathology, maladjustment, and monstrosity would be dispelled, if not for the general public at least for other lesbians who may never have knowingly met another lesbian in their lives. The presence of such an organization and others that followed consecrated a notion of lesbian group identity and provided the locus for a struggle for recognition (Martin and Lyon, *Lesbian/Woman*). The name of the group, synonymous with lesbian, signaled that there was indeed a group to name; the act of naming reified a social sexual identity just as it resulted from the idea that people with the same sexual preference had something to gain from identifying themselves as a group.

Toynbee originally used the term *postmodern* to characterize what he saw as a "decline . . . into irrationality and relativism."[4] Designating at the beginning a less-than-positive concept of historical and cultural change, the postmodern has only in the seventies come to signify a more specifically promising literary practice understood in relation to modernism. Within the broad parameters of Toynbee's application of the term and its apparent relevance to a wide variety of cultural practices, the postmodern's critical field has been almost entirely a project focused on the definition and differentiation of this intellectual/aesthetic/cultural "shift." Because of the ambivalence that attends the reception of the postmodern, like the lesbian, the postmodern becomes the terrain for definitional anxieties—for a literary style made up of styles, for a practice, a subjectivity, an identity—that can no longer be fixed. Since its crystallization in the seventies the postmodern has proliferated in essays that define and enlarge it, which themselves become impossible to manage except under the rubric postmodern.

The fifties' movement toward a positive lesbian self-recognition and the institutionalization of an apparently radical new worldview become very different gestures in the seventies and eighties. The name *lesbian* comes out, and *lesbian* and *postmodern* become parts of critical usage in different venues, both piquing anxieties about definition, not only of the specific terms but of the spheres—feminism, gay studies and activism, or literary and cultural theory—in which they operate. In the seventies the lesbian becomes synecdochal of the category feminist within the popular imagination as well as in Adrienne Rich's theorizing of a lesbian "continuum" which labels as *lesbian* a wide variety of women-centered relationships. In the early eighties Monique Wittig questions the epistemological gender bases for our understanding of sexual categories, claiming that because women are understood as women only within a heterosexual matrix, the "subject lesbian is *not* a woman" ("One Is Not Born a Woman," 53). Bonnie Zimmerman points to a critical obsession with lesbian definition in her pioneering essay "What Has Never Been." But even within the lesbian's apparent challenges to heterosexuality and gender thrives an urge to establish a distinct lesbian identity, aesthetics, and critical practice, a self-affirming drive to fix a lesbian essence. At the same time, the postmodern becomes a stylish moniker signaling critical currency and often standing opaquely for an undifferentiated set of contradictory and very "modernist" traits.

And yet all is not just a name. Instead, the terms *lesbian* and *postmodern* harness a series of traits that would otherwise disallow any naming at all within philosophical binaries as they have been utilized. Both embody a paradoxical containment of the uncontainable, preserving a status quo while pinpointing what might challenge it. The nominal gestures of containment, however, function differently in the cases of the lesbian and the postmodern. The lesbian's configuration of unrepresentability is a product of a heterosexual weltanschauung. Its exceptional quality relies entirely upon the heterosexual categories it appears to challenge. Naming and defining it makes sense of the lesbian position as both an exception to and mimetic of a heterosexual rule. To avoid the inevitable straitjacket of a heterosexual paradigm, the lesbian must be defined in such a way as to avoid gendered categories. Otherwise, the lesbian becomes simply an echo of a heterosexual structure, a pose instead of a position, the lesser version of the same instead of a difference. Because this difference would seem to endow the lesbian with a privileged perspective outside of a heterosexual system, the very definition of lesbian becomes a crucial political issue in the domain of sexual gender politics and as those politics affect knowledge.

The name *postmodern* operates in a field apparently beyond the "local" intrigues of gender and sexuality. A convenient shorthand for managing sets of dislodged eccentricities, the term *postmodern* enables a sense of a traditional oedipal historical literary movement. The sociohistorical terms of the postmodern have to do with anxieties about the loci of knowledge and power as they affect both institutions and subjectivity. Uneasiness about a postmodern loss of center is related to a possible dissolution of identity and position, but, as with the lesbian, naming the postmodern is imbricated with defining. Together, naming and defining the postmodern enact a kind of displaced power—the power of naming and fixing—both in the place of the namer and in the name of the postmodern. The postmodern thus intimates a disorder its naming orders and defers. In this sense, by delineating its differences from modernism, the definition of the postmodern effects a conservative opposition contained by a scheme of a dialectically ordered historical movement.

While distinctions in their fields of play would tend to separate them, lesbian and postmodern rejoin in the realm of gender, where the lesbian's gender challenge meets the postmodern's gender usurpation. The hidden agenda of ostensibly neuter postmodern denomination, like that of most official literary cadres, obscures its stake in gendering and heterosexual norms. Postmodern disruption of identity categories and certainty suggests a disturbance of gender certainty that supplants the gender challenge posed by the lesbian by seeming to dispense with gender altogether. But this apparent disruption of categories is represented in a pattern of stereotypically gendered binaries. Not only does the idea of the postmodern as a flexible, multiple, decentered, split-subjected condition (to extract from its proliferated definitions) look like stereotypical assignations of femininity, its dialectical representation as counter to a centered, certain, identity-enforcing modernism reiterates a familiar opposition applied to stereotypes of feminine and masculine though the familiarity of this almost hackneyed feminine/masculine opposition is rarely acknowledged by the postmodern's namers.[5] Assigning itself the stereotypically "feminine" position against a threatened, but logos-bound "masculine" modernism, the postmodern appropriates the now desirable locus of flexibility and uncertainty. Rather than dispensing with gender ideologies, the postmodern simply displaces the locus of knowledge games to the level of the name, taking flux and change as content, relegating feminist challenge to the realm of the surmounted obsolete, and appropriating the margins for the center in a manner typical of philosophies that appeal to the "human" condition. The "feminine" emotional illogic previously tacked onto feminism is displaced onto an unstylishly stolid, centered search for concrete experience and to a kind of plodding and misleading modernist captivation with a material reality upon which the feminist community and its political impetus depend. This unacknowledged gender flip works, as Nancy Fraser and Linda Nicholson point out, against feminist praxes that depend upon institutional location and identity, casting feminist political activities as primitive and anachronistically naive.

The Postmodern Lesbian Body

It is logical that if the postmodern is a general cultural trend that does indeed stand for some shift in cultural/aesthetic conditions, lesbian work would participate in that shift. But actually linking the lesbian and the postmodern in some essential relationship imparts more than the associations of history and cultural change. Despite what might be seen as an antipathy between the position of the lesbian and the post-modern—or perhaps because of a kind of competition between them over the position of the challenger to gender and logos—the associa-tion of the lesbian and the postmodern can actually benefit both. For example, to prevent the postmodern from usurping the position of marginal challenge, one simply names it lesbian. To transform the covert gender politics of the postmodern, one simply appends it to a lesbian category understood to challenge gender binaries. To avoid the frustrating denial of the bases of identity politics and experiential discourse so necessary to the mustering of feminist institutional posi-tion, one links oneself to the postmodern critique of those practices as an effective identity politic.

The coalescence of lesbian and postmodern makes perfect sense, then, if the stake of lesbian definitions is to avoid recontainment by the binary sex/gender system and if the postmodern is seen as a gener-ic category of flexibility, challenge, and decenteredness endowed with the magical power of contemporary poststructuralist understandings. Bringing the two terms together as the foundation for a definition of lesbian identity appears to extend the sex/gender challenge offered by the lesbian. Linking the lesbian and the postmodern could thus be an empowering gesture that simultaneously defines a lesbian position and identity and makes the position significant in broader issues of cultural praxis. It also manages to define the lesbian as simultaneous-ly liberating (unbound by ordered differences, i.e., binaries) and as the end result of a desirable overthrow of patriarchal (paternal) power.

While the logic of empowerment and association would seem to spark the definition of the lesbian as postmodern, the drive for lesbian self-definition—for certainty, identity, and position appended to issues of libidinal organization—also works against such an associa-tion, denying and negating the connection between the lesbian and the postmodern even as it is made. This definitional tension exists in two places: (1) between more traditional structural understandings of the lesbian as woman-centered and postmodern ideas of the lesbian as gender challenge and mutability; and (2) in the paradox of a post-modern "definition" that limits by defining as unlimited. The problem of postmodern flux versus epistemological certainty that characterizes criticism of the work of such overtly lesbian writers as Monique Wittig and Nicole Brossard reveals a critical anxiety about the relationship between the lesbian and the postmodern. In the criticism of the work of these two authors, the term *postmodern* plays a significant definitional role, but is also subject to a tremendous ambivalence and shifting that might be ironically characterized as postmodern. At least this postmodern anxiety reveals precisely how problems of definition and the postmodern cooperate in the reestablishment of identity and certainty even as they suggest there is none.

Monique Wittig's novels, *Les Guerillères* (1969), *L'Opoponax*, and *The Lesbian Body* (1973), and her *Lesbian Peoples: Material for a Dictionary* (1978, with Sande Zeig), all challenge the notion of a speaking subject organized under the aegis of heterosexuality, enact a broad intertextuality, and fragment narrative—in other words (except for the heterosexual part), they seem to embody the superficial features of postmodern literature. In her essay, "Lesbian Intertextuality," Elaine Marks attributes Wittig with revolutionary accomplishment, declaring Wittig's "J/e" "the most powerful lesbian in literature . . . the only true anti-Christ" (376) and crediting Wittig with effecting an escape from "male literary culture" (375). Namascar Shaktini, in her essay "Displacing the Phallic Subject," claims that Wittig accomplishes an "epistemological shift" away from phallocentrism through her "reorganization of metaphor around the lesbian body" (29). Marilyn Farwell believes that Wittig's textual practice "undercuts dualism" in its creation of a "lesbian narrative space," as she put it in her essay, "Toward a Definition of the Lesbian Literary Imagination" (98). Diane Griffith Crowder, equating the lesbian with a political position in "Amazons and Mothers," sees Wittig's work as having already eluded a phallocentric weltanschauung by virtue of its lesbian standpoint: "'lesbian writing' restructures the meanings of words and of literary forms because it is written from a social position in which masculinist thought has been nullified." (127).

Though none of these assessments describes Wittig's work as postmodern (a term rarely used in feminist criticism before the late eighties), all of these critics clearly position Wittig in the place of a successful challenge to identity, truth, power, and knowledge as those are constructed within a heterosexual system. Because she seems to call into question the very categories by which the lesbian can be known in the first place, Wittig's work seems to create a kind of lesbian postmodern in the field of lesbian writing characterized by a primary gender struggle. Wittig herself characterizes the relationship between language and materiality as a gender struggle, seeing language as a material means for effecting structural and ideological change. In her 1980 essay, "One Is Not Born a Woman," Wittig insists on the material basis for any challenge to gender oppression, locating the lesbian at the point of that challenge. Perceiving the oppressiveness of the gender system as a system, challenging the very epistemological basis of naturalized gender categories, Wittig pits the material experience of lesbians against the heterosexual hegemony: "Lesbian is the only concept I know of which is beyond the categories of sex (woman and man), because the designated subject (lesbian) is *not* a woman, either economically, or politically, or ideologically" (53).

Wittig's deft transition from materiality to a categorical confrontation with gender skips over one of her problematic underlying assumptions: that language can transparently represent experience and can thus directly transform ideology. By eliding the practical difficulty of getting from imagined materiality to representation, Wittig can offer the act of rejecting gender as a way of surmounting it. This utopian gap in Wittig's otherwise perceptive critique of the ideology of gender exposes her very traditional reliance on the originary existence of a subject outside of ideology. Wittig assumes a "pre-social ontology of unified and equal persons," as Judith Butler points out in *Gender Trouble* (115). Wittig's notions of gender and sexuality rely upon what Butler calls "the systemic integrity" of both heterosexuality and homosexuality, with homosexuality "conceived as radically unconditioned by heterosexual norms" (121).

Though Wittig's writing *looks* postmodern (it would fit nicely into Hassan's list of postmodern traits), its covert reliance upon the very categories it rejects, its appeal to a preexistent nongendered, pure lesbian identity, and its uncritical belief in the power of language are, as Butler suggests, "a modernist" practice. The figure of the lesbian in Wittig's oeuvre is anything but postmodern, functioning as it does to moor and stabilize challenges to gender that result in the celebration of a lesbian persona liberated from the hegemony of heterosexuality— a persona fixed in her fluid subjectivity, interpenetration, and capacity to wield the language of desire and ferocity. Even Penelope Engelbrecht, the most fervent advocate of the lesbian *as* postmodern finally must decide that Wittig is not really completely postmodern, since, as Engelbrecht observes in "'Lifting Belly Is a Language,' " Wittig's "concentration on essence limits her postmodern strategy" (96).

The logic by which Engelbrecht concludes that Wittig fails in her postmodernity itself reiterates the tension between notions of identity and the rejection thereof that characterizes the complex relationship between the category lesbian and ideas of the postmodern. Following Wittig's assertion that material lesbianism can provide a platform for transforming oppressive gender systems, Engelbrecht reiterates Wittig's assumptions about the relationship of language to experience on the one hand and to power on the other. Seeing the postmodern as a way to "subvert the linguistic and literary conventions of phallogocentrism" (94), Engelbrecht hypothesizes that this postmodernism might also serve as a more accurate vehicle for the representation of a lesbian materiality, because the postmodern, like the lesbian, offers "an alternative literary mode, an alteration of patriarchal literary conventions" (93). Understanding Wittig's fictions as displacing the male subject with a specifically lesbian one (as does Shaktini), Engelbrecht characterizes Wittig's work as bringing "the real body violently to life in the words of the book" (95). Engelbrecht imagines that this Frankensteinian inscription of the lesbian body somehow bypasses the problems of language and representation as well as the restraints of binary structure. But despite the liberationist ethic of Wittig's alchemy, Engelbrecht has trouble with Wittig's split pronoun "J/e," describing it as postmodern while also criticizing its literal split of the lesbian subject and concluding that Wittig's linguistic violence is a "characteristically phallic intention antithetical to lesbian[ism]" (96).

While Wittig sees the material existence of the lesbian as a category whose very presence undermines the truth of gender and the heterosexuality upon which it depends, Engelbrecht materializes this lesbian challenge, defining lesbian identity (she calls it "a metaphysic" or "truth") by literalizing literary metaphors: "It [a lesbian metaphysic] must be active, not static; must be relational, not absolute, not least because lesbian[ism] itself is something consisting of activity, constituted by dynamic social relationships of women, rather than a state of being or mere thought" (86). At the core of Engelbrecht's evocation of the postmodern is an identity politics playing in a scenario where a preexisting material set of lesbian qualities seeks an aesthetics appropriate to it and finds the postmodern. Coagulating identity, sexuality, and aesthetics in this heartily certain manner is itself anything but postmodern or even anything like the lesbian aesthetic Engelbrecht outlines. Repeating the problem of a belief in a preexisting, radically pure lesbian subject and an even more severe case of essentialism than she attributes to Wittig, Engelbrecht, like Wittig, bares the underlying modernist urge toward lesbian identity and essence hiding within the postmodernist lesbian impetus.

Thoroughly Postmodern Lesbians

Wittig's postmodern breakdown enables Engelbrecht to make way for what she considers to be the truly postmodern lesbian literary texts: those of Nicole Brossard and Gloria Anzaldúa. The privileged sites of the intersection of the lesbian and the postmodern, both Brossard, a Québecoise, and Anzaldúa, a Chicana, write mixed-genre, consciously lesbian texts. With these writers, the stake in aligning the lesbian and the postmodern becomes clearer. Mere intertextuality and linguistic games do not suffice; rather, radical difference and multiple media are necessary to convey the specifically lesbian desire central to a postmodern practice seen as a "true" lesbian practice. That Engelbrecht replaces her earlier focus on naming, language, and subjectivity with lesbian desire suggests a promising shift from content and structure to a process that operates in an economy of radical ethnic and racial differences.

Engelbrecht defines Brossard's desire as a "bi-directionality" (103), "the search for that which one finds always already gone, but gone *somewhere*—perhaps to the Other/self" (102). This mutual mutable desiring *is* writing and reading, an identity between text and psyche that would seem to embody the kind of self-conscious performative strategies often attributed to postmodern texts. But even if Brossard's writings exemplify this desiring process and even if her *Aerial Letter* proposes a radical lesbian textual practice, Engelbrecht's understanding of it as postmodern is based on a rigidly conservative notion of lesbian identity operating in a very circumscribed field of lesbian desire locked into material experience—into a lesbian common knowledge. Engelbrecht interprets Brossard's transparent link between sexuality and textuality as a literal lesbian erotic experience, finding in Brossard's work the postmodern allegory of lesbian materiality and language she seeks: " 'reading' [on the body of the woman] is possible only for those who comprehend and speak the same language, in this case the language of lesbian[ism], which is enabled by the (erotic) event of mutual Desire" (102). Engelbrecht thus delimits the desire enacted by the text, binding it to a specific lesbian experience (here opposed to a process that might open up desire) fixed in a knot of encoded identity.

That this identity-linked desire as a measure of a common definitive experience constitutes Engelbrecht's version of a lesbian postmodern becomes clear in her dismissal of Gloria Anzaldúa's attempt to enlarge issues of desire and sexuality into a broader, more diverse, cultural context. Engelbrecht sees Gloria Anzaldúa's *Borderland: La Frontera* as stylistically postmodern because its mixture of languages and genres—its outline of a metaphorical borderland—provides another version of Brossard's desire for Other/self. But after disqualifying Anzaldúa from the truly lesbian (and postmodern) on the ground that her borderland consists of too many conflicting "binaries" (105), Engelbrecht finally salvages a lesbian postmodern feature in Anzaldúa's figure of Coatlicue as the "sign for the intertext of 'I' and 'She' " (105). This recognizable figure of a common lesbian desire survives Engelbrecht's critique of style, binary structure, and social commentary, and it endures as the nexus of a lesbian postmodern, represented again by a name.

Lesbian desire transformed into the knowledge of an identity is the real locus for the lesbian postmodern. This makes sense if we understand Engelbrecht's project as an attempt to construct a legitimating metanarrative for lesbian identity in the face of a potential loss of gender categories and the threat of uncontrollably multiplied differences. And this works only if we accept Lyotard's analysis of the postmodern as a loss of the metanarratives legitimizing knowledge. Engelbrecht's transitive connection of certain traits she defines as postmodern to a lesbian epistemology and textual practice defines lesbian as postmodern in a very nonpostmodern fix on identity. Paradoxically situating the postmodern *as* identity begins the circular narrative by which the lesbian gains the politically desirable traits of the postmodern—fluidity, interpenetrability, mutability—that seem to evade knowledge and fixation, while positing them as the certain knowledge of lesbian material existence. That these same traits are seen as virtuous in the feminist praxis of the late eighties—a practice that seeks to avoid binaries, objectification, and phallogocentrism—makes their application to the lesbian both desirable and politically legitimating. Why then doesn't Engelbrecht simply claim the lesbian as embodying the saving graces of feminist philosophical progress? Naturalizing lesbian traits through an appeal to lesbian materiality and proving the truth of that naturalization through the discovery of a tradition of lesbian postmodern aesthetics that extends from Stein to Brossard claims the postmodern for the lesbian and extends the importance of lesbian identity beyond the realm of feminist politics. Arriving at the conclusion with which it began, the metanarrative of a lesbian postmodern, thriving on an experiential analogy that still assumes a natural relationship between language and experience, situates itself in the position of cultural currency, correctness, and radicality—in the appropriated "feminine" position of challenges to knowledge itself. The appeal to desire at the center of this decentered centering masks a desire for identity rather than a desire for flux or uncontrollable process; the desire of this lesbian postmodern is a desire for legitimation and community in a world of disrupted categories.

Desperately Seeking Metanarratives

The irony of this version of a lesbian postmodern is that it is, despite itself, quite postmodern, but postmodern in the way theorists of the postmodern are also anxious about legitimation. For example, Lyotard's account of postmodern conditions of knowledge valorizes what he sees as a loss of the legitimating metanarratives of scientific knowledge in favor of diversity and a rejection of totality that might enable radical change through "paralogy," or the insights of an accidental illogic. But like Engelbrecht's ultimate search for identity, Lyotard's analysis of this loss of metanarrative relies upon an unrecognized legitimating metanarrative that establishes the "truth value" of no truth. If we know that we cannot know, if we distrust representation and understand that the value of knowledge has become linked to its performativity, then our knowing that we cannot know becomes the point of knowing, becomes the legitimating uncertainty about knowledge that provides us with a certainty about knowledge's uncertainty. To see paralogy as desirable—to see a lack of totality as a condition for potential change—is to inscribe uncertainty in the place of truth in the same liberating metanarratives about knowledge that see truth as human liberation. Like looking for a lesbian identity in the place of uncertainty, the assignation of uncertainty as the definition for a position or condition simply displaces certainty and identity to another place and another legitimizing metanarrative more obscured by the performative panegyric of an apparent multiplicity. Those who know their uncertainty become the liberated—the point of human truth and understanding—like the lesbian or the postmodern theorist.

Without subscribing to the truth of Lyotard's theory, we can see how the anxiety about knowledge in both the lesbian and postmodern suggest their analogy to one another, their status as products of the same uneasiness. In his analysis of knowledge, Lyotard identifies two originary versions of legitimating metanarratives. The first is a populist and democratic narrative of the relation of knowledge to freedom that casts "humanity as the hero of liberty. All peoples have a right to science"; access to knowledge makes freedom possible (31). The second, a more nationalist moralist version, legitimizes knowledge as the means to an end: the better building of "character and action," based on the totalizing ideal of a truth that founds a more just government run by better individuals (32). These legitimating metanarratives of democratic freedom ("emancipatory") and the service of an "autonomous collectivity" lose their credibility in the face of a proliferation of technologies that shift "emphasis from the ends of action to its means" (37). Unifying metanarratives of social utility give way to notions of the legitimation of knowledge through its performativity— its ability to fuse "wealth, efficiency, and truth" (45). But the legitimizing metanarrative that underwrites performativity is power, a power that is not only "mastering reality," but also "good performativity . . . effective verification and good verdicts" (47). This performativity of knowledge is self-legitimating: its ends justify its means which justify its ends. The metanarrative of performativity finally breaks down at this point of self-legitimation when the automatic relationship between means and end—the reality of reality—is brought into question. The questioning of reality results, according to Lyotard, in a science concerned with "undecidables, the limits of precise control, conflicts characterized by incomplete information, . . . producing not the known, but the unknown" (60).

Lyotard attends to the historical contingency of these metanarratives, seeing them as both products of and responses to cultural and technological change. While the period Lyotard considers spans three centuries, the question of lesbian legitimation narratives occurs only within the twentieth century, and they are raised most acutely after 1970, the period when the postmodern—and its retrospective vision of a knowledge crisis—comes to the fore. The trajectory of Lyotard's metanarratives ranges from the legitimating value of effect to that of means to the power of performativity to the paradoxical conflation of knowledge and power conferred by knowing the dislocation of knowledge, a path paralleled by a similar series of metanarratives that legitimize lesbians as a subgroup. I would suggest that the prevailing concern of the last twenty years with legitimating lesbian metanarratives has to do precisely with the crisis of knowledge addressed by Lyotard but approaches it from a slightly different perspective. Lacking legitimation, lesbian theorists attempt to establish both history and transcendence by constructing metanarratives of self-definition. Potential political power is achieved through knowledge of identity, through an appeal to a lesbian "real," while Lyotard's postmodern discards certainty for a knowledge of the unknown. The way that the lesbian and the postmodern come together signals a kind of closure for both series of metanarratives—an end in triumphant dis-closure.

Lesbian metanarratives, entwined with issues of knowledge, simultaneously legitimate the lesbian and dislocate gender. They must surmount problems of gender and heterosexuality, since the problem with defining the lesbian, as is evident in the work of Wittig, is that our understanding of the position of the lesbian is somehow dependent upon both. As long as this is the case, the lesbian is illegitimate— a variant rather than an authorized entity. Parallel to Lyotard's two versions of the legitimating effects of social utility, the lesbian metanarrative of the foremother tradition recounts the liberating narrative of the relationship between lesbian self-identification and a positive, self-sustaining tradition. Founding itself in the imaginary of the great goddess, this foremother narrative produces a lesbian history traced through figures of women who create a separate and separable lesbian culture. *Knowing* this history makes possible the legitimation of lesbian identity that leads to liberation; the *fact* of this history legitimizes a specifically lesbian identity by producing a literal parallel to patriarchal descent that affords a documentary nonpatriarchal reality. Built on a list of names laboriously recovered like a lost Atlantis, this metanarrative of tradition and continuity arrives with modernism and Natalie Barney and continues in the work of Jeannette Foster, Judy Chicago, and Elaine Marks.

Lyotard's shift from the effects of knowledge to its means and performativity appears in the lesbian trajectory in Wittig's questioning of the very terms by which histories and categories are constructed. Wittig relies upon a metanarrative of triumphant gender disruption where the means—language and consciousness—authorize their lesbian source. Speaking as a lesbian means challenging gender categories, which means speaking as a lesbian. Reflecting the self-legitimation of performativity, Wittig's textual practice relies upon a naturalized relation between language and status in which lesbian status is authorized by self-evident shifts in language and structure and vice versa that indicate the efficient truth value of lesbian knowledge. Lesbian knowledge places the lesbian outside and beyond the gender limitations of others' knowledge: the lesbian knows gender because she is beyond it. This metanarrative sustains what appears to be postmodernity in its style and apparent transgression of gender and personal boundaries, but rather than refusing gender categories, it tends to reify them and its graphic violence seems to reiterate them.

Lyotard's final apparent dissolution of legitimating metanarratives comes with the simultaneous recognition of the unreliability of reality and the power inherent in knowing that one doesn't know. The lesbian metanarrative linking the lesbian to the postmodern through an essential identity reflects this step in a very odd way. Engelbrecht relies heavily upon what she calls "lesbian material existence," a kind of appeal to a reality situated as *the* authorizing factor of a lesbian postmodern. But Engelbrecht literally appends lesbian material reality to the postmodern power of knowing that a dispersed and paradoxical knowledge is the final condition of knowledge. In this way, the lesbian is legitimated both through a knowledge of identity and by being located in the most "legitimate" place in culture: the place of knowing, the place of naming, the place of controlling any unknowing. Both the lesbian and the postmodern rely upon a metanarrative of empowerment that underlies the apparent denial of legitimation and power. But the lesbian metanarrative also brings together the epistemological certainties of real experience with the uncertainties of discredited knowing, symptomatically revealing the postmodern (and lesbian) stake not in knowledge, but in legitimating the position from which one sees it.

Understanding both lesbian identity and the postmodern status of knowledge in terms of these legitimating metanarratives reveals not a liberation but a kind of conservatism focused on power and certainty, which is the response to an anxiety about legitimation that affects both. Though Lyotard analyzes the legitimating metanarratives of scientific knowledge and the legitimating metanarrative of the lesbian refers to lesbian identity as a kind of knowledge both of self and of the heterosexual, gendered nature of Western culture, the problem of power as expressed in legitimating metanarratives is a problem provoked by the very fear of a loss of power and knowledge. If knowledge has granted power and if knowledge is lost, then knowing about that loss inscribes a new kind of power as it does in Lyotard's evocation of paralogy and Engelbrecht's association of the lesbian with flexibility and mutuality. This shift in an understanding of knowledge responds directly to tensions created by diversities, by the dissolution and multiplication of categories. If, for example, gender is brought into question or its possibilities multiplied, where does the lesbian fit? How can a specifically lesbian material reality survive the onslaught of many other realities that might stake an equal claim to gender challenge, mutuality, flexibility, etc.? Linking a lesbian identity to the postmodern offers a tentative defense against the dissolution of identity, against the potential irrelevance of the category, against a loss of specificity and an authorization to speak in a world of multiplied gender and sexual variations.

Not Playing Postmodern

Without evoking the name postmodern and the authorizing power it conveys, a praxis linked to several possible ideas of the lesbian—the potentially affirmative disturbances of the binary and oppositional categories by which identity itself is constituted, the substitution of a desiring process for knowing—might avoid and dissolve the identity crisis that underlies formulations of a lesbian postmodern. For example, Brossard's enactments of a lesbian-linked theory/writing shaped around a desiring process rather than a definition of desire may make possible a relinquishment of the urge to power that characterizes naming gestures, not in opposition to or in a linear sequence with the postmodern, but playing elsewhere with different rules that decenter naming by drawing attention to it, proliferating, estranging, and deprivileging it. In *Surfaces of Sense*, Brossard plays with what looks like a tradition of lesbian writers that might appear to authorize Brossard's own practice. Speaking to and about "Gertrude, Adrienne, and Yolande," Brossard alludes to the foremother tradition but undoes its legitimating power by using the names as indefinite referents, as dislocated points in a net of desire that constitutes writing itself. Displaced from any authorizing function, the names serve to remind rather than license or explain; Brossard's repetition of them both enlarges the temporal and spatial range of her writing and reduces naming to only one among a number of other strategies that play the desire for desire.

Perhaps even Brossard's practice is just another version of a performative self-legitimation that corrects for the absence of any locus of reality. Perhaps it is the idea of legitimation behind all of this, what Alice Jardine identifies as a paternal function, that makes it difficult to escape legitimizing processes. Perhaps it is the attraction of power and mastery that makes it difficult to relinquish the powers of naming without reiterating them elsewhere. Maybe one clue lies in seeing legitimation for what it is—not power or authorization, but anxiety and emptiness—and this can happen not through its willed absence or denial but only through its irrelevance. Wishing does not make it so, but maybe freeing a politics of desire can, a desire with many names and none, that plays upon and acknowledges the presence of legitimating metanarratives as one dynamic of desire, that relinquishes lesbian as an identity in favor of identities, places, a process of roving and coming, textually and otherwise.

Perhaps there is value in the sustained tension of an undefined and unlocated term, not as an indeterminacy that reiterates a cultural paradigm, but as one that plays within and beyond such paradigms—there and not there, not working as a name but as a suggestion. But is relinquishing the name like permitting the collapse of "the distinction between speaker and interlocutor," which threatens, as Jane Gallop suggests, "the risk of death—loss of self, loss of identity" (*The Daughter's Seduction*, 115)? Or might it not inaugurate a different dynamic that allows for interplay and layering so that the necessity of unified identity gives way to a more generous practice not marked by loss but by exchange? "What is it, after all," Elizabeth Meese asks, "to be a (lesbian) without the word, without writing *l-e-s-b-i-a-n* or something like it? It seems like nothing" ("Theorizing Lesbian," 79). And maybe everything—everything that shifting the locus of the name might mean.

Notes

1. John D'Emilio, *Sexual Politics, Sexual Communities: The Making of a Homosexual Minority in the United States, 1940–1970*, 103.

2. John McGowan, *Postmodernism and Its Critics*, 1.

3. For a general argument about cultural configurations of lesbian sexuality, see Roof, *A Lure of Knowledge*.

4. Steven Connor, *Postmodernist Culture: An Introduction to Theories of the Contemporary*, 65.

5. In *Gynesis*, Alice Jardine notes the role of woman within certain discussions about the postmodern, including that of Jean Baudrillard in *Seduction*, whom she paraphrases as saying, "The only recognition that can help us return to this ritual state . . . is that of 'femininity as the principle of uncertainty'—femininity as *seduction*" (67).

Works Cited

Anzaldúa, Gloria. *Borderlands/La Frontera: The New Mestiza*. San Francisco: Spinsters/ Aunt Lute, 1987.

Baudrillard, Jean. *Simulations*. Translated by Paul Foss, Paul Patton, and Philip Beitchman. New York: Semiotext(e), 1983.

——. *Seduction*. Translated by Brian Singer. New York: St. Martin's, 1990.

Brossard, Nicole. *The Aerial Letter*. Translated by Marlene Wildeman. Toronto: The Women's Press, 1988.

——. *Surfaces of Sense*. Translated by Fiona Strachan. Toronto: Coach House Press, 1989.

Butler, Judith. *Gender Trouble: Feminism and the Subversion of Identity*. New York: Routledge, 1990.

Connor, Steven. *Postmodernist Culture: An Introduction to Theories of the Contemporary*. Oxford: Blackwell, 1989.

Crowder, Diane Griffith. "Amazons and Mothers? Monique Wittig, Hélène Cixous, and Theories of Women's Writing." *Contemporary Literature* 24(2) (1983): 117–44.

D'Emilio, John. *Sexual Politics, Sexual Communities: The Making of a Homosexual Minority in the United States, 1940–19707*. Chicago: University of Chicago Press, 1983.

Engelbrecht, Penelope. " 'Lifting Belly is a Language': The Postmodern Lesbian Subject." *Feminist Studies* 16(1) (Spring 1990): 85–114.

Farwell, Marilyn. "Toward Definition of the Lesbian Literary Imagination." *Signs* 14 (1988): 100–18.

Foster, Jeannette. *Sex Variant Women in Literature*. Tallahassee, Fla.: Naiad, 1985.

Fraser, Nancy, and Linda Nicholson. "Social Criticism Without Philosophy: An Encounter Between Feminism and Postmodernism." In Linda Nicholson, ed., *Feminism/Postmodernism*, pp. 19–38. New York: Routledge, 1990.

Gallop, Jane. *The Daughter's Seduction: Feminism and Psychoanalysis*. Ithaca: Cornell University Press, 1982.

Hassan, Ihab. *The Dismemberment of Orpheus: Toward a Postmodern Literature*. New York: Oxford University Press, 1971.

Jameson, Fredric. *Postmodernism; or, The Cultural Logic of Late Capitalism*. Durham, N.C.: Duke University Press, 1991.

Jardine, Alice. *Gynesis: Configurations of Woman and Modernity*. Ithaca: Cornell University Press, 1985.

Lyotard, Jean-François. *The Postmodern Condition: A Report on Knowledge*. Translated by Geoff Bennington and Brian Massumi. Minneapolis: University of Minnesota Press, 1984.

McGowan, John. *Postmodernism and Its Critics*. Ithaca: Cornell University Press.

Marks, Elaine. "Lesbian Intertextuality." In George Stambolian and Elaine Marks, eds., *Homosexualities and French Literature*, pp. 353–77. Ithaca: Cornell University Press, 1979.

Martin, Del, and Phyllis Lyon. *Lesbian/Woman*. San Francisco: Glide, 1972.

Meese, Elizabeth. "Theorizing Lesbian: Writing—A Love Letter." In Karla Jay and Joanne Glasgow, eds., *Lesbian Texts and Contexts: Radical Revisions*, pp. 70–87. New York: New York University Press, 1990.

Roof, Judith. *A Lure of Knowledge: Lesbian Sexuality and Theory*. New York: Columbia University Press, 1990.

Shaktini, Namascar. "Displacing the Phallic Subject: Wittig's Lesbian Writing." *Signs* 8(1) (Autumn 1982): 29–44.

Wittig, Monique. *l'Opoponax*. Paris: Editions de Minuit, 1964.

——. *Les Guerillères*. Translated by David Le Vay. New York: Viking, 1971.

——. "The Straight Mind." *Feminist Issues* 1(1) (1980): 103–11.

——. "One Is Not Born a Woman." *Feminist Issues* 1(3) (Winter 1981): 47–54.

——. *The Lesbian Body*. Translated by David Le Vay. Boston: Beacon Press, 1986.

Wittig, Monique, and Sande Zeig. *Lesbian Peoples: Material for a Dictionary*. New York: Avon, 1978.

Zimmerman, Bonnie. "What Has Never Been: An Overview of Lesbian Feminist Literary Criticism." In Elaine Showalter, ed., *The New Feminist Criticism: Essays on Women, Literature, Theory*, pp. 200–24. New York: Pantheon, 1985.

4   Refiguring Lesbian Desire

Elizabeth Grosz

> *I knew you'd be a good lover when I noticed you always smelt*
> *books before you read them—especially hardbacks . . . now make*
> *love to me.* Mary Fallon, *Working Hot*, 86

Experimental Thought

A great deal of work has been published in the last decade in the area
now known as lesbian and gay studies. Much of this work has been
exceptionally powerful and worthwhile in both political and intellectual terms. A whole series of issues vital not just for lesbian and gay
studies but also for understanding the structures of heterosexuality
and, indeed, for understanding the notion of subjectivity or identity in
broader terms have been engaged with, analyzed, and discussed.
Many of these key issues center around questions of the structures of
social power, of sexuality and the processes involved in the production of an identity: essentialism versus constructionism[1]; coalitionist
politics versus separatism; the alignments of lesbians with feminists
versus their alignments with gay male activists; the entwinement of
'alternative' sexual and lifestyle practices with what it is they attempt

to challenge and move beyond (for example, the current debates about the political status of lesbian s/m, of drag, and issues in what is now understood as lesbian or sexual ethics and whether these are transgressive or recuperative practices) have now been fairly thoroughly debated, if not entirely successfully resolved.[2] I do not plan to make any particular contribution to the richness and complexity of these debates. While I am impressed with the scholarship, knowledge, and political sense made by many working in this area, these issues will not be the ones that concern me here.

In the framework of this volume, I have, for once, the luxury of being able to undertake a wildly speculative paper, one that is openly experimental (in concepts, if not in style) and in which I have no guarantee that my claims will make sense, that my arguments are cogent, or that my position is "politically correct." I figured that at least once in my professional life I could—indeed, I must—take the risk of being totally wrong, of committing some heinous theoretical blunder, of going way out on a limb, instead of being very careful, covering myself from rearguard criticism, knowing in advance that at least some of my claims have popular support or general credibility. Why now? Because it seems to me that in a topic as personally important to me as refiguring and rethinking lesbian desire I need to go beyond the more typical theoretical models and paradigms used to explain and assess the social, political, sexual, and economic positions of lesbians and gay men in order to see if something different, something new, another way of seeing things, might serve to characterize lesbian desire beyond its usual models of representation.

Thus I don't really want to talk about lesbian or gay "identities," whether these are considered as unified, a priori totalities (the essentialism position) or as "fractured or dislocated multiplicities" (the so-called postmodern and/or psychoanalytic positions). I don't want to talk about lesbian psychologies, about the psychical genesis of lesbian desires, or about the meaning, signification, or representation of these desires (this already differentiates my paper from the vast bulk of material now beginning to pour out of the lesbian and gay studies industry, including my own previous forays into the terrain).[3]

In short, I don't want to discuss lesbian identity or desire in terms of a psychical depth or interiority, or in terms of a genesis, development or processes of constitution, history or etiology. I am much less interested in where lesbian desire comes from, how it emerges, and the ways in which it develops than in where it is going to, its possibilities, its open-ended future. I am interested in how to embrace this openness, to welcome unknown readings, new claims, provocative analyses—to make things happen, to move fixed positions, to transform our everyday expectations and our habitual conceptual schemas.

Nor am I here interested in notions of sexual morality, in discovering a "true" sexuality or an "ideologically sound one." I am not interested in judging the sexual practices, fantasies, and desires of others—but I am interested in what kinds of terms may be appropriate for understanding my own. Thus I am not concerned with adjudicating what is transgressive or recuperative or to what extent drag, sexual role playing, butch-femme relations, etc., etc., participate in phallocentrism or heterosexism or serve to undermine them. *All* sexual practices, in any case, are made possible and function within the constraints of heterosexism and phallocentrism, but this indeed is the condition of any effective transgression of them: we must no longer understand them as megalithic systems that function in immutability and perfection. Rather, they are contradictory systems, fraught with complexities, ambiguities, and vulnerabilities that can and should be used to strategically discern significant sites of contestation. My project is thus not to analyze or explain lesbian desire but rather to experiment with an idea, or a series of them, to see how far they can go, what they enable us to rethink, to recontextualize, to see in a different way—a kind of excessive analysis, one that goes beyond a well-charted terrain with Nietzschean joy.

I want to explore here two issues that I believe are deeply interrelated: can feminist theory sustain its ability to think innovatively and experimentally, playing with views, positions, models, frameworks—even frameworks that may be treated with caution or suspicion—in order to see how far they take us in rethinking what has been taken for the truth or orthodoxy (even if it is now feminists who, at least in some cases, supply and validate these truths or orthodoxies), in redoing the social and cultural order? And can feminist theory find an adequate, i.e., an experimental or hitherto unworked-out, way of (re)thinking lesbianism and lesbian desire? In short, can feminist theory move beyond the constraints imposed by psychoanalysis, by theories of representation and signification, and by notions of the functioning of power relations—all of which implicitly presume the notion of a masculine or sexually neutral (which also means masculine) subject and the ontology of lack and depth? Can feminist theory eschew the notion of depth? Can we think desire beyond the logic of lack and acquisition, a logic that has rendered women the repositories, the passive receptacles of men's needs, anxieties, and desires? Can desire be refigured in terms of surfaces and surface effects?

The Ontology of Lack

My problem is how to conceive of desire, particularly, how to think desire as a "proper" province of women. The most acute way in which this question can be formulated is to ask the question: How to conceive lesbian desire given that lesbian desire is the preeminent and most unambiguous exemplar of *women's* desires, women's desire(s) for other women? In what terms is desire to be understood so that it can be attributed to and conceived of in terms of women? This is not really an idle or perverse question though it may seem so at first sight. I am asking how it is that a notion like desire, which has been almost exclusively understood in male (and commonly heterocentric) terms, can be transformed so that it is capable of accommodating the very category on whose exclusion it has previously been based. Desire has up to now functioned only through the surreptitious exclusion of women (and hence lesbians). How can this concept be dramatically stretched to include as subject what it has previously designated only by the position of object, to make what is considered passivity into an activity?

There are, in my understanding, three irresolvable problems associated with the notions of desire we have generally inherited in the West. These three problems signal that desire must be thoroughly overhauled if it is to be capable of accommodating women's desires and those desires—whatever they might be—that specify and distinguish lesbianism. These I can indicate only briefly although they clearly warrant a much more thorough investigation.

In the first place, the concept of desire has had an illustrious history beginning with the writings of Plato, especially in *The Symposium*, where Plato explains that desire is a lack in man's being, an imperfection or flaw in human existence. For him, desire is both a shortcoming and a vindication of human endeavor. Desire is considered a yearning for access to the good and the beautiful, which man lacks. It is thus simultaneously the emblem of atrophy and of progress toward the Idea. Born of *penia* (poverty) and *poros* (wealth), of inadequacy and excess together, this Platonic understanding of desire remains the dominant one within our received history of thought, even today. This trajectory for thinking desire reaches a major, modern turning point in Hegel's understanding of desire in *The Phenomenology of Spirit*, where Hegel conceives of desire as a unique lack that, unlike other lacks, can function only if it remains unfilled. It is therefore a lack with a peculiar object all its own—its object is always another desire. The only object desire can desire is an object that will not fill the lack or provide complete satisfaction. To provide desire with its object is to annihilate it. Desire desires to be desired. Thus, for Hegel, the only object that both satisfies desire yet perpetuates it is not an object but another desire. The desire of the other is thus the only appropriate object of desire.

Freud himself and the psychoanalytic theory following him are the heirs to this tradition of conceiving of desire in negative terms, in terms of an absence, and it is largely through psychoanalytic theory— in which, for example, Lacan reads Freud quite explicitly in terms of Hegel's understanding of desire—that this conception of desire continues to be the dominant one in feminist, lesbian, and gay studies. Freud modifies the Platonic understanding of desire while nonetheless remaining faithful to its terms: the lack constitutive of desire is not an inherent feature of the subject (as Hegel assumed) but is now a function of (social) reality. Desire is the movement of substitution that creates a series of equivalent objects to fill a primordial lack. In seeking to replace an (impossible) plenitude, a lost completion originating (at least in fantasy) in the early mother/child dyad, desire will create a realm of objects that can be substituted for the primal (lost, forbidden) object. Desire's endless chain is an effect of an oedipalizing process that requires that the child relinquishes its incestual attachments through creating an endless network of replacements, substitutes, and representations of the perpetually absent object.

Now this notion of desire as an absence, lack, or hole, an abyss seeking to be engulfed, stuffed to satisfaction, is not only uniquely useful in capitalist models of acquisition, propriety, and ownership (seeing the object of desire on the model of the consumable commodity), but it also inherently sexualizes desire, coding it in terms of the prevailing characteristics attributed to the masculine/feminine opposition, presence and absence. Desire, like female sexuality itself, is insatiable, boundless, relentless, a gaping hole that cannot be filled or can only be temporarily filled; it suffers an inherent dependence on its object(s), a fundamental incompletion without them. I would suggest that the metaphorics of desire on such models[4] are in fact coded as a sexual polarization. Where desire is given a negative status, it is hardly surprising that it becomes or is coded in terms similar to the ones attributed to femininity. Moreover, it is precisely such a model, where desire lacks, yearns, seeks, without ever being capable of finding itself and its equilibrium, that enables the two sexes to be understood as (biological, sexual, social and psychical) complements of each other— each is presumed to complete, to fill up, the lack of the other. The model of completion provided here corresponds to or is congruent with the logic regulating the goal posited by Aristophanes's hermaphrodite. Such a model, in other words, performs an act of violence: for any consideration of the autonomy of the two sexes, particularly the autonomy of women is rendered impossible within a model of complementarity. It feminizes, heterosexualizes, and binarizes desire at an ontological and epistemological level. The activity of this model of complementarity is merely a reaction to its perceived shortcomings, its own failure to sustain itself.

If this is the primary model of desire we in the West have inherited over millennia, this problem seems to me to be complicit with a second problem, a problem that can, this time, be more narrowly circumscribed and represented by a single corpus of writing. This second problem I see with the notion of desire as it is commonly understood can be most readily articulated with reference to a psychoanalytic account of desire, which in this context can be used as a shorthand version for—indeed, as a symptom of—a broader cultural and intellectual tradition. In such models—the most notable certainly being Freud's—desire is, as he describes it, inherently masculine. There is only male or rather masculine libido; there is only desire as an activity (activity being, for Freud, correlated with masculinity); in this case, the notion of female desire is oxymoronic.

Freud does get around this complication in a variety of ingenious ways: for him the so-called normal or heterosexual response on the part of woman is to give up the (masculine, phallic, anaclitic) desire to love and to substitute for it the passive aim of being loved and desired. This constitutes women's adult, secondary version of their primary narcissism;[5] by contrast, the woman suffering from the "masculinity complex" retains an active relation to desire at the cost of abandoning any self-representation as feminine or castrated. In exchange for the activity and phallic status she refuses to renounce—and while retaining the structure of virile desire—she abandons femininity. When she loves and desires, she does so not as a woman but as a man.

This understanding of female "inversion" (both literally and metaphorically) permeates the two case studies of female homosexuality Freud undertook—his study of Dora (1905) (which he recognized too late as a study of *homosexual* desire, that is, well after Dora had left him) and the study of the young female homosexual (1920), in which he can only represent the young woman's love relations to "her lady" on the model of the chivalrous male lover. In short, insofar as the woman occupies the feminine position, she can only take the place of the object of desire and never that of the subject of desire; insofar as she takes the position of the subject of desire, the subject who desires, she must renounce any position as feminine.[6] The idea of feminine desire or even female desire is contradictory. It is thus rather surprising, given the inherent impossibility of psychoanalysis to adequately provide the terms by which an analysis of women and of female desire is possible, that it nevertheless provides the basis for a disproportionately large number of texts within the field of lesbian and gay studies.

The third problem with this dominant notion of desire is of course bound up with the other two. It could be described as the implicit "hommo-sexuality"[7] of desire. Here the claim is not, as I have just argued, that desire is inherently masculine insofar as it is defined as necessarily active; in addition to its phallocentrism there is a claim about the circuits of exchange in which desire functions. Irigaray argues that what psychoanalysis articulates as the imposition of oedipalization is in fact the (re)production of a circuit of symbolic exchange in which women function only as objects, commodities, or goods. In this circuit women, as it were, serve as the excuse, the intermediary, the linkage point between one man and another. As evidence, she cites the fascination of many men with prostitution, with the idea of sharing a woman that other men have "had."[8]

Moreover, gay male relations are partly persecuted in our culture, she claims, because they (or many of them) make explicit the fundamentally *hommo-sexual* nature of exchange itself—including the exchange constituted as desire—that is, they make clear that the stakes do not involve women themselves. If desire is a lack, and if it functions by way of the substitution of one impossible/unsatisfying object after another, then what is significant about desire is not the objects to which it attaches itself but rather the flows and dynamics of its circulation, the paths, detours, and returns its undergoes. If Irigaray is correct in her readings of psychoanalytic discourse as representative of

Western philosophical thought, and more generally in terms of its underlying investments in phallocentrism, then it also follows that these circuits of exchange are, like desire and sexual difference itself in patriarchal cultures, governed and regulated with respect to the phallus. These circuits are hommo-sexual, for and between men.

It is now clear, I hope, why there may be a problem using theories like psychoanalysis—as many lesbian theorists have done[9]—to explain the psychic and sexual economies of lesbians even if psychoanalysis could provide an explanation/account of male homosexuality (which seems dubious to me, given Freud's presumption of the primitive, maternally oriented heterosexuality as the "origin" of male desire). In the terms we have most readily available, it seems impossible to think lesbian desire. To think desire is difficult enough: desire has never been thoroughly reconsidered as an intensity, innervation, positivity, or force. Women's desire is inconceivable within models attributing to desire the status of an activity: women function (for men) as objects of desire. To think lesbian desire thus involves surmounting both of these obstacles; while it is possible to experience it, to have/to be it, psychoanalysis, theories of interiority, and, indeed, sociological, literary, and representational accounts—accounts that attempt to explain or assess it—are all required to do so in the very terms and within the very frameworks making this unthinkable. For this reason I would propose a temporary abandonment of the attempt to understand and explain lesbian desire and instead propose the development of very different models by which to experiment with it, that is, to understand desire not in terms of what is missing or absent, not in terms of a depth, latency, or interiority but in terms of surfaces and intensities.

Refiguring Desire

If the dominant or received notions of desire from Plato to Freud and Lacan have construed desire as a lack or negativity, there is a minor or subordinated tradition within Western thought that has seen desire in quite different terms. In contrast to the negative model that dooms desire to consumption, incorporation, dissatisfaction, destruction of the object, there is a tradition—we may for our purposes date it from Spinoza[10]—of seeing desire primarily as production rather than as lack. Here, desire cannot be identified with an object whose attainment provides satisfaction but with processes that produce. In contrast to Freud, for Spinoza reality does not prohibit desire but is produced by it.[11] Desire is the force of positive production, the energy that creates things, makes alliances, and forges interactions between things. Where Hegelian desire attempts to internalize and obliterate its objects, Spinozist desire assembles things, joins, or unjoins them. Thus, on the one hand, desire is a pure absence striving for an impossible completion, fated evermore to play out or repeat its primal or founding loss; on the other hand, we have a notion of desire as a pure positivity, as production, forging connections, making things, as non-fantasmatic, as real. If Freud and psychoanalytic theory can act as representatives of the first and dominant understanding of desire as a lack, then Deleuze and Guattari can be seen to represent the second broad trajectory. And it is to some of their work I now wish to turn, acknowledging that in the space that I have here, I am unable to do justice to the richness and complexity of their works. What follows must therefore be considered as notes pointing toward a further investigation.

At first sight it may appear that I am simply substituting one evil (Deleuze and Guattari's rhizomatics) for another (Freudian and Lacanian psychoanalysis), that I am throwing away what feminists, and many lesbian feminists, have found the most appealing of all theoretical models. I do not do so lightly, having myself invested a great deal of time in psychoanalytic theory. In spite of well-recognized problems—problems I have discussed elsewhere and that others have dealt with as well[12]—I believe that their work does not have to be followed faithfully to be of use in dealing with issues that they do not, or perhaps even cannot, deal with themselves, most specifically the question of lesbian desire. Nevertheless, because they refuse to understand desire in negative terms, because they refuse to structure it with reference to a singular signifier—i.e., the phallus—and because they allow desire to be understood not just as feeling or affect but also as doing and making, I believe that Deleuze and Guattari may have quite a lot to contribute to refiguring lesbian desire.

Following Nietzsche and Spinoza, Deleuze understands desire as immanent, positive, and productive, as inherently full. Instead of a yearning, desire is seen as an actualization, a series of practices, action, production, bringing together components, making machines, creating reality: "Desire is a relation of effectuation, not of satisfaction," as Colin Gordon put it ("The Subtracting Machine," 32). Desire is primary, not lack. It is not produced as an effect of frustration but is primitive and given; it is not opposed to or postdates reality, but it produces reality. It does not take a particular object for itself whose attainment provides it with satisfaction; rather, it aims at nothing in particular, above and beyond its own self-expansion, its own proliferation. It assembles things out of singularities and breaks down things, assemblages, into their singularities: "If desire produces, its product is real. If desire is productive, it can be so in reality, and of reality" (Deleuze and Guattari, *Anti-Oedipus*, 26).

As production, desire does not provide blueprints, models, ideals, or goals. Rather, it experiments, it makes: it is fundamentally aleatory, inventive. Such a theory cannot but be of interest for feminist theory insofar as women are the traditional repositories of the lack constitutive of desire and insofar as the oppositions between presence and absence, between reality and fantasy, have conventionally constrained women to occupy the place of men's other. Lack only makes sense to the (male) subject insofar as some other (woman) personifies and embodies it for him. Such a model of desire, when explicitly sexualized, reveals the impossibility of understanding lesbian desire. Any model of desire that dispenses with a reliance on lack seems to be a positive step forward and for that reason alone worthy of further investigation.

Lesbian Bodies and Pleasure

The terms by which lesbianism and lesbian desire are commonly understood seem to me problematic: it is no longer adequate to think them in terms of psychology, especially given that the dominant psychological models—psychoanalytic ones—are so inadequate for thinking femininity. So, in attempting to go the other way, I want to be able to provide a reading of lesbianism, or at least of lesbian sexuality and desire, in terms of bodies, pleasures, surfaces, intensities, as suggested by Deleuze and Guattari, Lyotard, and others.

There are a number of features of lesbian theory and of characterizations of lesbian desire that I would consequently like to avoid. In the first place, I wish to avoid the sentimentality and romanticism so commonly involved in thinking lesbian relationships. While I can understand the political need to validate and valorize lesbian relations in a culture openly hostile to lesbianism, I think it is also politically important to remain open to self-criticism and thus to change and growth. Lesbian relationships are no better, nor any worse, than the complexities involved in all sociosexual interrelations. Nor are they in any sense a solution to patriarchal forms of sexuality, because lesbianism and gay male sexuality are, as much as heterosexuality, products of patriarchy. There is no pure sexuality, no inherently transgressive sexual practice, no sexuality beyond or outside the limits of patriarchal models. This is not, however, to say that all forms of human sexuality are equally invested in patriarchal values, for there are clearly many different kinds of subversion and transgression, many types of sexual aberration that cannot be assimilated into historically determinate norms and ideals. It is not only utopian but also naive to take the moral high ground in proclaiming for oneself the right to judge the transgressive or other status of desire and sexuality: the function of moral evaluations of the sexual terrain can only be one of policing and prohibition, which does not deal with and does not explain the very desire for and energy of transgression.

In the second place, I would like to avoid seeing lesbian relations in terms of a binary or polarized model: this means abandoning many of the dominant models of sexual relations between women. In short, I want to avoid seeing lesbian sexual partners either as imaginary, mirror-stage duplicates, narcissistic doubles, self-reflections, bound to each other through mutual identification and self-recognition or in terms of complementarity with the lovers complementing each other's sexual style and role—butch-femme and bottom-top couplings.

In the third place, I would also like to avoid models that privilege genitality over other forms of sexuality. While it is clear that genitality remains a major site of intensity, in a phallic model it is the only true sexuality. I would like to use a model or framework in which sexual relationships are contiguous with and a part of other relationships—those of the writer to pen and paper, of the body-builder to weights, of the bureaucrat to files. The bedroom is no more the privileged site of sexuality than any other space; sexuality and desire are part of the intensity and passion of life itself.

In the fourth place, I want to avoid the kinds of narrow judgmentalism that suggest that any kind of sexuality or desire is better, more political, more radical, more transgressive than another and the kinds of feminist analysis that seek to judge the morality and ethics of the sexual practices of others, adjudicating what is wrong if not what is right.

And fifth, I want to look at lesbian relations and, if possible, at all social relations in terms of bodies, energies, movements, and inscriptions rather than in terms of ideologies, the inculcation of ideas, the transmission of systems of belief or representations, modes of socialization, or social reproduction, flattening depth, reducing it to surface effects.

Sexuality and desire, then, are not fantasies, wishes, hopes, aspirations (although no doubt these are some of their components), but they are energies, excitations, impulses, actions, movements, practices, moments, pulses of feeling. The sites most intensely invested always occur at a conjunction, an interruption, a point of machinic connection; they are always surface effects between one thing and another—between a hand and a breast, a tongue and a cunt, a mouth and food, a nose and a rose. In order to understand this notion, we have to abandon our habitual understanding of entities as the integrated totality of parts, and instead we must focus on the elements, the parts, outside their integration or organization; we must look beyond the organism to the organs comprising it. In looking at the interlocking of two such parts—fingers and velvet, toes and sand—there is not, as psychoanalysis suggests, a predesignated erotogenic zone, a site always ready and able to function as erotic. Rather, the coming together of two surfaces produces a tracing that imbues both of them with eros or libido, making bits of bodies, its parts, or particular surfaces throb, intensify, for their own sake and not for the benefit of the entity or organism as a whole. In other words, they come to have a life of their own, functioning according to their own rhythms, intensities, pulsations, and movements. Their value is always provisional and temporary, ephemeral and fleeting; they may fire the organism, infiltrate other zones and surfaces with their intensity, but they are unsustainable—they have no memory. They are not a recorded or a recording activity.

These body relations are not (as much of gay male culture presumes) anonymous, quick encounters; rather, each is a relation to a singularity or particularity, always specific, never generalizable. Neither anonymous nor yet entirely personal, each is still an intimacy of encounter, a pleasure/unpleasure of and for itself. Encounters, interfaces between one part and another of bodies or bodies and things, produce the erotogenic surface, inscribe it as a surface, linger on and around it for their evanescent effects: like torture, diet, clothing, and exercise, sexual encounters mark or inscribe the body's surface, and in doing so they produce an intensity that is in no way innate or given. Probably one of the most interesting and undervalued theorists of the erotic and of desire is Alphonso Lingis, whose wonderful texts shimmer with the very intensity he describes:

> The libidinal excitations do not invest a pregiven surface; they extend a libidinal surface. This surface is not the surface of a depth, the contour enclosing an interior. The excitations do not function as signals, as sensations. Their free mobility is horizontal and continually annexes whatever is tangent to the libidinal body. On this surface exterior and interior are continuous; its spatiality that of a Moebius strip. The excitations extend a continuity of convexities and concavities, probing fingers, facial contours, and orifices, swelling thighs and mouths, everywhere glands surfacing, and what was protuberance and tumescence on the last contact can now be fold, cavity, squeezed breasts, soles of feet forming still another mouth. Feeling one's way across the outer face of this Moebius strip one finds oneself on the inner face—all surface still and not inwardness. (Lingis, *Libido*, 76)

To relate through someone to something else, or to relate through something to someone: not to relate to some one and only one, without mediation. To use the machinic connections a body part forms with another, whether it be organic or inorganic, to form an intensity, an investment of libido, is to see desire and sexuality as productive. Productive, though in no way reproductive, for this pleasure can serve no other purpose, can have no other function than its own augmentation, its own proliferation: a production, then, that makes but reproduces nothing—a truly nomad desire unfettered by anything external, for anything can form part of its circuit and be absorbed into its operations.

If we are looking at intensities and surfaces rather than latencies and depths, then it is not the relation between an impulse and its absent other—its fantasies, wishes, hoped-for objects—that interests us; rather, it is the spread or distribution, the quantity and quality of intensities relative to each other, their patterns, their contiguities that are most significant. It is their effects rather than any intentions that occupy our focus, what they make and do rather than what they mean or represent. They transform themselves, undergo metamorphoses, become something else, never retain an identity or purpose. Others, human subjects, women, are not simply the privileged objects of desire: through women's bodies to relate to other things to make connections.

While I cannot give a "real life illustration," I can at least refer to one of Australia's few postmodern lesbian writers, Mary Fallon:

> Stroking my whole body all night long until your fingers became fine sprays of white flowers until they became fine silver wires electrifying my epidermis until they became delicate instruments of torture and the night wore on for too many hours and I loved you irritably as dawn reprieved us we are two live-wire women wound and sprung together we are neither of us afraid of the metamorphoses transmogrifications the meltings the juices squelching in the body out of the body—a split fruit of a woman we are neither of us is afraid to sink our teeth into the peach it's not love or sex it's just that we are collaborating every night on a book called The Pleasures of the Flesh Made Simple. (Fallon, *Working Hot*, 87)

One "thing" transmutes into another, becomes something else through its connections with something or someone outside. Fingers becoming flowers, becoming silver, becoming torture instruments. This is precisely what the Deleuzian notion of "becoming" entails: entry into an arrangement, an assemblage of other fragments, other things, becoming bound up in some other production, forming part of a machine, becoming a component in a series of flows and breaks, of varying speeds and intensities. To "become animal" (or, more contentiously, to "become woman") does not involve imitating, reproducing, or tracing the animal (woman) and becoming like it. Rather, it involves entering into relation with a third term and with it to form a machine that enters into relations with a machine composed of "animal" components.[13] Becomings then are not a broad general trajectory of development but always concrete and specific, becoming something, something momentary, provisional, something inherently unstable and changing. It is not a question of being (animal, woman, lesbian), of attaining a definite status as a thing, a permanent fixture, nor of clinging to, having an identity, but of moving, changing, being swept beyond one singular position into a multiplicity of flows or into what Deleuze and Guattari have described as "a thousand tiny sexes": to liberate the myriad of flows, to proliferate connections, to intensify.

Becoming lesbian, if I can put it this way, is thus no longer or not simply a question of being lesbian, of identifying with that being known as a lesbian, of residing in a position or identity. The question is not am I—or are you—a lesbian but, rather, what kinds of lesbian connections, what kinds of lesbian-machine, we invest our time, energy, and bodies in, what kinds of sexuality we invest ourselves in, with what other kinds of bodies, with what bodies of our own, and with what effects? What it is that together, in parts and bits and interconnections, we can make that is new, that is exploratory, that opens up further spaces, induces further intensities, speeds up, enervates, and proliferates production (production of the body, production of the world)?

While what I am putting forth here is a positive view, it is not, in my opinion, a utopian one: it is not a prophecy of the future, a vision of things to come, an ideal or goal to aspire to. It is a way of looking at things and doing things with concepts and ideas in the same ways we do them with bodies and pleasures, a way of leveling, of flattening the hierarchical relations between ideas and things, qualities and entities, of eliminating the privilege of the human over the animal, the organic over the inorganic, the male over the female, the straight over the "bent"—of making them level and interactive, rendering them productive and innovative, experimental and provocative. That is the most we can hope for from knowledge. Or desire.

Notes

1. In my understanding, a mistaken bifurcation or division is created between so-called essentialists and constructionists insofar as constructionism is inherently bound up with notions of essence. To be consistent, constructionism must explain what the "raw materials" of the construction consist in; these raw materials must, by definition, be essential insofar as they precondition and make possible the processes of social construction.

2. The work of a number of feminists in this area is clearly laudable and provides a model or ideal for politically engaged knowledges. In this context, see the work of Butler, de Lauretis, and Fuss.

3. See, for example, my paper "Lesbian Fetishism?" (1991).

4. Such models are of course not the only ones spawned by Western thought; alternative models, which see desire as a positivity, a production or making, while considerably rarer in our received history, nonetheless still develop and have exerted their influence in the writings of, among others, Spinoza, Nietzsche, Deleuze, and Lyotard, as I will discuss in more detail below.

5. I have tried to elaborate in considerable detail the differences between masculine, anaclitic forms of love/desire and feminine/narcissistic forms in *Jacques Lacan: A Feminist Introduction*, ch. 5.

6. This idea has been effectively explored in Jacqueline Rose's penetrating analysis of Freud's treatment of Dora (1985).

7. See Irigaray, *This Sex Which Is Not One*; Grosz, *Sexual Subversions*, and Whitford, *Luce Irigaray*.

8. See Irigaray, "Commodities Among Themselves" and "Women on the Market" (in *This Sex Which Is Not One*).

Implicitly condemned by the social order [the prostitute] is implicitly tolerated. . . . In her case, the qualities of woman's body are "useful." However, these qualities have "value" only because they serve as the locus of relations—hidden ones—between men. Prostitution amounts to the *usage that is exchanged*. Usage that is not merely potential: it has already been realized. The woman's body is valuable because it has already been used. In the extreme case, the more it has served, the more it is worth. . . . [It] has become once again no more than a vehicle for relations among men. (186)

9. See the works of Butler, De Lauretis, and Fuss.

10. I am grateful to Moira Gatens for her research on Spinoza, which has been invaluable to me in this paper and in reconceiving corporeality. See Gatens, *Feminism and Philosophy*.

11. The mind endeavours to persist in its being for an indefinite period. . . . This endeavour . . . when referred to the mind and the body in conjunction . . . is called *appetite*; it is, in fact, nothing else but man's essence, from the nature of which necessarily follow all those results which tend to its preservation. . . . Further, between appetite and desire, there is no difference . . . we deem a thing to be good, because we strive for it, wish for it, long for it or desire it. (Spinoza, *The Ethics*, 3:ix)

12. Rosi Braidotti articulates with considerable subtlety and sophistication many common reservations regarding Deleuze and Guattari's work, most especially concerning their appropriation of the metaphorics of femininity ("becoming-woman") as a kind of betrayal of feminist interests:

Deleuze's desiring machines amalgamate men and women into a new supposedly gender-free sexuality; . . . this drive towards a post-gender subjectivity, this urge to transcend sexual difference to reach a stage of multiple differentiation is not fully convincing. . . . Is the bypassing of gender in favour of a dispersed polysexuality not a very masculine move? . . . When this "becoming-woman" is disembodied to the extent that it bears no connection to the struggles, the experiences, the discursivity of real-life women, what good is it for feminist practice? Deleuze's multiple sexuality assumes that women conform to a masculine model which claims to get rid of sexual difference. (*Patterns of Dissonance*, 120–21)

13. "The actor Robert De Niro walks 'like' a crab in a certain sequence: but, he says, it is not a question of his imitating a crab; it is a question of making something that has to do with the crab enter into composition with the image, with the speed of the image" (Deleuze and Guattari, *A Thousand Plateaus*, 274).

Works Cited

Braidotti, Rosi. *Patterns of Dissonance: A Study of women in Contemporary Philosophy*. Translated by Elizabeth Guild. Cambridge: Polity Press, 1991.

Butler, Judith. *Gender Trouble: Feminism and the Subversion of Identity*. New York and London: Routledge, 1990.

——."Imitation and Gender Insubordination." In Diana Fuss, ed., *Inside/Out: Lesbian Theories, Gay Theories*, pp. 13–31. New York and London: Routledge, 1991.

Creet, Julia. "Daughter of the Movement: The Psychodynamics of Lesbian S/M Fantasy." *differences* 5(2) (1991): 135–59.

de Lauretis, Teresa. "The Female Body and Heterosexual Presumption." *Semiotica* 67(3–4) (1987).

——."Sexual Indifference and Lesbian Representation." *Theatre Journal* 40(2) (1988).

Deleuze, Gilles. *Masochism: Coldness and Cruelty*. Translated by Jean McNeil. New York: Zone Books, 1989.

Deleuze, Gilles, and Felix Guattari. *Anti-Oedipus: Capitalism and Schizophrenia*. Vol. 1. Translated by Mark Seem. Minneapolis: University of Minnesota Press, 1977.

Deleuze, Gilles, and Felix Guattari. *A Thousand Plateaus: Capitalism and Schizophrenia*. Vol. 2. Translated by Brian Massumi. Minneapolis: University of Minnesota Press, 1987.

Fallon, Mary. *Working Hot*. Melbourne: Sybella Press, 1989.

Freud, Sigmund. "Fragment of an Analysis of a Case of Hysteria." In *The Standard Edition of the Complete Psychological Works of Sigmund Freud*. Translated and edited by James Strachey. Vol. 7 (1905), pp. 1–122. London: Hogarth Press, 1953–1974.

——. "The Psychogenesis of a Case of Homosexuality in a Woman." In *The Standard Edition of the Complete Psychological Works of Sigmund Freud*. Translated and edited by James Strachey. Vol. 18 (1920), pp. 145–72. London: Hogarth Press, 1953–1974.

Frye, Marilyn. *The Politics of Reality: Essays in Feminist Theory*. Trumansburgh, N.Y.: Crossings Press, 1984.

Fuss, Diana. *Essentially Speaking: Feminism, Nature, and Difference*. New York and London: Routledge, 1989.

——, ed. *Inside/Out: Lesbian Theories, Gay Theories*. New York and London: Routledge, 1991.

Gatens, Moira. *Feminism and Philosophy: Perspectives in Equality and Difference*. Cambridge: Polity Press, 1991.

Gordon, Colin. "The Subtracting Machine." *I & C* 8 (1981).

Grosz, Elizabeth. *Sexual Subversions: Three French Feminists*. Sydney: Allen and Unwin, 1989.

——. *Jacques Lacan: A Feminist Introduction*. New York and London: Routledge, 1990.

——. "Lesbian Fetishism?" *differences* 5(2) (1991): 39–54.

——. (Forthcoming) "A Thousand Tiny Sexes: Feminism and Rhizomatics." In Constantin Boundas and Dorothea Olkowski, eds., *Gilles Deleuze: The Theater of Philosophy.*

Irigaray, Luce. *This Sex Which Is Not One.* Translated by Catherine Porter. Ithaca: Cornell University Press, 1985.

King, Katie. "Producing Sex, Theory, and Culture: Gay/Straight Remappings in Contemporary Feminism." In Marianne Hirsch and Evelyn Fox Keller, eds., *Conflicts in Feminism*, pp. 82–101. New York and London: Routledge, 1990.

Lingis, Alphonso. *Libido: The French Existential Theories.* Bloomington: Indiana University Press, 1985.

Rose, Jacqueline. "Dora: Fragment of an Analysis." In Charles Bertheimer and Claire Kahane, eds., *Dora's Case: Freud—Hysteria—Feminism*, pp. 128–47. New York: Columbia University Press, 1985.

Whitford, Margaret. *Luce Irigaray: Philosophy in the Feminine.* London and New York: Routledge, 1991.

5   The Postmodern Lesbian
Position: *On Our Backs*

Colleen Lamos

The phrase *lesbian postmodern* is an odd conjunction, suggesting that
there might be a peculiarly lesbian version of the widely recognized
and presumably heterosexual postmodern. Yet even its promoters
admit that there is something queer about postmodernism, beginning
with the fact that it is notoriously difficult to define. Postmodernism's
lubricous heterogeneity, its celebration of artificiality and commodification, and its association with a camp aesthetic lend it a sodomite
cast.[1]

How, then, can we conceive of a specifically lesbian postmodernism or a postmodern lesbianism? What can lesbianism and postmodernism reveal about each other, and what can their conjunction
produce? These questions may evoke the image of rather odd bedfel-
lows, the lesbian perversely united with a seductive and wily old
French intellectual or perhaps with an American drag queen. Within
feminist theory, the metaphor of matrimony is frequently used to

describe the relation between feminism and other critical practices (Gallop, *Around 1981*, 177–205). The oft-proposed marriage of feminism and postmodernism has been variously conceived of as a fruitful and episodic "affiliation" (Singer, "Feminism and Postmodernism," 467–68), as a serious and dangerous commitment hedged about by prenuptial conditions (Fraser and Nicholson, "Social Criticism Without Philosophy"), or—perhaps most commonly—as a disaster.[2] Rather than joining two separate critical discourses, though, I will try to show that the juxtaposition of the terms *lesbian* and *postmodern* tends to erode the conceptual coherence of each, specifically, that of lesbianism as a distinct sexual orientation and that of postmodernism as a distinct historical epoch.

The obscurity of the phrase *the lesbian postmodern* is partially due to the vagueness of the latter term. *Postmodern* is common currency in many fields—including architecture, art history, the performing arts, philosophy, literary theory and criticism, the history of science, Marxist theory, ethical-political reflection, and cultural studies—where it refers to different phenomena, for different reasons, and is assumed to have quite different implications, ranging from the end of life as we know it to more reruns of "The Donna Reed Show." These diverse phenomena, however, are often lumped together by commentators under the general heading of postmodernism and either rejected as decadent nihilism or embraced as the coming revolution. Given the lack of definitional clarity of postmodernism and acknowledging its many other significations, I take it here to refer to poststructuralist thought, especially to the work of Michel Foucault, Judith Butler, and Eve Kosofsky Sedgwick.

Considerations of postmodernism typically begin by distinguishing it from its predecessor, listing its characteristics, and then setting a date for the break between the two epochs. One of the most influential theorists of postmodernism, Fredric Jameson, thus announces that, whereas "in modernism . . . some residual zones of 'nature' or 'being' subsist," in postmodernism "nature is gone for good. . . . 'Culture' has become a veritable 'second nature' " (*Postmodernism*, ix). Jameson attributes this shift to alterations in the economic infrastructure of capitalism that generated superstructural, cultural changes by the early 1970s. Like modernism, postmodernism is a historical period with discernible origins and traits.

Such a framework could provide an explanation of the postmodern lesbian, offering the coherence and lucidity of a historical narrative and placing lesbianism within a determined context. Indeed, this narrative is especially attractive since it accounts for the birth of the lesbian at the start of the modern era around the turn of the twentieth century. As is well known, the modern lesbian or female invert was the discovery (or invention) of sexologists who distinguished her from heterosexual women and gave her a psychology and an etiology. Coinciding with the emergence of feminism as well as with major socioeconomic changes affecting women, the lesbian as a female whose being—whether psychologically, hormonally, or genetically determined—is by nature abnormal was born. Lesbianism also became a social problem for governments, schools, religious leaders, the military, and vigilant parents in the modern era. Today, though, we are witnessing the demise of the modern lesbian, replaced by the postmodern lesbian: thoroughly constructed, nonessentialist, perhaps even postlesbian.

There is much to be said for this account, nor do I think that it is wrong, strictly speaking. Yet such a history remains curiously modern in its belief that the historian knows what a lesbian is, indeed, that lesbians exist as a distinct category of persons. The current heated debate over "the death of the subject" concerns precisely the possibility of thinking about persons as ontological substances or subjects. While a history of lesbianism may be a politically admirable way of trying to grant lesbians full status as human beings instead of simply as mutilated or unauthorized subjects, it nevertheless begs the question of the constitution of subjectivity raised by postmodern thought and evades the challenge of postmodernism in general by situating it as another historical era, mapped by the historian's surveying eye. I would like to describe the postmodern lesbian from a different perspective—from *On Our Backs*—a position within the poststructuralist critique of the stable subject, and by focusing on the way the lesbian body is represented or made discursively intelligible within the pages of the leading lesbian pornographic magazine in the United States. In short, I would like to go beyond historicizing lesbianism to analyzing the concept of lesbian sexual orientation and its discursive production. A reading of *On Our Backs* and of contemporary butch/femme sexual styles may flesh out the heretofore shadowy figure of the postmodern lesbian as well as shed some light on that obscure phrase *the lesbian postmodern*.

Describing itself as "entertainment for the adventurous lesbian," *On Our Backs* is a racy blend of photospreads, erotic fiction, sex advice, personal narratives, and advertisements for, among other things, sex toys, piercing services, phone sex, spanking videos, and custom-made Victorian corsets. Born during the porn wars of the early 1980s, this San Francisco-based magazine straddles the divide between feminism and commercial (that is, male and largely straight) pornography. Its title explicitly defies the antipornography position espoused by *Off Our Backs*, the leading lesbian newspaper of the 1970s, which had become the voice of lesbian-feminist orthodoxy by 1984 when *On Our Backs* began publication. The latter flaunts its bad-girl attitude, echoing the liberation rhetoric of the sexual revolution and rebelling against what Julia Creet calls the maternal authority or "Law of the Mother" of orthodox feminism ("Daughter of the Movement," 397).[3]

On Our Backs is, relatively speaking, a success story. Now in its ninth year of publication, with thirty thousand subscribers, a paid staff of about ten people, and a booming business in porn videos, *On Our Backs* has carved a niche for itself in the commercial porn industry, almost single-handedly serving the lesbian market for sexually explicit materials. On one level, the success of *On Our Backs* demonstrates the unflagging ability of capitalism to respond to changing demands from emerging consumer groups, however queer. (There are, of course, significant differences in the production and consumption of lesbian and male (both gay and straight) pornography as well as distinctions in content and graphic design, which I cannot explore here.) Produced by lesbians for a lesbian audience, *On Our Backs* is nonetheless also read by straight women and men, as the letters to the editor reveal. For instance, when a female subscriber complained that "Men who read your magazine are no better than rapists," a flood of responses gushed in from apparently inappropriate readers protesting their right to look at it, wondering "What does it mean to be a magazine FOR a particular audience?" Matt, a heterosexual man, wrote in the March/April issue of 1991 that "your magazine . . . appeals to an audience beyond the lesbian community. . . . I buy *On Our Backs*, read it, and give it to some women I know" (7). According to Steven Bonvissuto, another letter writer, the women who appear in it "dare to topple the mold . . . created for the female sex, and gleefully blow away the illusion and facade. That's a real turn-on." He added that "more than one issue of *On Our Backs* has disappeared into the hands of girls I know" (May/June 1991:7).

The spectacle of these undesignated readers peering into the pages of *On Our Backs* poses some unsettling problems. To begin with, pornography is typically classified according to genres that are targeted at particular audiences, distinguished by gender and sexual orientation as well as by a variety of erotic tastes. These distinctions are blurred in the case of *On Our Backs*, however. As Linda Williams notes in her landmark study, *Hard Core*, the "polar opposites of a soft . . . women's erotica and a hard . . . phallic pornography have begun to break down" into a "multiformity" of pornographies (6) although neither she nor anyone else has analyzed the overlapping audiences of magazines like *On Our Backs*. Instead, she says that she decided not to examine gay and lesbian porn films *because* they are "not aimed primarily at" her, "a heterosexual woman." Yet, I would argue that the generic differentiations within pornography are the residue of discredited sexological typologies and naive notions of a text's or film's implied reader or spectator as well as the effects of class- and sex-based production and distribution systems. These generic categories rest upon the presupposition of a clear, even innate, difference between hetero- and homosexual (or other) desires. If it turns out that we—women and men, gay and straight—are reading each other's mail, as it were, then at the very least the assumption of appropriate or intended audiences for various genres of pornography should be reconsidered.

Such a reconsideration has direct implications for the relations among sexual desire, fantasy, and actual behavior, relations that are largely organized around the concept of sexual orientation. Certain types of people are supposed to want to look at certain types of pictures and entertain certain types of fantasies. What about lesbians who enjoy photographs of men? Or straight women who like pictures of women? Confessing that she reads men's porn, Sandy Allen asks in a letter to the editor in the 1991 March/April issue of *On Our Backs*, "how many other women have ever thumbed through a magazine labeled *Entertainment for Men* looking for pictures of sexy women? Gay men must also think me evil for enjoying *Drummer*" (7). To be sure, many lesbians and their allies have fought hard for the acceptance of lesbianism as a legitimate but different sexual orientation; yet, the former editor of *On Our Backs*, Susie Bright (a.k.a. Susie Sexpert), acknowledges that while "straight" and "gay" are "shorthand" terms "we use . . . to communicate our desires and point of view," she doesn't "believe in" them (Jan./Feb. 1991:3). Unlike Williams, Bright takes the language of sexology as contingent and pragmatic signifiers, not exclusive categories. Moreover, if the personal ads (which are heavily butch/femme) and articles such as "Can Dykes Be Daddy's Girls?" and "Elvis is a Lesbian" are to be understood, the so-called lesbian readership of this magazine must be engaged in fantasies and practices that bear a perverse relation to heterosexuality. In short, *On Our Backs* is not just the lesbian version of or counterpart to straight male pornography, acceptable to liberal sensibilities as, perhaps, "different strokes for different folks." Instead, the magazine makes it all the more difficult to distinguish between "different strokes" and "different folks" or between heterosexuality and homosexuality.

The peculiar position of *On Our Backs*, with one foot in feminism and one in commercial pornography—at once asserting female sexual agency and subjectivity while embracing the commodification of female bodies as objects of pornographic display, available for your viewing pleasure at $5.95 per issue—raises the provocative and troubling question of what happens when women "take on the phallus." The magazine itself is an instance of women "taking on the phallus" in the sense that its readers have appropriated the previously male-only privilege of gazing at women's bodies for the purpose of sexual arousal. In a particular sense, simultaneously metaphorical and nakedly literal, *On Our Backs* represents women taking on the phallus by strapping on dildos. Each issue contains numerous advertisements for dildos along with a variety of other sex toys, including sado-masochistic and leather paraphernalia. Every number of the 1991 volume features stories about heroines with dildos, letters to the editor debating the merits of penetration, and photographs of women wearing and using dildos.

The prominence of the dildo in depictions of lesbian sexuality in the pages of *On Our Backs*—indeed, the very publication of lesbian pornography—is offensive to many, not only feminists and lesbians, because it represents dirty carnal lust instead of egalitarian, nonobjectifying eroticism.[4] By commodifying women's bodies and representing lesbian phallicism, *On Our Backs* explicitly rejects traditional feminist claims to a moral superiority based upon supposed female innocence, powerlessness, and purity from which has issued a politics of resentment and vengeance. Wendy Brown argues that, as feminists, "our nervousness about moving toward . . . postmodern political theory" stems from our fear of "giving up the ground of specifically *moral* claims against domination . . . and moving instead into the domain of the sheerly political" ("Feminist Hesitations, Postmodern Exposures," 75). Those moral claims, according to Brown, are rooted in feminism's conviction that it speaks the truth of "women's experiences, feelings, and voices" (71). By contrast, *On Our Backs* renounces authenticity and truth to contest the production of female sexual pleasure within that bastion of male power and artifice—pornography. Lesbian pornographic representation paradoxically denies the uniqueness of female or lesbian sexuality, reproducing it within the heretofore masculine discourse of active, visible potency. The most notorious instance of this redeployment of power, the dildo flaunts its phallicism and in so doing throws into doubt received distinctions between male and female as well as between hetero- and homosexuality. Borrowing many of the graphic conventions of *Penthouse* and *Playboy*, *On Our Backs* explicitly plays with—indeed, exploits—the traditional yet hotly contested butch/femme lesbian sex roles. The resurgence of interest in butch/femme and the increase in the use of dildos by lesbians is seen by many as at best a retro fad or at worst a dangerous return to the prefeminist model of the "mannish lesbian." Beyond being a simple sexual option, the dildo and butch/femme pose an especially embarrassing affront to normative heterosexuality and suggest its (possibly postmodern) subversion.

The image of the lesbian that is entertained by some Americans is that of the dildo-wielding butch. In part this is due to the popularization of turn-of-the-century sexological theories that held that female inverts, bent on playing the man, fashion an artificial penis, whose use, according to Havelock Ellis, is widespread. Although Ellis stresses that male homosexuals are not effeminate, he distinguishes between the congenitally "inverted woman [whose] masculine traits are part of an organic instinct" (*Studies in the Psychology of Sex*, 88) on the one hand and the only latently perverted, "womanly" female on the other hand who is seduced or coerced into lesbianism by the former. Ellis's theories, along with those of Krafft-Ebing, opened the door to what we now know of as butch/femme and to the ensuing definitional incoherence of the lesbian as someone who simultaneously is and is not a genuine woman (Sedgwick, *Epistemology of the Closet*, 158–59; Weeks, *Coming Out*, 66, 93).

The figure of the butch dyke is pervasive in twentieth-century literature and popular culture. Its proliferation implies that butch/femme was not just the work of the sexologists; rather, they merely responded and contributed to the paranoid formation of the lesbian as a doubled, duplicitous figure, either flagrantly obvious as a butch or suspiciously invisible as a femme. A 1961 mass-market paperback by Carlson Wade entitled *The Troubled Sex* tries to clarify this epistemological dilemma in its portrait of the lesbian. Wade provides his readers, "normal, heterosexual people," with a symptomatically incoherent but nevertheless thorough account of how to "detect" a lesbian. In the section entitled "Recognition Factors" (90–95), Wade explains that his task is difficult because "body build is . . . no indication of sexual characteristics"; yet he happily goes on to explain that there are in fact two kinds of female homosexuals, "the weaker, passive types and the aggressive, eager lesbians," with opposing and complementary physiques. Wade lavishes obsessive attention on the butch, detailing with horrified fascination the shape of her body and the manner of her dress as though she were a bizarre species under zoological inspection. "The aggressive lesbians of the masculine kind" have wide shoulders and narrow hips, "more than the usual amount of hair," a "sultry," "sharp" voice, "thick fingers" and ankles, "strong, sturdy, and rather bony" arms, and a "short, thick" neck; the lesbian "walks with a broad gait, and is somewhat ape-like in appearance." Her clothing is "mannish," unsurprisingly, but Wade notes a few telltale signs: "In warm climates, lesbians often wear Bermuda shorts." Like the men they wish to be, "Lesbians have an attraction toward dogs. . . . Lesbians do not scare easily from such things as mice, bugs, or snakes. Many can ride horses." And, of course, they use dildos (16). The femmes are scarcely mentioned by Wade and are given only a couple of lines in this section. Those "innocent girls," who are not "'gay' in the true sense of the word," but are seduced into "the strange practices of lesbian love," have "narrow shoulders, full hips, and *rather pleasing breast form*" (emphasis mine). Although she is the victim of the predatory butch, the femme "can defy detection"; a traitor to the heterosexuality within her grasp, the femme unaccountably accepts her femininity while at the same time desiring another woman.

Wade's elaborately constructed, monstrous image of the butch is typical of the representation of lesbians in popular culture and medicoscientific discourses of the early and mid-twentieth century[5] and has been extremely effective as a disciplinary technique in the Foucauldian sense. The high and low lesbian subcultures that emerged during this period were structured by the fundamental binarism of butch/femme, the anchor of the lesbian semiotic code through which lesbians signified their desires.[6] Members of these closeted subcultures shared the medical and popular public discourse of female inversion in which "the lesbian" was a double figure, split into masculine and feminine types, the former a tiny, visibly offensive minority and the latter a hidden threat because so seemingly normal; the femme was at once necessary and incomprehensible to sexologists (Sedgwick, *Epistemology of the Closet*, 87–88).

It is little wonder that lesbian feminists of the 1970s denounced butch/femme as a recidivist mockery of a heterosexual model and a distorted representation of actual lesbian practices. If the figure of the monstrous, deformed butch was the nightmare fantasy of a culture fascinated and repulsed, like Wade, by the lesbian body, then surely the thing for lesbians to do was to make themselves over as proper women. The construction of the "woman-identified woman" by the 1970s radical lesbians was a political coup that turned the feminist critique of the patriarchy to the service of a vision of lesbian sexuality that had nothing whatsoever to do with masculine lust and everything to do with female friendship.[7] As recently as 1990 Marilyn Frye announced, remarkably, that "'sex' is an inappropriate term for what lesbians do"; lesbians don't "have sex," because that is a "phallic concept" implying coitus ("Lesbian 'Sex,'" 305). Indeed, "lesbian 'sex' . . . is utterly *in*articulable"; lesbians lack an appropriate language for their bodily experience, "which is not in any way phallocentric" (311–12). Attempting to define this sisterly love, Nett Hart states that lesbian desire is not directed at individuals but "is for the community formed by the self/mutual love of women" ("Lesbian Desire as Social Action," 297). While successful in gaining respectability for lesbians within the feminist movement, the lesbian-feminist "deal" (as JoAnn Loulan puts it) has nevertheless come undone.

In a sense, lesbian feminists put the homo back into homosexuality.[8] Rejecting the sexologists' notion of sexual inversion, they argued that lesbian desire was based not on gender difference (as in butch/femme) but on gender identification. As Sedgwick notes, this version of homosexuality "must have been attractive for the protective/expressive camouflage it offered" (160–61); yet it, too, suffered from definitional incoherence as did the older inversion model. Indeed, the lesbian-feminist consolidation of female gender and female sexuality ("feminism is the theory; lesbianism is the practice") curiously reiterates the sexist ideal of an essential, pure femininity. Thus, the move that was to strike the deathblow to patriarchy has betrayed itself as yet another ruse, and the political force of feminism has increasingly dissolved into cultural celebrations of the feminine as well as divisive quarrels over lesbian identity and membership in the sisterhood.

The demise of lesbian feminism may be seen as the end—the climax and collapse—of modern lesbianism, ushering in the new day of the postmodern lesbian. The commercialization and aestheticization of lesbian sexuality, manifest in the proliferation of sex toys, pornography, butch/femme sexual styles, s/m sexual practices, and phone sex— many of which have been adopted from gay men—attest to a queer lesbian culture that blurs distinctions between masculine and feminine and between gay and straight sexuality. Certainly, butch/femme and related practices have resexualized lesbianism. Although, as many are quick to caution,[9] "new" butches and femmes take an ironic, campy stance toward the gender roles they imitate, butch/femme always runs the risk of becoming naturalized, either by being reduced to male/female heterosexual norms or by being adopted as the psychological, inner truth of a person. Hence, the postmodern butch/femme lesbian may turn out to be just another essentialist identity, postmodern lesbian culture another gay ghetto, and postmodern lesbianism itself another moment in the history of sexuality rather than a challenge to it.

The most cogent and daring approach to these problems is offered by Judith Butler, who argues, following Foucault, that "the affirmation of 'homosexuality' is itself an instance of a homophobic discourse" ("Imitation," 14), so that even a "lesbian" identity is inevitably reinscribed within hegemonic heterosexual norms. Instead of defending homosexuality as a legitimate minority sexual orientation, Butler turns the tables and convincingly argues that heterosexuality, the supposedly natural expression of gender, "is always in the process of imitating and approximating its own phantasmatic idealization of itself—and *failing*" ("Imitation," 21). Heterosexuality is already "a constant parody of itself" (*Gender*, 122). The norms of heterosexuality are constituted through repeated performances that "mime" themselves and thereby produce the effect of being natural. The homosexual, inferior copy of heterosexuality is therefore "a copy of a copy" (22), a simulation of what is already a simulation. The now famous proposition Butler offers is to abandon the effort to base feminist politics on gender or sexual identity altogether, even as a "strategic essentialism," and to demonstrate the production of heterosex/gender through "parodic practices" that (re)produce "man" and "woman" as a pastiche or drag (*Gender*, 146). "The replication of heterosexual constructs in non-heterosexual frames brings into relief the utterly constructed status of the so-called heterosexual original" (*Gender*, 31). The most significant of the parodic practices that she proposes is the butch style, whose masculinity is set "against a culturally intelligible 'female' body," thereby denaturalizing male and female gender terms (*Gender*, 123).

This "dissonant juxtaposition" of masculinity and femininity functions, Butler implies, within an intersubjective erotic scene; specifically, "the object . . . of lesbian-femme desire is . . . the destabilization of both terms as they come into erotic interplay" (*Gender*, 123). The subversiveness of the butch's performance of gender impersonation appears to be contingent upon its being read as such, at least by her partner, the femme. Interestingly, while Butler clearly states that the object of desire is not the lesbian butch subject but rather the dissonance and "sexual tension" of her performance, a performance that *splits* the subject, Butler nevertheless presents the butch through the eyes of the femme and implies that the two form a couple—a butch/femme parody of heterosexual marriage.

Butler's theory of butch/femme as a "parodic repetition" of heterosexuality provides a sophisticated conceptual framework for understanding the dildo as the mime of the phallus/penis, a "fake or bad copy" (17) of the penis, but a derivative that shows the "original" penis is a reiterated and vain attempt to pass itself off as the phallus. Thus, the dildo, as the imitation of a penis, exposes the penis as itself "only" a representation or a failed imitation of the phantasmatic phallus. Alas, the dildo-bedecked lesbian may be disappointed that her parody of the phallus is interpreted differently by others, especially by heterosexuals who take the dildo or butch/femme straight, so to speak. To be sure, Butler qualifies her argument: "parodic replication . . . of heterosexual constructs" achieves the effects she claims "within nonheterosexual frames" ("Imitation," 23). But even within such frames—for instance, in the pages of *On Our Backs*—the significance of dildos and of butch/femme sexual styles are matters of intense interpretive debate.

The question of what is a real butch was one of the most controversial issues in the letters to the editor of *On Our Backs* throughout 1991. An angry Romey Smith wrote to complain:

All this talk about butches wanting to be fags with other butches because they aren't getting fucked with dildos is like going "from the sublime to the ridiculous." I am a butch and the last thing in the world I'd want to do is bend over for another butch! . . . So here's my advice to any boot stompin' or executive baby butch who claims she isn't having orgasms simply because her femme won't fuck her: trade in your jock strap for a garter belt, sweetheart, you ought to be a girl. (January/February 1991:5)

Ms. Smith is not the sort of woman for whom the dildo is an ironic, playful subversion of the penis with its phallic pretensions, but for her the dildo is the phallus. Her assertion that being penetrated by another woman would render her a faggot or a girl elicited several responses. D. K. Brown fired back in the July/August issue of 1991, "It's people like you, Romey, who promote the myth that because butches look a certain way, they have to have sex a certain way. I would love to bend over and give you some Daddy, but when you're done I expect to see you on all fours so I can do some cobweb bustin! This is give and take" (7). Other respondents to Brown, such as F. Fish, urged a pluralistic view: "Some of us [butch dykes] are faggots, some are boys, some are bitches with dicks, some are boys who love to get fucked or fuck their femme tops just the way she says" (May/June 1991:5).

As these letters testify, the butch/femme dichotomy has become complex and internally differentiated among, for instance, femme tops, butch bottoms, femmes butched-out (or cross-dressing) in (male) drag, butches femmed-out in drag, and even the butch fag in drag (the butch who, when she dresses in femme clothing, feels like a gay man dressing as a woman). These various mutations are explained by Fanny (of "Ask Fanny," a sex advice column in *On Our Backs*), who says that "genderbending is as malleable as Mr. Potato Head," so that "some butches [even] look like female sex goddesses" (July/August 1991:9). The personal ads reflect this heterogeneity of roles and desires, as well as a certain confusion; one writer says that she is "kinda butch, kinda femme," and another throws up her hands and offers, "[I] don't understand butch/femme but will do anything Susie Bright says." Leigh Crow, an Elvis impersonator whose drag-king name is "Elvis Herselvis," explains that she would sometimes "pretend that I was Elvis . . . but sometimes I'd pretend I was his costar. I couldn't decide which would be more fun," eventually settling on Elvis as the result of a dare (July/August 1991:27).

Within a lesbian setting, strapping on a dildo or playing the butch has various, conflicting meanings. The readers of *On Our Backs*—themselves not representative of lesbians in general—are divided regarding the significance of the dildo, including whether it distinguishes butch from femme or whether it is exchangeable and thus permits alternate roles. Nor is it clear if they see butch/femme as a sexual aesthetics or as an expression of the nature of a lesbian's desires. Of course, butch/femme roles have been uncritically adopted by many lesbians who view them as the enactment of a true but previously hidden identity. Although many personal narratives of butch/femme experience attest to the intuitively felt strength of these roles, they do not resolve the question of their validity. As Wendy Brown points out, the feminist—and lesbian—conviction of the truth of personal testimony as an epistemological foundation is at odds with the (also feminist) belief in the social construction of subjects ("Feminist Hesitations, Postmodern Exposures," 71–73). Like the coming-out story, butch/femme narratives tell a tale of denial followed by confession with an ensuing sense of relief at having secured a stable identity. However, as JoAnn Loulan discovered in her research, 95 percent of her lesbian respondents were familiar with butch/femme codes and had rated themselves or others in terms of those codes; yet the same percentage also felt that butch/femme was "unimportant in their lives" (*The Lesbian Erotic Dance*, 42–45). Herself a lesbian who had long "denied [her] femme self," Loulan interprets these findings as an indication of wholesale homophobic disavowal of stigmatized social roles. It is perhaps more plausible to take her respondents at their word; butch/femme may be a widely recognized set of conventions within lesbian culture, but it must not be assumed to be a constitutive or obligatory identification.

Like transvestism and other forms of camp, butch/femme provokes the desire for revelation. As Marjorie Garber notes, "What makes transvestism theoretically as well as politically interesting" is the way that it incites exposure while denying the interiority that it promises, thereby "undoing itself as part of the process of self-enactment" (*Vested Interests*, 149). The eroticism of butch/femme thus lies not in the so-called attraction of opposites, as though butch/femme were an ersatz version of heterosexual romance, but in its sexual *dea*uthorization of gender. Inverting the feminist tenet that, in Lynne Segal's words, "sex is the endorsement of gender," (quoted in Ehrenreich et al., *Remaking Love*, 202), butch/femme stages gender, manipulating its signs in a sexualized code that has everything to do with masculinity and femininity. Furthermore, the butch/femme stylization of gender conventions does not entail any particular sexual practice or position. Loulan was surprised to learn that there were "no significant differences" between the sexual activities of her respondents, including initiation of sex, use of dildos or vibrators, or frequency of orgasm. Indeed, "butches were the most likely to 'never' vaginally penetrate their lovers," while "femmes penetrate their lovers more frequently than anyone else" (*The Lesbian Erotic Dance*, 214, 207).[10] In short, butch/femme reverses the supposedly obligatory derivation of sex from gender and breaks the chain that links masculine/feminine with its associated binaries: top/bottom, penetrator/penetrated, active/passive, male/female, and subject/object of desire.

The results of Loulan's survey are, of course, the product of another sort of confession than the personal narrative. Like the latter, though, they do not offer the privileged, inside, "really true" story of butch/femme because no such story exists. Rather, the empirical particulars of Loulan's report, as well as the passages I have cited from *On Our Backs*, throw into sharp relief the status and stakes of theory in its relation to "the facts." The epistemological grounds for any explanation of the lesbian as such are inherently uncertain inasmuch as this figure was born from a paranoid incoherence. Hence, Sue Ellen Case's complaint that gay camp has been misappropriated by straight postmodernists who ignore "homosexual realities" ("Toward a Butch-Femme Aesthetic," 288) would bear more weight if those "realities" were not already confused by the theoretical difficulty of distinguishing "homosexual" from "heterosexual" ones. Indeed, Case's advocacy of butch/femme as providing "the strong subject position the [feminist] movement requires" and her description of "the combo butch/femme as subject," as a couple or "dynamic duo" (283), is already implicated within the heterosexism that her essay bravely disputes.

As Case demonstrates, the subversiveness of butch/femme is contingent upon its discursive articulation within specific contexts—for particular people, under particular circumstances, for particular ends. It is perhaps most effective as a deconstructive strategy not within a nonheterosexual framework but on the boundary between queer and straight cultures, and even there its effects are unpredictable. The consequences of disarticulating gender identity from its sexual performance cannot be governed and may often—perhaps always—turn out not to be what one had planned. In a word, butch/femme always works at least two ways, to confirm and to unsettle the naturalness of gender and the heterosexual norms it subtends, because the simulacrum of gender can always be naturalized as the real. The multivalent, contingent, and unintended—indeed, aleatory—consequences of parodic repetition mean that it cannot serve as the means to universal political salvation, but perhaps it can work in these postmodern times.[11]

The conjunction of lesbianism and postmodernism is no accident for, as Sedgwick has argued, the epistemological grounds of Western culture in our century "are structured—indeed fractured—by a chronic, now endemic crisis of homo/heterosexual definition" (*Epistemology of the Closet*, 1). Postmodernist skepticism toward historical metanarratives could be shown to issue from the recognition that those narratives are based upon the rotting foundation of a discredited natural sexual order. Jameson decries the postmodern "penetration and colonization of Nature and the Unconscious" (*Postmodernism*, 36), yet nature and the unconscious were already colonized. Lesbianism is not the product of late capitalist decadence but attests to the internal failure of heterosexual patriarchy to account for itself and its excluded others. Moreover, attempts to offer historical explanations of lesbianism encounter the intractable problem of definition; the difficulty of determining what a lesbian is, including whether she was discovered or invented, casts doubt upon the assumption of a normal or natural heterosexuality as well as upon the traditional claims to knowledge by historical inquiry. The lesbian postmodern thus signifies not just a revision in the history of sexuality but an interrogation of the sexuality of history.

Similarly, the postmodern lesbian is not another lesbian but the end of lesbianism as we know it—as a distinct, minority sexual orientation. Lesbianism was born in the panic of sexual/gender definition at the turn of the twentieth century. As we approach our own fin-de-siècle that panic has not subsided; rather what Sedgwick terms "the crisis of homo/heterosexual definition" has reached a boiling point in which it is no longer theoretically feasible nor politically practical to demarcate lesbianism as a unique identity. The widely feared loss of lesbianism as an identity presents queer theorists with the opportunity to challenge the constitution of sexuality in general.

Notes

1. I gratefully acknowledge Elisabeth Ladenson's assistance with this paper.

2. In her essay "Feminist Hesitations, Postmodern Exposures," Wendy Brown remarks that "postmodern deconstruction of the subject incites palpable feminist panic" (71). For instances of this panic, see Nicholson, *Feminism/Postmodernism*. For more positive views see Butler and Scott as well as the special issue of *differences*, "Politics/Power/Culture: Postmodernity and Feminist Political Theory" (3 [1], Spring 1991).

3. Creet's claims are anticipated by, among others, B. Ruby Rich who claims that "feminism has become a mother figure, and what we are seeing is a daughter's revolt" ("Feminism and Sexuality in the 1980s," 529).

4. Gloria Steinem's formula became the feminist slogan: "Erotica is about sexuality, but pornography is about power" ("Erotica and Pornography," 24).

5. See Smith-Rosenberg, "Discourses of Sexuality and Subjectivity," 271f. Wade borrows heavily from Havelock Ellis.

6. The butch/femme lesbian subculture of aristocratic women in the 1920s and 1930s, especially in Paris, is widely known (Garber, *Vested Interests*, 152–56). Less public and less documented was the low butch/femme subculture of working-class dyke bars; in both instances, butch/femme provided public visibility for these lesbians, albeit at the price of persecution (Nestle, *Restricted*, passim; Newton, "The Mythic Mannish Lesbian," passim).

7. This vision of lesbian-feminist sexuality is in keeping with prefeminist, homophobic theories of lesbianism. The sexologist Charlotte Wolff claimed in 1971 that "It is not homosexuality but homoaffectionality which is at the centre and the very essence of women's love for each other. . . . The sex act . . . is always secondary with them" (*Love Between Women*, 70).

For differing views, see Elizabeth Wilson ("I'll Climb the Stairway to Heaven," passim). According to Beatrix Campbell, within lesbian feminism "*sisterhood* became transposed . . . into a cult of women" ("A Feminist Sexual Politics," 35). Gayle Rubin also argues that the women's movement shifted to the right in the 1970s and that "all of this celebration of femininity tends to reinforce traditional gender roles"; she calls this celebration "femininism" ("Leather," 216–17). The three collections of essays edited by Vance, Snitow, Stansell, and Thompson, and the Feminist Review Collective discuss the heated debates between cultural feminists and prosex feminists, a debate incited by the issue of pornography.

For a recent revisionist history of 1970s lesbian feminism, see Echols (*Daring to Be Bad*, passim).

8. *Homosexuality* has a double root: the Greek prefix *homo* (referring to "the

same") spliced onto the Latin substantive.

9. Faderman assures her readers that "neo-butch/femme . . . doesn't imply sexual inversion" and that the butch does not "take the part of the man" in contemporary lesbian sex (*Odd Girls and Twilight Lovers*, 264–65); rather, quoting Phyllis Lyon, "women 'play at it' rather than 'being it' " (268).

10. Loulan unexpectedly found that, "when the question of attraction was raised, almost half of the femmes were attracted to butches; almost half of the butches were attracted to femmes. . . . However, one-third of the femmes were attracted to other femmes; one-fourth of the butches were attracted to butches" (*The Lesbian Erotic Dance*, 213).

11. I am indebted to conversations with Joseph Valente for these ideas.

Works Cited

Allen, Jeffner, ed. *Lesbian Philosophies and Cultures*. Albany: State University of New York Press, 1990.

Brown, Wendy. "Feminist Hesitations, Postmodern Exposures." *differences* 3(1) (1991): 63–84.

Butler, Judith. *Gender Trouble: Feminism and the Subversion of Identity*. New York: Routledge, 1990.

——. "Imitation and Gender Insubordination." In Diana Fuss, ed., *Inside/Out: Lesbian Theories, Gay Theories*, pp. 13–31. New York: Routledge, 1991.

Butler, Judith, and Joan W. Scott, eds. *Feminists Theorize the Political*. New York: Routledge, 1992.

Campbell, Beatrix. "A Feminist Sexual Politics: Now You See It, Now You Don't." Feminist Review Collective, eds., *Sexuality*, 19–39.

Case, Sue-Ellen. "Toward a Butch-Femme Aesthetic." In Lynda Hart, ed., *Making a Spectacle: Feminist Essays on Contemporary Women's Theatre*, pp. 283–99. Ann Arbor: University of Michigan Press, 1989.

Creet, Julia. "Daughter of the Movement: The Psychodynamics of Lesbian S/M Fantasy." *differences* 3(2) (1991): 135–59.

Duberman, Martin, et al., eds. *Hidden from History: Reclaiming the Gay and Lesbian Past*. New York: Penguin, 1989.

Echols, Alice. *Daring to be Bad: Radical Feminism in American, 1967–1975*. Minneapolis: University of Minnesota Press, 1989.

Ehrenreich, Barbara, Elizabeth Hess, and Gloria Jacobs. *Remaking Love: The Feminization of Sex*. Garden City, N.Y.: Doubleday, 1986.

Ellis, Havelock. *Studies in the Psychology of Sex*. Vol. 1. London: University Press, 1897.

Faderman, Lillian. *Odd Girls and Twilight Lovers: A History of Lesbian Life in Twentieth-Century America*. New York: Columbia University Press, 1991.

Feminist Review Collective, eds. *Sexuality: A Reader*. London: Virago, 1987.

Fraser, Nancy, and Linda J. Nicholson. "Social Criticism without Philosophy: An Encounter between Feminism and Postmodernism." In Nicholson, ed., *Femi-*

nism/Postmodernism, pp. 19–38.

Frye, Marilyn. "Lesbian 'Sex.' " In Allen, ed., *Lesbian Philosophies and Cultures*, pp. 305–15.

Gallop, Jane. *Around 1981: Academic Feminist Literary Theory*. New York: Routledge, 1992.

Garber, Marjorie. *Vested Interests: Cross-Dressing and Cultural Anxiety*. New York: Routledge, 1992.

Hart, Nett. "Lesbian Desire as Social Action." In Allen, ed., *Lesbian Philosophies and Cultures*, pp. 295–333.

Jameson, Fredric. *Postmodernism, or the Cultural Logic of Late Capitalism*. Durham: Duke University Press, 1991.

Loulan, JoAnn. *The Lesbian Erotic Dance: Butch, Femme, Androgyny, and Other*. San Francisco: Spinsters, 1990.

Nestle, Joan. *A Restricted Country*. Ithaca: Firebrand Books, 1987.

——, ed. *The Persistent Desire: A Femme-Butch Reader*. Boston: Alyson Publications, 1992.

Newton, Esther. "The Mythic Mannish Lesbian." In Duberman et al., eds., *Hidden from History*, pp. 281–93.

Nicholson, Linda J., ed. *Feminism/Postmodernism*. New York: Routledge, 1990.

Rich, B. Ruby. "Feminism and Sexuality in the 1980s." *Feminist Studies* 12 (1986): 525–61.

Rubin, Gayle. "Thinking Sex: Notes for a Radical Theory of Sexuality." In Carol S. Vance, ed., *Pleasure and Danger: Exploring Female Sexuality*, pp. 267–319. Boston: Routledge, 1984.

——. "The Leather Menace: Comments on Politics and S/M." In Samois, ed., *Coming to Power: Writing and Graphics on Lesbian S/M*. 3d ed. Boston: Alyson, 1987.

——, et al. "Talking Sex: A Conversation on Sexuality and Feminism." Feminist Review Collective, eds., *Sexuality: A Reader*, pp. 63–81.

Sedgwick, Eve Kosofsky. *Epistemology of the Closet*. Berkeley: University of California Press, 1990.

Singer, Linda. "Feminism and Postmodernism." In Butler and Scott, eds., *Feminists Theorize the Political*, pp. 464–75.

Smith-Rosenberg, Carroll. "Discourses of Sexuality and Subjectivity: The New Woman 1870–1936." In Duberman et al., eds., *Hidden from History*, pp. 264–80.

Snitow, Ann, Christine Stansell, and Sharon Thompson, eds. *Powers of Desire: The Politics of Sexuality*. New York: Monthly Review, 1983.

Steinem, Gloria. "Erotica and Pornography: A Clear and Present Difference." In Laura Lederer, ed., *Take Back the Night: Women on Pornography*, pp. 20–25. New York: Bantam, 1980.

Vance, Carole S., ed. *Pleasure and Danger: Exploring Female Sexuality*. Boston: Routledge, 1984.

Wade, Carlson. *The Troubled Sex*. N.p.: Beacon Envoy, 1961.

Weeks, Jeffrey. *Coming Out: Homosexual Politics in Britain from the Nineteenth*

Century to the Present. London: Quartet, 1977.

Williams, Linda. *Hard Core: Power, Pleasure, and the "Frenzy of the Visible."* Berkeley: University of California Press, 1989.

Wilson, Elizabeth. "I'll Climb the Stairway to Heaven: Lesbianism in the Seventies." In Sue Cartledge and Joanna Ryan, eds., *Sex and Love: New Thoughts on Old Contradictions*, pp. 180–95. London: The Women's Press, 1983.

Wolff, Charlotte. *Love Between Women*. New York: St. Martin's Press, 1971.

6 Irigaray's Female Symbolic in the Making of Chicana Lesbian *Sitios y Lenguas* (*Sites and Discourses*)

Emma Pérez

When I was nineteen in the mid-seventies, I came out as a lesbian, although like many lesbians I can trace my desire for women back to my mother's womb. I am a native of Texas, a state where homophobia is as severe as racism. To come out, I left Texas, moved to California, and within one month I met the woman of my dreams, the woman with whom I'd spend the rest of my life. We lasted six months. She was a year older than me, and I like to say she left me for a younger woman, a woman of eighteen. When we lived together those first glorious months, we endured a small yellow cottage with a black-and-white plaid couch, no bed, and no curtains. We slept on a cold, hard floor. One evening, as we finished shopping at a local market, a carload of young white boys barked words they imagined would lure us to them. We shouted we weren't interested, and they replied predictably. They screamed accusingly, "Lesbians!" and we blared, "Yeah, so what?" Luckily, they drove away, and, laughing, we walked to our curtainless yellow cottage feeling exposed to a hostile world but too young and in love to care.

I disclose this personal story to introduce my stand as a strategic essentialist. Deconstructive theorist Gayatri Chakravorty Spivak integrated these concepts when she wrote, "it is not possible not to be an essentialist, one can self-consciously use this irreducible moment of essentialism as part of one's strategy."[1] A strategic essentialist, then, is one who exercises political representation, or identity politics, within hegemonic structures. The strategy asserts countersites within dominant society. As a dynamic process, this tactic gives voices to each new marginalized social or political group, bonded temporarily at specific historical moments. French feminist Luce Irigaray, for example, exhorts women to "break away" into separate spaces as a political strategy to create a female imaginary resisting phallocentric representation.[2] Strategic essentialism is a type of caucusing with each new caucus making its own rules, agreeing upon its demands, restrictions, freedoms. The process is not permanent or fixed but instead somewhat dialectical, acknowledging irreducible differences within separate *sitios y lenguas* where the resolution of differences is neither desirable nor necessary.[3]

At this juncture in so many struggles for human rights, I essentialize myself strategically within a Chicana lesbian countersite as a historical materialist from the Southwest who dares to have a feminist vision of the future. My essentializing positions are often attacked by a sophisticated carload of postmodern, post-Enlightenment, Eurocentric men and by women who ride in the back seat, who scream epithets at those of us who have no choice but to essentialize ourselves strategically and politically against dominant ideologies that serve only to disempower and depoliticize marginalized minorities. Postmodernists accuse essentialists of being exclusionary and totalizing because we claim identities without regard for others. But as "marginalized others," essentializing ourselves within countersites thwarts cultural and political suicide. We must separate into decolonized third world spaces of our own making. Stragegic essentialism is practiced resistance against dominant ideologies that silence and/or model marginalized groups. The modeled minority, aware of the danger of being *the* token, knows that an invitation to the center serves to silence and disempower the group(s) she/he is invited to represent symbolically, individualizing a political cause. To survive, modeled minorities must assert self-identity among their own political, cultural, or social group, or face persistent, lonely fragmentation.

My reply to the more cultivated carload of men and women who accuse me of essentializing is like my reply to the young pestering boys when I was nineteen. I jeer, "Yeah, so what." This paper is a lengthy rejoinder to the accusation that categorizes marginalized groups into an essentialist camp without regard for the fact that in a postmodern world, where many of us speak as women of color, as ethnic white women, as lesbians of color and white lesbians, as third world people, as physically marginalized people, we construct creative, not reactive, countersites with multiple voices in mostly masculinist, Eurocentric colonizing institutions.[4] I believe, as Spivak argues, that representation cannot take place without essentialism.[5] If we do not identify ourselves as Chicanas, lesbians, third world people, or simply women, then we commit social and political suicide. Without our identities, we become homogenized and censored.

To speak as a woman or, more specifically, to speak as a Chicana lesbian who has inherited a history of conquest and colonization in the Southwest, to speak as myself with other women like myself, means that I seek decolonized spaces where discourse can unfold and flourish, where theories of Chicana lesbian representation can be launched among ourselves without the threat of appropriation from those who claim to want our words.

But we have entered a postmodern age, some say a postcolonial one. In the Southwest, however, I often feel we are still embedded in the colonial social relations we inherited in the sixteenth and nineteenth centuries. Postmodernists suspiciously glare at those of us who claim to speak as women, as third world people, or as lesbians. Being a woman, a lesbian, or a person of color does not ensure that one will speak as one, given our multiple identities and multiple voices. There is no "authentic" Chicana lesbian voice. But authenticity is hardly the issue. The real question, I believe, is posed by Nancy Hartsock who plainly and powerfully asks, "Why is it that just at the moment when so many of us who have been silenced begin to demand the right to name ourselves, to act as subjects rather than objects of history, that just then the concept of subjecthood becomes problematic?"[6] Why, indeed.

In the first part of this essay, I engage Luce Irigaray's theory of the female symbolic to argue for *sitios y lenguas* as a matrix of strategic essentialism. In the second part, I introduce examples of invasionary politics as experienced by third world women and Chicana lesbians who grapple with dominant discourses. Briefly, and at the end, I exemplify Chicana/Mexicana lesbian representation in Texas/Chihuahua with women who uniformly create social and political spaces.[7] Throughout, I'd like to suggest that safe, decolonized spaces where Chicanas, Mexicanas, and lesbianas interact follow Irigaray's scheme by contributing to a culturally specific female imaginary. A distinct, Chicana/Mexicana *lesbiana cultura* has been in the making, even if occasionally interrupted by exhausting, invasionary discourse and politics. This is also a call for coalition-building with other political and social groups who acknowledge a need for alternative strategies.

Can women speak as women, can Chicana lesbians speak as Chicana lesbians? Do hegemonic voices have to speak for the marginalized? By invoking Luce Irigaray whose work theorizes a definitive urgency for the construction of the female symbolic, I pose these questions. The French feminist does not want to "create a theory of woman," but instead, she is attempting to "secure a place for the feminine within sexual difference."[8] The female imaginary would persevere without being subsumed by the male imaginary. Women would stop masquerading for and as men.

A critic of Irigaray, Lisa Jardine, discusses the French feminist's strategy, a strategy that initiates female discourse to conceive of the female imaginary. Jardine notes "Here is Irigaray, speaking the female imaginary, leaving the (male) imaginary to his own devices."[9] Jardine claims that despite the trend to create fresh feminist psychoanalytic theory, the discourse falls prey to what it challenges, the male-symbolic order, and within that order, men argue, "feminists have got to give us some space."[10] Hence, appropriation of feminist discourse leads to the diffusion of women's language, women's story, her story, her space. I agree with Jardine's main premise, that feminist discourse is appropriated, therefore disempowered. I do dispute a secondary argument about Irigaray. She reduces the French feminist to a biological reading and criticizes her language, a female-centered language which makes Jardine "uncomfortable." Quoting from Irigaray's essay, "When Our Lips Speak Together," where the French feminist pronounces woman's pleasures as plural, Jardine omits phrases from the page because "if it deliberately discountenances the men, we too have always felt a certain uncomfortableness with it, (that's why I left a bit of the last passage out)."[11] The phrases, which make Jardine and other (perhaps hetero-sexual?) women uncomfortable, are the following:

> Fondling the breasts, touching the vulva, spreading the lips, stroking the posterior wall of the vagina, brushing against the mouth of the uterus, and so on. To evoke only a few of the most specifically female pleasures. Pleasures which are somewhat misunderstood in sexual difference as it is imagined—or not imagined.[12]

For some women—I would argue for some lesbians anyway—Irigaray's narrative offers a language of desire, even a seductive discourse. She constructs the female imaginary as she negotiates for its creation.

For Lisa Jardine, Irigaray's discourse reduces the theorist to biological essentialism. By placing women, women's bodies, and their sexualities at center, the feminist essentializes to achieve a specific task—the female imaginary. She seems aware of "biology is destiny" arguments hurled against her. However, Irigaray is nobody's fool, not Lacan's, and not that of the women who have come after him to footnote her text and place it in an essentialist category. She also seems cognizant of the female symbolic as a dynamic process, which leads me to the following section.

Why am I, a Chicana lesbian historical materialist appealing to French feminism? Can European feminist paradigms help to reconstruct Chicana (hi)stories? Does the female symbolic lead to an understanding of Chicana lesbian representation? Can Irigaray's discourse clarify the cultural construction of sexuality for Chicanas? I use Irigaray for a number of reasons. I subscribe to her contention that women need to create female discourses; however, as a historian, I have witnessed how women have always created their communities and discourses within phallocentric arenas. My point of departure argues for marginal marginalized lesbians and women of color to continue framing our decolonized spaces and languages, *sitios y lenguas*. We have done so within designated, colonial spaces. But, just as Jardine points out that men appropriate from feminists, women of color face the same appropriation when our spaces are invaded and penetrated, as we are discursively and territorially colonized. We seek decolonized spaces beyond the third world spaces of white women's kitchens and white men's cotton fields where we still find Chicanas.

I look to Irigaray to ask whether essentializing strategies, such as centering women—but in this case lesbians of color—inhibit or enhance social, historical, and cultural analyses. Is a socialist feminist lesbian of color an essentialist because she claims *sitios y lenguas*, spaces and languages, sites and discourses, apart from male-defined and/or Eurocentric arenas? Do essentializing strategies for radical socialist feminist lesbians of color confine us? Yes and no. Essentializing strategies are survival strategies, after all, and often the only means to an end for marginalized groups. These strategies are never the solution, but they are a process for finding and expressing one's multiple voices.

I am also intrigued by Irigarayan concepts because I believe that her probing of sexuality may provide lesbians with a language to decode sociosexual relations and then invert the language at our command. In her essay, "When Our Lips Speak Together," she uses transgressive female language. Her essay, as women's erotica, offers a site and language of deconstruction and reconstruction. As a lesbian of color, I borrow from Irigaray the advocacy of female discourses for communities of women of color; as a Chicana feminist, I adopt yet another language, European feminism, to understand how third world women are located by colonialists.

Margaret Whitford outlines two dominant readings of Irigaray, one is a biological reading, the other is a Lacanian reading, whether interpreting or misinterpreting Lacan. But a third, less popular reading is by North American feminists who read Irigaray as a feminist celebrating relationships between women.[13] My own reading probably falls into the second and third categories although I question what almost appears like an analysis of the universal woman.[14] Instead, I argue for historical, regional, and cultural specificity to celebrate relationships between women. For me, marginalized groups must have separate spaces to inaugurate their own discourses, *nuestra lengua en nuestro sitio*.

Celebrations are hardly an impulse when Euro-American, Eurocentric women and men, or even men of color, assume they have rights to Chicana lesbiana *sitios*, claiming they must have equal access to our spaces as if social relations are equal between people of color and Euro-Americans or between women and men, as if we no longer lived in a capitalist, patriarchally framed society that continues to dictate hierarchies. Even though postmodern theorists have retired hierarchies, domination, unequal socioeconomic relations, unequal gender relations, and unequal racial relations—all still thrive, and, totalizing as it seems, for the powerless and colonized only a powerful, colonizer exists. Subtleties and refined differences among the powerful are lost nuances to the powerless and the colonized.[15]

Invasionary Politics

I would like to present two examples of invasionary politics in the academic community. Invasive or invasionary politics are most often practiced under the guise of sisterhood or brotherhood. I want to critique these prototypes of sisterhood to exemplify the problems women of color face in the academy when asked to speak as women of color and are therefore essentialized from above. In the second personal illustration, I outline the political dynamics when Chicana lesbians speak as Chicana lesbians in the academy.

The first case is taken from an essay in the anthology *Conflicts in Feminism*. Marianne Hirsch, one of its editors, exposes her feminist politics and the way in which she came to terms with her racism.[16] She refers to the feminist theory group organized at the Bunting Institute in 1984 where one African-American member and one Chicana member led the first discussion on race and class. She claims she was prepared to accept criticism about her exclusionary practices concerning women of color, but she was not prepared for the women of color to ask, "Why should we talk about this with you? What purpose will it serve?" Hirsch was horrified when the Chicana said that she felt more deeply connected to Hispanic men than to white women. Hirsch responds,

> There I knew what to say, I argued back, heatedly, passionately, terrified that if what she said was true I would lose what I had been building—personally and theoretically—for fifteen years. It took a long time for me to acknowledge that I was trying to argue her out of her experience. Her experience threatened me profoundly, and with my defensiveness I was only confirming her point.[17]

She further rationalizes that during the next year, the women in the group built trust by thinking more seriously about the privileged positions of white middle class feminism. Hirsch also notes that they built "powerful coalitions, even lasting bonds."[18]

Both editors, Marianne Hirsch and Evelyn Fox Keller, theorize that conflict is essential and sometimes even a "source of pleasure" when feminist coalitions between Euro-American women and women of color are formed. I ask, pleasure for whom? If indeed we acknowledge inequality and unevenness, not to mention the cultural biases in a room where two women of color become the moral conscience—the cultural workers for white majority women—then we cannot assume the dynamic is good, enlightening, or pleasurable for the marginalized. Race, class, and ethnic equality is presumed. And I only name a few of the differences reduced by the dream of a common language. Women of color have been invited, but not to discourse with each other. They have been invited as reactors and resisters, who reveal discursive and territorial colonization, upon entering confrontations that presume equal sociopolitical relations between first- and third-world people. Unfortunately, only after abusive conflict do some Euro-American women begin to realize gender consciousness is irreducible and that coalition building is a delicate matter, to say the least. How can this pleasurable conflict be cast so lightly while the social relations between Euro-Americans and people of color in the United States remain historically incongruous? Inequality, historically inherited and materially grounded, impedes pleasure for the person lower on the socioeconomic, racial, patriarchal rung.

The question the women of color posed before Hirsch's group in 1984, "Why should we talk about this with you?" is the same question many women of color asked through the feminist movements of the 1960s and 1970s, and the question still remains in the 1990s. The practice of invasionary politics is reasserted under the guise of feminist discourse and under the guise of equal opportunity. Marginalized others are silenced, having no rights to spaces to construct creative rather than reactive discourses.

Social scientists and field workers have proven repeatedly that conflict with those who have more socioeconomic and political power places the disempowered in a peculiar position, a distrustful one, but certainly not one in which the colonized voluntarily bond with a discursive and territorial colonizer. The ground work laid by such discourses can be rather like false intimacies. Chandra Mohanty reminds us, "Sisterhood cannot be assumed on the basis of gender; it must be forged in concrete, historical, and political practice and analysis."[19] The praxis, after all, will serve to liberate us.

Theoretical commonalities, based on gender, do not negate irreducible differences. For one, the hierarchy within a capitalist, patriarchally framed society must be dealt with. And, in an ideal socialist feminist universe, differences would still exist, but they would be respected and admired, not trivialized. A racial economy, which benefits many Euro-American Eurocentric people and harms many people of color, can parallel an argument about a male-centered economy that damages women, an Irigarayan concept. But what is the reality? As a historical materialist, I observe race relations, and I observe social relations between women and men. A political, historical, and regional analysis of race and gender relations is imperative. The irreducible differences are centered in multiple *sitios y lenguas*, ongoing processes with little or no resolution. The mistake made within any arena, whether academic or political, is that a common enemy bonds "us" and makes "us" all the same, while "they," the common enemy, are also all the same. But strategic essentialism circumvents totalizing by implementing a political strategy that recognizes that political and cultural bonds and coalitions are based on identities in constant flux. At this juncture, I become a historian searching for specificity, regionally and locally, to ask how inherited sociosexual relations affect people. Historical specificity, then, is compulsory.

The next example of invasionary politics is a personal one about homophobia at home, to quote Gloria Anzaldúa.[20] When the few Chicana lesbians who are "out" in the academy decided to hold a closed panel at the National Association for Chicano Studies in spring 1990, a panel open to all women—physically challenged, lesbian, heterosexual, bisexual, homophobic, Latina, Euro-American, working class, middle and upper class, etc.—we expected criticism from some of our less supportive female and male colleagues, but we did not expect combat. The gentler comments ranged from "That's separatism" to "What do lesbians want anyway?" The harsher comments I'd prefer not to repeat. When a group of Chicana lesbians proposed the possibility of a lesbian caucus, the response from well-respected, Chicano professors was that "a marijuanista caucus" would have to receive equal time if a lesbian caucus was formed, linking lesbianism to deviance. Later, the men who made such comments denied them and pretended they had only been joking, unaware that lesbian and gay bashing are no more amusing than racial slurs. There were also those who sat passively while homophobic remarks flew.

After I confronted a heterosexual Chicana about her homophobia, she said, I was told, that a workshop open only to women was exclusionary. She denied her homophobic stance and later complained to other people that she had been "verbally raped" (interesting imagery). This "confrontation" would later earn me the title "lesbian terrorist" at a Chicana academic meeting in the summer of 1990. I also challenged Chicano males (one heterosexual and one gay) about their uninformed comments. My gay colleague quickly agreed; the heterosexual man listened and then admitted he had prejudged us. Despite my so-called terrorist tactics, both of these men communicate regularly with me. Along with my call for Chicana/Mexicana *sitios y lenguas*, I also see essentializing strategies as ways to open up dialogue between essentialist camps. (Such conflicts and confrontations, however, are hardly bliss.)

But getting back to the questions of who speaks as a lesbian or can lesbians speak? My experience has been that when Chicana lesbians speak politically, there are efforts to silence Chicana lesbian voices, and any effort to make spaces and create discourses is threatened by invasionary politics. The straight mind also denies the possibility of women's devotion to female-centered sexuality.[21] Heterosexual discomfort permeates critiques of women-loving women. Interestingly, Irigaray is herself a heterosexual, but it is my contention that within her female symbolic she centers women's bodies and sexuality to arouse heterosexual women to awaken from compulsory heterosexuality. In the case of Chicanas, the straight mind mostly disregards lesbian sexuality unless we look to Gloria Anzaldúa or Cherríe Moraga, both of whom are often trivialized because theirs is *just* a lesbian perspective and therefore a marginal one. In either case, the power dynamic I've spoken of earlier in the situations I outlined above is victimizing. Irigaray when speaking as a woman is trivialized, lesbians when speaking as lesbians become the heterosexual's victim discursively.

Those who read lesbians merely as essentialists, or Irigaray as a biological determinist, impose not only a heterosexist critique but reduce the experiences to univocality. I agree with Margaret Whitford's reading of Irigaray, which equivocates the male philosophers, who accuse Irigaray of essentialism, as the true essentialists.[22] Within a male symbolic, women have two choices: either practice strategic essentialism or embrace the male symbolic, which mimics women who mimic men who sometimes mimic women mimicking men. The mimicking men are the postmodernists who have entered feminist territory to invade, to appropriate, and to hurl accusations at women who claim essentialist strategies.

Sitios y Lenguas en Tejas y Chihuahua

As representations of Chicana/Mexicana lesbian sites and discourses, I would like to introduce briefly summaries of voices from these communities. I borrow partly from ethnographic methodology presenting anonymous informants. The women did not want to be identified from taped recordings and preferred to talk openly and freely in group sessions. I took notes but only after the sessions were over.[23] Anonymity for these women is culturally, regionally, and politically critical.

The topics at group meetings included sexual practices, multiple partners, monogamy, aging, mothers, dancing, dress, make-up, AIDS, safe sex, dental dams, lubricants, vibrators, families, married lovers, marriages, leather harnesses, sizes, colors, and shapes of silicone dildos, who did it to whom and how, Catholicism, Protestantism, films, writers, artists, the (not-so-) Free Trade Agreement, the border patrol, daily border crossings, the bar scene, the pick-up scene, tequila, racist customs officers, sobriety, butch/femme, coming out, cooking, jealousy, money and class distinctions, cars, fathers, children, and, finally, cultural differences and similarities between Chicanas and Mexicanas.

At one of the livelier sessions, women invented cultural vocabulary, making up words and poems with transgressive connotations. For example, *chingar* (fuck) has phallocentric implications. Tired of the phallologocentrism, the women improvised with *panochear*, from the Nahuatl root, *panocha*, which is contemporary slang for vagina. Instead of using *chingon*, which implies a herculean man, we invented *panochona*, representing a formidable, impressive, woman, whether lesbian or straight. At another meeting, one of the Mexicanas, whom I'll call Fulana, created the first lines of the following poem and then other women added more lines. Note the Nahuatl sounds.

> Machácame la panocha
> machácamela otra vez
> mi panocha machaca
> machácamela bien.[24]

My point is this: the discussions could not have been as open, as free, or as nurturing if "outsiders," e.g., non-Latina lesbians, had attended. Cultural affinities are part of the self-naming process. As

Chicanas and Mexicanas redefining ourselves, we felt empowered. I do not want to give the impression that we only gathered socially, to talk *tonterias*, nonsense. I only mean to argue that for third-world lesbians, a regionally and culturally specific female symbolic can be constructed in our own spaces. For me, this kind of bonding and nurturing makes it possible to embark upon struggles for social change.

Again, I ask myself, why I, a Chicana lesbian, am attracted to Irigaray's female symbolic, herself a Eurocentric feminist, although cognizant of historical materialism.[25] I find in her work an essentializing strategy, a point of departure for my own essentializing strategies as a historical materialist from a region twice conquered and colonized. I find in her work a method that strips away masks, and I find in her work the suggestion of a solution, the construction of female discourses. Our communities have always had a healthy degree of community separatism, spaces and languages apart from invasion, conquest, rape, and penetration, whether conquest is discursive—of the body of text—or territorial and physical—of the land and body. As an idealist, I continue to envision a future materially grounded in a female symbolic that appreciates irreducible differences.

Notes

1. Spivak, *The Post-Colonial Critic*, 109. In the same interview, Spivak notes that Stephen Heath has also been credited with first using "strategic essentialism."

2. Irigaray, *This Sex Which is Not One*, 160–61.

3. See my essay, "Sexuality and Discourse: Notes from a Chicana Survivor," 159–84, where I define *sitio y lengua* as self-constructed Chicana spaces to create Chicana discourses. This process is also what Homi Bhabha refers to as "sliding ambivalently from one enunciatory position to another" in an attempt to "articulate cultural differences." See Bhabha, "DissemiNation: Time, Narrative, and the Margins of the Modern Nation," 298.

4. See Chela Sandval's essay, "Third World Women and a Theory of Oppositional Consciousness," *Genders*, Fall 1991. She argues for third-world women's oppositional consciousness as the means by which they have survived dominant feminist spaces.

5. Spivak, *The Post-Colonial Critic*, 109.

6. Hartsock, "Foucault on Power: A Theory for Women?," 163.

7. This is part of an ongoing assessment of Chicana/Mexicana lesbiana voices in the El Paso/Juárez border where I have lived for three years. I thought it necessary to provide a few examples of how Chicana/Mexicana lesbiana *sitios y lenguas*

continue to thrive in a unique geographic area where homophobia could kill us, psychically and physically, but our lesbiana discourses nurture and enliven us.

8. Irigaray, *This Sex Which Is Not One*, 159.

9. Jardine, "The Politics of Impenetrability," 66.

10. Ibid., 63.

11. Ibid., 66–67.

12. Irigaray, *This Sex Which Is Not One*, 28. This is a different translation from the one Jardine uses.

13. Whitford, "Rereading Irigaray," 107.

14. I agree with Whitford's analysis that Irigaray is not a pre-Lacanian, but a post-Lacanian. She seems to understand profoundly his patriarchal bias where women are concerned. Ibid., 108.

15. Memmi, *The Colonizer and the Colonized*.

16. Hirsch and Fox Keller, "Conclusions: Practicing Conflict in Feminist Theory," 370–85.

17. Ibid., 383.

18. Ibid., 384.

19. Mohanty, "Under Western Eyes: Feminist Scholarship and Colonial Discourses," 333–58.

20. Anzaldúa, *Borderlands/La Frontera*.

21. Of course, I must cite Wittig, *The Straight Mind and Other Essays*, for her analysis of the "straight mind."

22. Whitford, *Philosophy in the Feminine*, 103.

23. I talked with ten to twelve women over less than a year, meeting with them weekly at first and then sporadically. Sometimes only four or five women would be at a rap session. Half of the women were native to Texas and the other half were native to Chihuahua, Mexico. I spoke with more women from each region but decided to narrow my notes to twelve. I use assumed names, given the delicate topics and their open dialogue. I am taping some women in one-to-one sessions but, again, only anonymously.

24. *Machaca* was redefined as "to embrace, squeeze, or hold firmly and passionately."

25. Irigaray speaks of women as commodities and surplus value for men in both *Speculum of the Other Woman* and *This Sex Which Is Not One*, clearly borrowing from Marx's theories.

Works Cited

Anzaldúa, Gloria. *Borderlands/La Frontera*. San Francisco: Spinsters/Aunt Lute, 1987.

Bhabha, Homi K. "DissemiNation: Time, Narrative, and the Margins of the Modern Nation." In Homi K. Bhabha, ed., *Nation and Narration*, pp. 291–322. New York: Routledge, 1990.

Hartsock, Nancy. "Foucault on Power: A Theory for Women?" In Linda J.

Nicholson, ed., *Feminism/Postmodernism*, pp. 157–75. New York: Routledge, 1990.

Hirsch, Marianne, and Evelyn Fox Keller. "Conclusions: Practicing Conflict in Feminist Theory." In Marianne Hirsch and Evelyn Fox Keller, eds., *Conflicts in Feminism*, pp. 370–85. New York: Routledge, 1990.

Irigaray, Luce. *Speculum of the Other Woman*. Translated by Gillian C. Gill. Ithaca: Cornell University Press, 1985.

——. *This Sex Which Is Not One*. Translated by Catherine Porter with Carolyn Burke. Ithaca: Cornell University Press, 1985.

Jardine, Lisa. "The Politics of Impenetrability." In Teresa Brennan, ed., *Between Feminism and Psychoanalysis*, pp. 63–72. New York: Routledge, 1989.

Mohanty, Chandra. "Under Western Eyes: Feminist Scholarship and Colonial Discourses." *boundary 2* 12–13 (Spring/Fall 1984): 333–58.

Memmi, Albert. *The Colonizer and the Colonized*. Boston: Beacon Press, 1967.

Pérez, Emma. "Sexuality and Discourse: Notes from a Chicana Survivor." In Carla Trujillo, ed., *Chicana Lesbians*, pp. 159–84. Berkeley: Third Woman Press, 1991.

Spivak, Gayatri Chakravorty. *The Post-Colonial Critic: Interviews, Strategies, Dialogues*. Edited by Sarah Harasym. New York: Routledge, 1990.

Whitford, Margaret. "Rereading Irigaray." In Teresa Brennan, ed., *Between Feminism and Psychoanalysis,* pp. 106–26. New York: Routledge, 1989.

——. *Luce Irigaray: Philosophy in the Feminine*. New York: Routledge, 1991.

Wittig, Monique. *The Straight Mind and Other Essays*. Boston: Beacon Press, 1992.

7 Lesbian Bodies in the Age of (Post)Mechanical Reproduction

Cathy Griggers

What signs mark the presence of a lesbian body?

Writing the lesbian body has become more common of late, making reading it all the more difficult. Less hidden, and therefore more cryptic than ever, the lesbian body increasingly appears as an actual variability set within the decor of everyday discourse. Signs of her presence appear on the cover of *ELLE*, for example, or in popular film and paperback detective mysteries as both the sleuth *and* femme fatale, in texts that range from Mary Wings's overt lesbian thriller *She Came Too Late* (1987) to the conflicted, symptomatic lesbian subplot in Bob Rafelson's *Black Widow* (1986). She appears disguised as a vampire in Tony Scott's *The Hunger* (1983), and masquerading as the latest American outlaw hero in *Thelma and Louise* (1991). On television, she's making her appearance on the evening soap "L.A. Law," and she virtually made MTV via Madonna's "Justify Your Love" music video (1990). When MTV censored the video, she appeared on

ABC's "Nightline" instead under the guise of "news." Elsewhere, in the latest lesbian mail-order video from Femme Fatale—a discursive site where the lesbian imaginary meets the sex industry—you can find her on all fours and dressed in leather or feathers, or leather *and* feathers, typically wearing a phallic silicone simulacrum. Amidst controversy, she appeared in the trappings of San Francisco's and London's lesbian bar culture passing as a collection of art photographs in Della Grace's *Love Bites* (1991). In the summer of 1992, PBS broadcast a BBC production depicting the torrid affair between Violet Treyfusis and Vita Sackville-West into the living rooms of millions of devoted public-broadcasting viewers as part of the "Masterpiece Theatre" series, with an introduction by Alistair Cooke. Meanwhile, Susie Bright, author of *Susie Sexpert's Lesbian Sex World* (1990), made more lesbian sexual reality in 1992 with her new *Susie Bright's Sexual Reality: A Virtual Sex World Reader*, published by Cleis Press and quickly selling out of its first printing. Lesbian computer nerds quietly wait for Bright to assist in the world's first virtual sex program designed by a lesbian. Same-sex sex between women is already a menu option on the popular on-line *Virtual Valerie*, along with a menu for a variety of sex toy applications. Let's face it; lesbian bodies in postmodernity are going broadcast, they're going techno-culture, and they're going mainstream.[1]

In the process of mainstreaming, in which minoritarian and majoritarian significations intermingle, the lesbian body of signs is exposed as an essentially dis-organ-ized body.[2] *The* lesbian is as fantasmatic a construct as *the* woman. There are women, and there are lesbian bodies—each body crossed by multiplicitous signifying regimes and by different histories, different technologies of representation and reproduction, and different social experiences of being lesbian determined by ethnicity, class, gender identity, and sexual practices. In other words, as lesbian bodies become more visible in mainstream culture, the differences among these bodies also become more apparent. There is a freedom and a loss inscribed in this current cultural state of being lesbian. On the one hand, lesbians are given greater exemption from a categorical call that delimits them from the cultural spaces of the *anytime, anywhere*. On the other hand, the call of identity politics becomes increasingly problematic.

The problem of identity is always a problem of signification in regard to historically specific social relations. Various attempts have been made to locate a lesbian identity, most inculcated in the grand nominalizing imperative bequeathed us by the Victorian taxonomies of "sexual" science. Should we define the lesbian by a specific sexual practice or by the lack thereof? By a history of actual, or virtual, relations? Can she be identified once and for all by the presence of a public, broadcast kiss, by an act of self-proclamation, or by an act of community outing? Should we know her by the absence of the penis or by the presence of a silicone simulacrum? Surely this material delimitation may go too far—for shouldn't we wonder whether or not a lesbian text, for all that, can be written across the body of a "man"? I can point to the case of male-to-female transsexuals who cathect toward women, but why should we limit the problematic to its most obvious, symptomatic manifestation?[3]

The question of a lesbian body of signs always takes us back to the notion of identity in the body, of body as identity, a notion complicated in postmodernity by alterations in technologies of reproduction. Benjamin observed in "The Work of Art in the Age of Mechanical Reproduction" that mechanical reproduction destroyed the aura of the original work of art and, more important, provided a circuit for mass mentalities and thus an access code for fascism in the twentieth century.[4] In regard to this observation, we might recall Hitler's admission that without the electronic reproduction of his voice over the radio, he could never have conquered Germany. For the sake of thinking the future of lesbian bodies in postmodernity, I want to recall Benjamin's critique of the state's techno-fetishization of technologies of reproduction in the context of contemporary lesbian bodies—bodies working under a signifying regime of simulation and within an economy of repetition. Baudrillard (*Simulations*, 1983) has defined (post)mechanical reproduction as the precession of simulacra, the accession of post–Second World War, postindustrial culture to a state of hyperreality. This state is reached when cultural reproduction begins to refer first and foremost to the fact that there is no original. For Attali (*Noise*, 1985) (post)mechanical reproduction marks the difference between an economy of representation, in which representative power is used to maintain belief in the harmony of the socius, and an economy of repetition, which is characterized by the repetitive mass production of all social relations and the silencing of disorder by a bureaucratic power operating in the ambiance of a deafening syncretic flow of mass productions. The cultural reproduction of lesbian bodies in the age of (post)mechanical reproduction, that is, in an economy of simulacral repetition, has more than ever destroyed any aura of an "original" lesbian identity while exposing the cultural sites through which lesbianism is appropriated by the political economy of postmodernity.

Benjamin noted that the aesthetic debates over the status of photography as "art" obscured the more crucial question of whether the invention of photography had transformed the very nature of art. Similarly, the appearance of the public lesbian, particularly after World War II liberated her from a depression economy, raises the question of whether the "nature" of the feminine hasn't substantively changed in postmodern culture. The point is that the political economy of (post)mechanical reproduction is altering traditional values and expressions of gendered social identities as subjects of history.

The subjective transformation that Benjamin was on the verge of articulating in the years just before the Second World War involved the relationship between technologies of representation and the human body in regard to identification. In Benjamin's reading of the broader effects of photography and film, the audience's identification had shifted from the actor (Hitler) to the camera (technology). Technical reproduction not only changes the reaction of the masses to art, it calls the masses into being in their late modern and postmodern forms as subjects, not of nature, but of technology.[5]

We are at a moment of culture, for example, when phallic body prostheses are being mass-produced in the merger of the sex industry with plastics technologies. *On Our Backs* is not the only photojournal to market artificial penises. Even *Playgirl*, marketed primarily to straight women, carries pages of advertisements for a huge assortment of phallic simulacra. We're left to wonder what these women might eventually think to do with a double-ended dildo. But there's no mistaking that the lesbian assimilation of the sex toy industry is reterritorializing the culturally constructed aura of the phallic signifier. By appropriating the phallus/penis for themselves, lesbians have turned techno-culture's semiotic regime of simulation and the political economy of consumer culture back against the naturalization of masculinist hegemony. Once the penis is mass-reproduced, any illusion of a natural link between the cultural power organized under the sign of the phallus and the penis as biological organ is exposed as artificial. The reproduction of the penis as dildo exposes the male organ as signifier of the phallus and not vice versa, that is, the dildo exposes the cultural organ of the phallus as a simulacrum. The dildo is an artificial penis, an appropriated phallus, and a material signifier of the imaginary ground for a historically manifest phallic regime of power.

The effect on lesbian identities of this merger between the sex industry and plastics technologies is typical of the double binds characteristic of lesbianism in postmodernity. Ironically, the validity of grounding phallic power and gendered identity in the biological sign of difference in the male body is set up for cultural reinvestigation and reinvestment once the penis itself is reproduced as signifier, that is, in the very process of mass-producing artificial penises as a marketable sign for the consumption of desiring subjects, including subjects desiring counterhegemonic identities. At the same time, the commodification of the signifier—in this case the penis as signifier of the phallus—obscures the politico-economic reproduction of straight class relations by channeling lesbian signification from the unstable and uncertain register of the *real* to the overly stable, imaginary register of desire for the fetish-sign (i.e., the repetitive channeling of desire into the fixed circuit that runs from the penis as phallus to the phallus as penis in an endless loop). In other words, if working-class and middle-class urban lesbians and suburban dykes can't afford health care and don't yet have real national political representation, they can nonetheless buy a ten-inch "dinger" and a matching leather harness, and they can, with no guarantees, busy themselves at the task of appropriating for lesbian identities the signs of masculine power. This situation provides both a possibility for self-reinvention and self-empowerment and an appropriation of lesbian identities—and their labor, their leisure, and their purchasing power—into the commodity logic of techno-culture.

At the same time, new reproductive technologies, including artificial insemination by donor (AID), in-vitro fertilization (IVF), surrogate motherhood, Lavage embryo transfer, and tissue farming as in cross-uterine egg transplants, are both reterritorializing and reifying biological relations to gendered social roles.[6] The "body" is breaking up. I'm not talking just about the working body, the confessing body, the sexual body. These are old tropes, as Foucault showed us. In postmodernity, even the organs are separating from the body. That these organs are literal makes them no less organs of power. The womb is disjunct from the breast, for example, the vagina from the mouth that speaks, the ovaries and their production from the womb, etc. The lesbian body's relation to these reified technologies is entirely representative of the contradictions of lesbian subject positions in postmodernity. While new reproductive technologies generally reinforce a repressive straight economy of maternal production, body management, and class-privileged division of labor, the technology of cross-uterine egg transplants finally allows a lesbian to give birth to another lesbian's child, a fact that to date has gone entirely unmentioned by either the medical community or the media.[7]

The point is that the bodies that are the supposed ground of identity in essentialist arguments—arguments that assert we are who we are because of our bodies—are both internally fragmented in response to the intrusions of biotechnologies and advanced surgical techniques, including transsexual procedures, and externally plied by a variety of technologically determined semiotic registers ranging from the sex toy industry to broadcast representation. As a result, lesbian identities are generating a familiar unfamiliarity of terms that San Francisco's lesbian sexpert, Susie Bright, has been busily mainstreaming on the "Phil Donahue Show"—terms as provocative as female penetration, female masculinity, s/m lipstick dykes, and lesbian phallic mothers.

While all social bodies are plied by multiple regimes of signs, as Deleuze and Guattari as well as Foucault have repeatedly shown, lesbian bodies in the age of (post)mechanical reproduction are particularly paradigmatic of a radical semiotic multiplicity. This situation is hardly surprising. That lesbians are *not* women because women are a class defined by their relation to men—a statement Monique Wittig (1992) has popularized—doesn't mean we know exactly what a lesbian is. The "lesbian," especially the lesbian who resists or slips the always potential sedimentarity in that term, marks a default of identity both twice removed and exponentially factored. Lesbians in the public culture of postmodernity are subjects-in-the-making whose body of signs and bodies as sign are up for reappropriation and revision, answering as they do the party line of technology and identity.

This double call of technology and identity complicates our understanding of lesbian bodies as minority bodies—a definition that locates lesbians within the discourse of identity by their differences from the majority bodies of the hetero woman and man. If Wittig (*The Straight Mind*, 1992) wants to envision lesbians as "runaway slaves with no other side of the Mississippi in sight," perpetual and permanent fugitives, it's also undeniable that lesbians are at the same time, and often in the same bodies, lesbians bearing arms, lesbians bearing children, lesbians becoming fashion, becoming commodity subjects, becoming Hollywood, becoming the sex industry, or becoming cyborg human-machinic assemblages. And from the alternative point of view, we are also bearing witness to the military becoming lesbian, the mother becoming lesbian, straight women becoming lesbian, fashion and Hollywood and the sex industry becoming lesbian, middle-class women, corporate America, and techno-culture becoming lesbian, etc. That is, the lesbian body of signs, like all minority bodies, is always becoming majority, in a multiplicity of ways. But at the same time, in a multitude of domains across the general cultural field, majority bodies are busy *becoming lesbian*.[8] This notion of the transsemiotics of identities follows from Deleuze and Guattari's schizoanalysis of the postulates of linguistics, in which the linguistic notion of minority language produces its meaningful variance from a rhizomatic, not oppositional, relation to its majority others.

In the lesbian cultural landscape of postmodernity, essentialist arguments about feminine identity are more defunct than ever, while Wittig's lesbian materialist analysis of straight culture is more urgent than ever and more problematic. Even if the first social contract underlying dominant class relations in later industrial capitalism is still the heterosexual contract, as Wittig premises in *The Straight Mind*, the cultural variables for negotiating the space of that social contract are undergoing reconfiguration in postmodernity in ways that Wittig overlooks. This is why it's crucial to think the question of contemporary lesbian bodies in the specific context of the breakdown of ontological discourses in the shift from modernity to postmodernity, because in that shift the Cartesian, total subject that Wittig wants to claim as a right and as the political goal of lesbian identity politics is more and more manifestly undergoing splittings and fragmentations.[9] The decentralization of the post-Cartesian subject of postmodern culture is not antithetical to the dis-organ-ized political economy of postindustrial society, as Deleuze and Guattari have argued in the two volumes of *Capitalism and Schizophrenia* (1983, 1987). Indeed, capitalism itself produces schizoid subjectivity as a cultural state of being. For example, the notion of self in consumer discourse as a state that can be perpetually reconstructed according to one's desire and the reification of that desire into the reproduction of class relations has, in the case of lesbians, set a political economy of signs based on the commodification of selves in contention with compulsory heterosexuality and the cultural function it and the nuclear family serve in reproducing the labor force.

Setting lesbian identities first within the context of postmodern culture suggests two further clarifications of Wittig. First, any materialist analysis of a lesbian revolutionary position in relation to straight women as a class has to begin with one irreducible conundrum of postmodernity in regard to lesbian identities. The cultural space for contemporary lesbian identities to exist—economic freedom from dependence on a man—is a historical outcome of late industrial capitalism's commodity logic in its total war phase in the first half of the twentieth century.[10] In *Odd Girls and Twilight Lovers* (1991) Faderman has thoroughly documented this historical occurrence and its outcomes for urban lesbian identities, particularly during recruitment for World War II and during the military purges of homosexuals in the decade following the war that sent large numbers of lesbians to urban port cities. Women, particularly single women, comprised a large proportion of the substitute bodies required by the state to maintain performativity criteria established before each world war or to meet the accelerated industrial needs of total war and reconstruction. This is one of the undeniable conditions of women's entry into the workforce and the professions in the U.S., including the academy, and of their assimilation into the commodity marketplace beyond the domestic sphere, and this, along with the civil rights movement of the 1960s, helped to set up the possibility of the women's movement of the 1970s.[11] This is also part of the history of the cultural production of lesbian bodies as we know them today.

In other words, and this is my final clarification of Wittig's reading of lesbian positionality, lesbians are becoming nomad runaways *and* becoming state *at the same time*. And it's at the various sites where these interminglings of bodies take place that the cultural contradictions will be most apparent and therefore the political stakes greatest. These sites include any becoming majoritarian of the minoritarian as well as the becoming minoritarian of majority regimes of signs, and in each of these sites the political stakes may not be equivalent. This political complication results from the theoretical challenge to materialist social analysis presented by the failure of poststructural linguistics to adequately map cultural dialects *except* as unstable and constant sites of transformation. These kinds of subcultural variance and continuous historical transformation have to be factored into any lesbian materialist modeling system if we are to continue the work Wittig has launched toward a lesbian materialist critique of straight class relations and toward a materialist critique of lesbianism itself.

A discursive multiplicity of differences has to be seen as *both* a pragmatics of appropriation by straight culture and as signs of actual historical and material differences within subcultural groups. It's not enough to say that our discursive differences obfuscate the material reproduction of our class relations. Yet the material manifestations of the discourse of technology have made the lines between discourse, culture, and actual social bodies increasingly difficult to distinguish. If Wittig would identify lesbians by their refusal to take on the identity of the class that provides the labor and bodies for reproducing the labor force, for example, that distinction can no longer be so easily made. Reproductive technologies and economic independence have made it even more common for lesbian bodies to be maternal bodies, if not maternal bodies bearing the phallus. The materialist mapping of lesbian identities in postmodernity will therefore have to calculate relations among commodity logic, racially segmented and gendered classes, technologies of reproduction and simulation, and a war-machine partially exterior to the state in spite of its historical appropriation under the regime of global security and within the military-industrial-foreign-aid complex. Consider, for example, the yet hypothetical but virtually real instance of the feminine cyborg assemblage made manifest in a female F-16 pilot executing desert bombing raids. When this virtual state of events becomes actual, my first question will be "Is she a lesbian body?"

Cultural mappings of lesbian bodies will also have to include interminglings among minorities. These specific sites of mixing and transformation will shape the political stakes and the political strategies for a lesbian-feminist-queer-nation alliance and any possible alliance between that configuration and ethnic minorities. Take the case, from the 1950s to the present, of lesbians becoming only with much difficulty lesbian-feminists and then becoming, after even more struggle, lesbian-feminists-of-color (these hybridities were always present, of course, but for years remained invisible within the "minority" social bodies of feminism or African-Americanism or Hispanic-Americanism). The history of this particular struggle over the interminglings of minoritarian social bodies is entirely representative of the dilemmas facing the traditional political notion of identity politics grounded in a totalized, stable, and fixed subject. In a parallel though disjunct cultural scene, there is the instance of lesbians assimilating gay male sexual practices and the identities they mobilize—which San Francisco knows better than any other North American city. Such states of hybridity are made visible respectively by Audre Lorde's biomythography as a black-lesbian-feminist in *Zami* (1982) and Della Graces's photographs for a leather-lesbian identity-politics in *Love Bites* (1991), a book seized by U.S. Customs for its so-called obscenity. In Grace's portrait of "Jane, Jane, Queen of Pain" we see a lesbian body appropriating the codes of straight porn while assimilating s/m sexual practices arising specifically out of the situationality of gay male bar culture. Grace's images and Lorde's candid self-portrayal, along with all the other mass-produced representations of lesbian bodies currently circulating in popular culture, remind us of the ways in which lesbian bodies are crossed by multiplicitous regimes of signs.

Indeed, the potential power of lesbian identity politics in the current historical moment comes from its situatedness and alliances in feminist, gay male, and civil rights activism. Some lesbian bodies are a current site of contention in the women's movement, particularly over the issue of s/m practices and porn, because of their greater affinities with gay males than with straight women. Furthermore, the activist politics of ACT-UP in the face of the ideological epidemic of significations surrounding AIDS represent for many lesbians a better strategy of cultural politics than the consciousness-raising discourses traditionally authorized by NOW. But in the face of direct losses of ground gained in the sixties, seventies, and eighties on women's issues—right to abortions and birth-control information, right to protection from sexual harassment in the workplace, right to have recourse to a just law in the case of rape—the Queer Nation/straight feminism alliance will be crucial to the future of lesbian cultural politics.

This state of being lesbian in the age of postmechanical reproduction does not eradicate radical politics but asks that we refigure our understanding of identity politics as a politics of transformation and hybridity as well as resistance—indeed a politics working from both inside and outside straight techno-culture and the race and class structures it reproduces. Haraway's "A Cyborg Manifesto" (1991) theorizes one direction that lesbians can mobilize for further developing alliance-based, unintegrated networks of power in the cultural game of identity politics. The strategy of making cyborg assemblages of bodies and technologies proposed by Haraway should have a special valence for lesbians, who as a group have a history of playing with body assemblages against which straight women's masqueradings pale by comparison.

If feminisms and Marxisms have run amok on continental theoretical imperatives to construct a revolutionary subject that premises metaphysical identity closure, as Haraway argues, cyborg bodies, "stripped of identity," are free to rewrite the texts of their bodies and societies without the limit-texts of god/man, self/other, culture/nature, m/f (*Simians, Cyborgs, and Women*, 176). Bearing the banner of subjects-as-etching-machines, cyborg politics would be the politics of multiplicitous coding practices and noise in a system of perfect communication, a politics of many in the place of one, of hybrids in the place of boundaries. For those who have experienced the dominations of the "autonomous" self, to etch the microsurfaces of the encoding social body as something less and more than a "One" may be an empowering reconceptualization of the "Family of Man."

Take camp struggles over straight semiosis, for example, which gay and lesbian subcultures have always understood as a style of everyday cultural politics and survival and not as prepolitical, a reading commonly produced by straight "politicized" subjects. If we premise that the body is not outside textuality, that the body is itself a field of signification, a site for the production of cultural meanings and ideological reifications, then we have to admit that we can play the game this way or that, we can choose to pass or not within this scene and the next, but we can't choose to stop playing with signs, with our own *material* production as a cultural (i.e., visibly signifying) body.

If we admit that social bodies only exist in a process of constant historical transformation, then there are only hybrid bodies, moving bodies, migrant bodies, becoming bodies, machinic-assemblage bodies. And in relation to bodies of signs in postindustrial capitalism, even in the case of the most organ-ized signifying regimes, Deleuze and Guattari insist there are only *trans*semiotics. It's futile then to ask what subjectivities *essentially* exist inside and alongside the transversed social bodies of postmodernity. Too many challenges facing lesbian cultural politics are rendered invisible by a discourse of essentialism. It is in this regard that Haraway's vision of unnatural, hyperconstructed social bodies in their potential, if blasphemous, positivity provides an empowering alternative strategy for thinking lesbian bodies and organ-izing lesbian cultural politics into a material (if monstrous) body of power. But thinking this circuited body that might order lesbian organs of power with and within other assemblages of identity and being will require not only Benjamin's critique of the state's techno-fetishization of technologies of reproduction but also Wittig's lesbian materialism as well as Deleuze and Guattari's schizoanalysis of being in capitalism.

When we take up Haraway's cyborg project *for* lesbianism, for example, Wittig's essays on the political economy of lesbianism should remind us that the sites of political struggle over lesbian cyborg affinities will solidify around the historically and materially determined pragmatics of *who* gets to produce cyborg bodies, who has access, who provides the laboring and component bodies, and who becomes and who buys the commodities reproduced. If we accept that the body exists in an assemblage with technology, the "human" body itself may well appear subordinate to the cyborg body of which it is a part. Thus cultural politics not only come in conflict with the ideal of the totalized bourgeois subject, but they come into being encrypted in and by dominant signifying regimes of the state (such as media politics, the commodification of desires, new reproductive technologies, Star Wars, techno-progress, C^3I, and globalization). The problem of organ-ized agency will take on a dimensionality involving spatial and temporal coordinates of multiplicitous, rhizomatic collective social "identities." In each case, we'd have to reconsider where a cyborg body begins and ends (the limits of the text), for example, or when an exteriority is also an interiority. And who will have ownership of the means of cyborg production and reproduction?

Lesbian bodies are not essentially counterhegemonic sites of culture, as Wittig might like to theorize. The lesbian may not be a woman, as she argues in "One is Not Born a Woman" (1992); yet she is not entirely exterior to straight culture. Each lesbian has a faciality touching on some aspect of a majority signifying regime of postmodernity, whether that be masculinity/femininity, motherhood, race, or the nation-state, the sex industry, technologies of simulation, surgical techno-plastics, the commodification of selves and knowledges, reproductive technologies, or the military under global capitalism. Lesbians are inside and outside, minority and majority, *at the same time*.

Lesbian bodies have always presented a challenge to essentialist notions of feminine identity and never more so than when lesbians are set in the historical context of postmodernity. The cultural period in late industrial and postindustrial society during World War II and in the fifty years since is their historical heyday. Lesbian bodies came of age under the specter of a holocaust that could reach finality only by the injection into the global symbolic of a nuclear sublime so horrific as to arrest all prior signification. Their agencies must be agencies that work with the reduced political rights of a worldwide civilian population under the new military regime of global security (Virilio, *Popular Defense and Ecological Struggles*). They are proffered a variety of prostheses and self-imaging technologies—in fact, a variety of bodies—as long as they meet the performativity criterion of commodity logic. And if they are runaways, they're running from the very political economy that produced their possibility. This is their double bind. For all these reasons, the immediate challenge facing lesbian bodies in postmodernity is how to make a dis-organ-ized body of signs and identities work for a progressive, or even a radical, politics.

Notes

1. Photographic and electronic imaging media—including photojournals, popular film, broadcast and cable TV, home-video and on-line transmissions—have mainstreamed lesbian images by disseminating them to broadcast audiences. The popular controversy over Madonna's "Justify Your Love" music video, which appeared in late 1990, exemplifies the continual process of semiotic assimilation. In this postmodern conundrum, Madonna not only *becomes lesbian* for a portion of the tape, but the lesbian subtext becomes, if not MTV, then broadcast news—specifically on ABC's "Nightline," which aired the video in its entirety for millions of late-night television viewers. *ELLE*'s butch-femme aesthetic—which has managed not to "go too far," as Madonna's video did—is successfully becoming majority fashion-feminine for a growing segment of the middle-class and upper-middle-class women's market. "L.A Law" in the meanwhile is mainstreaming for prime-time soap audiences the everyday aporias of how to comport oneself with, as, and for a lesbian. *Thelma and Louise*, making the cover of *Time* the summer of its release with a photograph of Susan Sarandon and Geena Davis looking both butch *and* exactly like each other under the heading "Why *Thelma and Louise* Strikes a Nerve" (June 24, 1991), is just another event in a long series of discursive assimilations that are producing the popular cultural generation of the new butch-femme. Lesbians are both out and "passing" as versions of normative femininity.

2. The dis-organ-ized body, in Deleuze and Guattari's (1987) micromental study of capitalism and schizophrenia, is the Body without Organs (BwO).

3. See Sandy Stone's account of and critique of the "gender dysphoria syndrome" in "The Empire Strikes Back: A Posttranssexual Manifesto" in *Body Guards*.

4. According to Ong, mechanical production began with the reification of the oral world/word into print.

5. Benjamin's discourse comes close to a discourse of degeneracy and deca-

dence anchored in a notion of the natural when he reads mechanical reproduction as a process of cultural "liquidation" and when he approaches the historical object as if it were analogous to the aura of the "natural" object. He's reluctant to let go of the modern notion of history as comprised of objects bearing the same permanence and value as nature, and for good reason—fascism was obviously in its pragmatics a project of rewriting history. This is the contradiction of any nationalist totalitarian regime of signs: its fetishization of technologies at the very same time that it mobilizes remnant traces of a romantic notion of the "natural" socius. Perhaps Benjamin couldn't bring himself to say in public that the "authority" of the traditional cultural heritage he appeals to in the face of fascism is itself purely constructed—depending on its own class structures and techniques of representation for reproduction and enforcement. The (constructed) authority of this "original" heritage in the minds of the masses would be appropriated more easily than anyone could have imagined by fascist dream machines using the new technologies of mass reproduction, epitomized in the Nazi's use of broadcast radio and the newsreel—media that Benjamin correctly recognized as new forms of armaments (*Illuminations*, 213). The Nazi's genocidal program would demonstrate that history *could* be rewritten in a matter of a few years and that the "real" history that should have saved the world from the kind of contorted fantasy of national history and identity that was cathected onto Hitler had no *essential* authority whatsoever. Fascism, in fact, becomes possible from the very moment that the masses come to perceive themselves as the technologized subject of nature and no longer as the object of nature.

6. See Gena Corea's *The Mother Machine: Reproductive Technology from Artificial Insemination to Artificial Wombs* and Christine Overall's *The Future of Human Reproduction*.

7. The legal implications of this scenario await testing in regard to the law recognizing both the biological mother and birth mother as legal parents bearing full rights. I'm assuming in the scenario an artificial insemination by an anonymous donor (AID).

8. The more this process of becoming minority occurs, however (and, of course, it's always occurring), the more difficult it becomes for the majority body to "resist infiltration," and the more necessary it becomes for dominant straight culture ("Traditional Values Coalitions," etc.) to protect all borders fronting on otherness. "Resisting infiltration" suggests a paranoid posture—one that denies the constant process of psychic auto-organization and reorganization—a process made visible particularly by subcultural collective identities organized around the erotic cultivation of the intersubjective transactions and psychic instabilities common to amatory relations. For this reason, Kristeva (*Tales of Love*, 1987) describes amorous relations as the *vertigo of identity*. Rather than return the gaze of a body functioning manifestly as a collapsed inside/outside system in interaction with a multidimensional and fluid (i.e., excessive, unnatural, monstrous) psychic system, the paranoid will take flight to a prolapsed symbolic, thereby stabilizing the illusion that identity is a stable relation to a fixed sign formation, (i.e., a natural signatory relation of self to others).

9. See Wittig's argument for a lesbian total subject in "The Mark of Gender" for example (1992).

10. See Rudy Willis's *Total War* (1991), particularly the chapter "Substitute Bodies," and Lillian Faderman's *Odd Girls and Twilight Lovers: A History of Lesbian Life in Twentieth-Century America* (1991), particularly the chapter " 'Naked Amazons and Queer Damozels': World War II and Its Aftermath."

11. The women's movement of the 1970s and the African-American civil-rights movement of the 1960s shared some of the same problematic ties to the war machine through the substitute bodies recruitment policy in U.S. universities during the Second World War and through the G.I. Bill.

Works Cited

Attali, Jacques. *Noise: The Political Economy of Music.* Translated by Brian Massumi. Minneapolis: University of Minnesota Press, 1985.

Baudrillard, Jean. *Simulations.* Translated by Paul Foss, Paul Patton, and Philip Beitchman. New York: Autonomedia, 1983.

Benjamin, Walter. *Illuminations.* Translated by Harry Zohn. New York: Schocken, 1978.

Bright, Susie. *Susie Bright's Sexual Reality: A Virtual Sex World Reader.* Pittsburgh: Cleis Press, 1992.

Corea, Gena. *The Mother Machine: Reproductive Technology from Artificial Insemination to Artificial Wombs.* New York: Harper and Row, 1986.

Deleuze, Gilles, and Félix Guattari. *Anti-Oedipus: Capitalism and Schizophrenia.* Minneapolis: University of Minnesota Press, 1983.

——. *A Thousand Plateaus: Capitalism and Schizophrenia.* Minneapolis: University of Minneapolis Press, 1987.

Faderman, Lillian. *Odd Girls and Twilight Lovers: A History of Lesbian Life in Twentieth-Century America.* New York: Columbia University Press, 1991.

Grace, Della. *Love Bites.* London: GMP Publishers, 1991.

Haraway, Donna. *Simians, Cyborgs, and Women: The Reinvention of Nature.* New York: Routledge, 1991.

Kristeva, Julia. *Tales of Love.* Translated by Leon S. Roudiez. New York: Columbia University Press, 1987.

Lorde, Audre. *Zami: A New Spelling of My Name.* Watertown, Mass.: Persephone Press, 1982.

Ong, Walter. *Orality and Literacy: The Technologizing of the Word.* New York: Routledge, 1982.

Overall, Christine, ed. *The Future of Human Reproduction.* Ontario: The Women's Press, 1989.

Stone, Sandy. "The Empire Strikes Back: A Posttranssexual Manifesto." In Julia Epstein and Kristina Straub, eds., *Body Guards*, pp. 280–304. New York: Routledge, 1991.

Virilio, Paul. *Popular Defense and Ecological Struggles.* New York: Autonomedia,

1990.

Willis, Rudy. *Total War and Twentieth Century Higher Learning: Universities of the Western World in the First and Second World Wars*. Cranbury, N.J.: Fairleigh Dickinson University Press, 1991.

Wittig, Monique. *The Straight Mind*. Boston: Beacon Press, 1992.

Part Two

Textual and
Performative Strategies

8   Jeanette Winterson's Sexing the Postmodern

Laura Doan

In Jeanette Winterson's witty and exuberant autobiographical first novel *Oranges Are Not the Only Fruit* (1985) the protagonist Jeanette, an adolescent who decrees confidently that heterosexuality is beastly, confusing, and utterly unappealing, ponders why her passionate involvement with members of her own sex causes so much disruption in her family and church: "It all seemed to hinge around the fact that I loved the wrong sort of people. Right sort of people in every respect except this one; romantic love for another woman was a sin" (127). The problem, as Jeanette sees it, stems not from her exquisite longings for women, but from others' inability to recognize and acknowledge the loveliness of sexual love shared between women. Jeanette's strength and the strength of this coming-of-age/coming-out novel, emerges from a profound and unshakeable conviction that her lesbianism is right and that any attempt to condemn or despise her— a celebrant of the most natural of passions—constitutes perversion.

Winterson totally redefines normal and renders heterosexuality as unintelligible for Jeanette.

Three novels later the women of Jeanette Winterson's imagination still discover ecstasy with one another rather than with the male companion a conventional telos demands. None of the twelve dancing princesses in *Sexing the Cherry* (1989) finds ultimate happiness with a prince. When the prince isn't homosexual himself and when princely husbands aren't murdered in a surprising and grotesque manner, the princesses explore, in richly poetic imagery, a startling array of unconventional liaisons, from "salty bliss" with a mermaid to a happy lesbian arrangement in Rapunzel's tower (happy, that is, until an insensitive and intrusive prince arrives on the scene). As with *Oranges*, where the reconceptualization of the normal makes lesbian existence possible by, in effect, reversing the dominant culture's definition of natural and unnatural, in her more recent work Winterson stalls any potential charge of transgression, or label of transgressor, by appropriating the very terms that legitimize heterosexual union—thus one princess comments that "the man I had married was a woman" (*Sexing the Cherry*, 54)—and positing merely an innocent switch of the acceptable terms and conditions of that contract. Eschewing realism, Winterson constructs her narrative by exploiting the techniques of postmodern historiographic metafiction (such as intertextuality, parody, pastiche, self-reflexivity, fragmentation, the rewriting of history, and frame breaks) as well as its ideology (questioning "grand narratives," problematizing closure, valorizing instability, suspecting coherence, and so forth) in order to challenge and subvert patriarchal and heterosexist discourses and, ultimately, to facilitate a forceful and positive radical oppositional critique.

Winterson's attempt to insert lesbian desire and thereby profoundly upset and unsettle heterosexual hegemony is clearly political, so political in fact that reviewer Rosellen Brown laments that Winterson's "stories feel like pretexts" for her "vengeful hostility to men and marriage, her fascination with androgyny, and her compensatory vision of women as the stronger, more sane, and even physically dominating sex" ("Fertile Imagination," 10). Brown's reading may be less than acute in drawing out the subtleties of Winterson's complex handling of issues relating to sexual politics and gender construction, but she nevertheless discerns that Winterson pursues her own peculiar vision of a lesbian feminist political agenda. Noticeably absent from Brown is an attentiveness to Winterson as a practicing postmodernist.

Reviewer Michael Gorra, on the other hand, seems less interested in Winterson's sexual politics than in her investment in the postmodern, even proffering what might be regarded as the highest compliment paid to a metafictional writer: the materials of her fiction, he maintains, "seem the clichés of postmodernism" ("Gender Games," 24). A conflation of two such diverse critiques might logically suggest that Winterson pursues her political agenda through a postmodern writing practice, though few critics of postmodern literary representation would credit its producers with much more than the capacity to wreak playful havoc in the social and cultural order.

Critics such as Linda Hutcheon insist with some urgency that the feminist writer (and presumably also the lesbian feminist writer) who effectively plunders postmodern writing strategies for her own political ends, ends up herself in an ambivalent and problematic space. Hutcheon presents her case on the dangers of a convergence between feminism and postmodernism vis-à-vis representation most forcefully in *The Politics of Postmodernism*. She contends that metafictional writing practices—and, by extension, Winterson's delightful and rapturous style—are by definition superbly qualified to pose challenging questions to patriarchal discourses and consequently execute the first critical step toward disruption, but they are also superbly disqualified from going any further. The tactics so prevalent in metafiction (all supremely evident in Winterson's work) offer endless possibilities for the feminist writer to foreground provocative questions that, according to Hutcheon, "reveal art as the place where values, norms, beliefs, actions are produced; [the postmodern] deconstructs the processes of signification. But it never escapes its double encoding: it is always aware of the mutual interdependence of the dominant and the contestatory" (*Politics of Postmodernism*, 157). For Hutcheon, the problem is quite simply that feminism is political whereas postmodernism is not, or, more accurately, postmodernism is "politically ambivalent, doubly encoded as both complicity and critique" (168). Above all, she argues, "postmodernism has not theorized *agency*; it has no strategies of resistance that would correspond to the feminist ones" (168, emphasis mine). The distinction is critical, of course, because according to this view feminist writers can make good use of various metafictional strategies (which can challenge and destabilize patriarchal discourses through questioning, ambivalence, contradiction, parody and paradox, and through its fetishizing of difference), but feminist use of such techniques constitutes only the first step, as Hutcheon puts it, in a "move towards change (a move that is not, in itself, part of the post-modern)" (149). Hutcheon concludes her book with the unequivocal assertion that "there is . . . no way in which the feminist and the post-modern—as cultural enterprises—can be conflated" (167).

The relationship between feminism and postmodernism is uneasy and highly problematic (as is the case with postmodernism and any sort of oppositional politics). Many postmodern theorists have been largely uninterested in questions pertaining to gender and some femi-nist theorists regard postmodern theory with wariness at best and dis-trust and hostility at worst; as Christine Di Stefano argues,

> [The] postmodernist project . . . would make any semblance of a feminist politics impossible. To the extent that feminist politics is bound up with a specific constituency or subject, namely, women, the postmodernist prohibition against subject-centered inquiry and theory undermines the legitimacy of a broad-based organized move-ment dedicated to articulating and implementing the goals of such a constituency. ("Dilemmas," 76)

For Di Stefano and others, feminism as a social movement with a transformative political agenda is basically at odds and fundamental-ly incompatible with postmodern theory. Wendy Brown's elaboration on "feminist anxieties" toward postmodernity casts the theoretical net of objections still further:

> Postmodernity unnerves feminist theory not merely because it deprives us of uncomplicated subject standing, as Di Stefano sug-gests, or of settled ground for knowledge and norms, as Hartsock argues, or of "centered selves" and "emancipatory knowledge" as Benhabib avers. Postmodernity unsettles feminism because it deprives us of the *moral* force that the subject, truth, and normativ-ity coproduce in modernity. ("Feminist Hesitations," 78)

Yet feminist neglect of, or indifference toward, the postmodern is equally dangerous, for in embracing all ideological discourses and therefore none, it can undermine the feminist project.

Feminism and its critique of patriarchal hegemony, it would seem, has been very good for postmodernism by focusing its attention on sexual difference and the body, but postmodernism is inherently lim-ited in what it might offer feminists who have "distinct, unambiguous political agendas of resistance" (Hutcheon, *Politics of Postmod-ernism*, 142). Winterson does not compromise her political agenda by choosing to negotiate a postmodern terrain and to delve into a cache of metafictional techniques, but for Hutcheon and others, Winterson does compromise her postmodernist stance, which, while itself political, can never be politically committed. Such a predicament raises two important, interrelated questions: what are the limits and possibilities of the intervention of lesbian feminist representation in the postmodern cultural domain and what might postmodernism offer the lesbian feminist writer? In other words, must we rule out completely the possibility of a lesbian postmodern that in turn envisions a politicization of the postmodern cultural domain by collapsing binaries and boundaries, demanding the reconfiguration of gender constructions and deregulating heteronormativity through the genesis of pluralistic sexual identities? That is, in effect, an oppositional lesbian feminist representation that undermines controlling repressive hegemonies through reconceptualizing the sexing of the postmodern?

In a 1990 interview Jeanette Winterson ascribed political efficacy to narrativity; the invention of stories is a political act and she's "hoping all the time that it will challenge people, both into looking more closely at these things they thought were cut and dried and also, perhaps, into inventing their own stories" (Marvel, "Winterson," 168). The following year, in a conversation with Helen Barr, Winterson explained that both the novel and her screenplay for the BBC television version of *Oranges Are Not the Only Fruit* "look at the way that the Church is offered up as a sacrament of love when really it is an exercise in power. They look at the hypocrisy of family life and they suggest very strongly that heterosexuality is not the only way to live and, indeed, might not always be the best way to live" (Barr, "Face to Face," 30). In both texts, the protagonist's rebellion against such inextricably connected and powerful institutions as church, family life, and heterosexuality entails coming to terms with larger ideological struggles, the wrestling with epistemological questions, and the deconstruction of patriarchal and heterosexual hegemony. This difficult process of growing up and eventual "coming out" constitutes a quest modestly equated to that of Perceval and the Holy Grail (a "miniseries" interpolated sporadically within the larger narrative); such a journey allows the protagonist, Jeanette, new adventures and alternative visions.

The novel opens with a description of a lower middle-class family in a working-class area of northern England where Winterson, writing in the first person, introduces Jeanette's parents and immediately switches the ordinary gender division of labor, relegating the passive role of watching the proceedings to Jeanette's nearly absent father and assigning the vastly more active, indeed interventionist, role to the mother, who imposes a philosophy of life of frightening clarity:

> My father liked to watch the wrestling, my mother liked to wrestle; it didn't matter what. . . . She had never heard of mixed feelings. There were friends and there were enemies.
>
> Enemies were: The Devil (in his many forms)
>   Next Door
>   Sex (in its many forms)
>   Slugs
> Friends were: God
>   Our Dog
>   Auntie Madge
>   The Novels of Charlotte Brontë
>   Slug pellets
>   and me, at first.
> (*Oranges Are Not the Only Fruit*, 3)

It is no accident that only Jeanette fails to fall neatly into one of the two lists that, from macrocosm to microcosm, embody the significant separation of all things into two discrete categories, defining the positive and strong against the negative and weak, from evil to sinful, sinful to perverse, perversities to pests. This maternal version of the "natural order" is one permeated with oppositions reminiscent of Genesis, the title of the novel's first section: light/dark, good/evil, believer/heathen, order/disorder, lost/found, saved/fallen. Jeanette learns at an early age that such oppositions provide the faithful and vigilant with the strategies and weapons necessary to wage battle; thus slug pellets destroy slugs and the dog attacks Next Door. The devil and sex are singled out as especially pernicious for either can appear in "many forms" (3). While God promises to be a powerful force for the righteous, a monolithic construct available to repel the devil's onslaught, nothing in this scheme offers protection from what is most dangerous and wicked: sex, which is only feebly and inadequately countered in the list by familial support (Auntie Madge, a character who appears rarely) and Brontë novels that valorize romance and passion.

Plucking her daughter from an orphanage (adoption distances

Jeanette from her biological or "natural" parents and instead positions her artificially as the offspring of a union outside of the requisite marital consummation), Jeanette's mother proceeds to inculcate in her child a worldview based on her rather eccentric interpretation of God's word. Jeanette's adoption is the first stage of a more elaborate scheme on the part of her mother, a Pentecostal Evangelical Christian, who has promised God that she would "get a child, train it, build it, [and] dedicate it to the Lord: a missionary child, a servant of God, a blessing" (10) (the gender-neutral "it" is more than convenient). Her mother even adjusts the ending of *Jane Eyre*—the only "non-Bible" literature she reads to her young daughter—so that, in conformity with the grand design, the narrative culminates in a celibate marriage akin to that of Jeanette's parents. Years later, "literate and curious," Jeanette is deeply disappointed to discover her mother's fabrication, a betrayal and a lie: Jane, in fact, does not marry St. John Rivers to become a missionary in India (74). Sex, even in marriage, must be avoided at all costs, and her mother warns her never to "let anyone touch [her] Down There" (88)—with any luck, Jeanette would emerge from childhood and enter adulthood with the requisite purity, sanctity, devotion, and perfection to serve God and the church and to fulfill her mother's ambitious and ostensibly natural/divine plan.

Yet, ironically, this very education, preparation, and experience as a child (and later teenage) preacher, are precisely what compel Jeanette to challenge and turn topsy-turvy the so-called natural plan. Even Jeanette's very willingness to fulfill the vocation chosen for her by her mother works to overturn those intentions. The church grants Jeanette power—and lots of it; she not only survives in the religious institution but positively flourishes. As Jeanette puts it: "If you want to talk in terms of power I had enough to keep Mussolini happy" (124). In the view of the church fathers, Jeanette's masculine access to the religious domain—the privilege to preach to the congregation and thereby influence its members—is what allows her to usurp masculine power in the sexual domain. According to their logic, at once perceptive and blind, Jeanette's "unnatural passions" stem, as Jeanette explains, from "allowing women power in the church. . . . [in taking] on a man's world in other ways I had flouted God's law and tried to do it sexually. . . . So there I was, my success in the pulpit being the reason for my downfall. The devil had attacked me at my weakest point: my inability to realise the limitations of my sex" (134). In this passage Winterson launches a sophisticated attack on the church and its masculine hegemony. Inevitably, the church must strip away Jeanette's power by rescinding masculine privilege, a punishment that will leave her defenseless and without resources or community.

Such an emphatically dogmatic education (maternal and ecclesiastical) provides, in a most surprising way, an unusual interpretive framework for Jeanette to negotiate the predicament of her own lesbianism, manifested by an intense love for Melanie. To Jeanette, her relationship with Melanie is unquestionably natural and right precisely *because* "everything in the *natural* world was a symbol of the Great Struggle between good and evil" (16, emphasis mine). Trapped in a binary schema that offers an extremely limited number of options rather than an array of subtle distinctions, Jeanette reaches what seems a sensible conclusion: if her love is not evil, it must be good. Jeanette experiences neither guilt nor self-doubt—let alone second thoughts. Her lovers attend her church, listen to her preach—they pray together before going home to make love. By embracing a credo ("To the pure all things are pure") that assures her of the rightness of her love, she reconciles her private involvement with women and her public position in the church. She perceives no discrepancy, moral or otherwise, between her sexual preference (natural and essential) and the prescriptions of the church (cultural and social) because she believes, like Winterson, that love shouldn't be "gender-bound." As Winterson herself explains, "It's probably one of the few things in life that rises above all those kinds of oppositions—black and white, male and female, homosexual and heterosexual" (Marvel, "Winterson," 165). Winterson's claim on behalf of the transcendence of love—rendering whichever way one is *born* inconsequential—seems to sidestep neatly the question of whether such categories of oppositions are themselves natural or cultural. The claim undoes itself, however, for asserting that anything can "rise above" such oppositions is an act of cultural intervention, revealing those oppositions as cultural fictions; "*constructs*," as theorist Judith Butler puts it, "socially instituted and socially regulated fantasies . . . not *natural* categories, but *political* ones (categories that prove that recourse to the 'natural' in such contexts is always political)" (*Gender Trouble*, 126). In *Oranges*, Jeanette may view her lesbianism as—essentially—natural (she was just born that way), but at the same time she recognizes that whoever holds the power to categorize can establish a claim for the label "natural."

Jeanette's potential as a successful, full-fledged missionary is, quite obviously, jeopardized by her confusion about, and ultimate rejection

of, the missionary position once she concludes at an early age that heterosexuality, distasteful and uninteresting, is made possible only
through conspiracy and coercion. When Pastor Spratt announces to
the entire congregation that Jeanette and her lover "have fallen under
Satan's spell," asking "Do you deny you love this woman with a love
reserved for man and wife," Jeanette answers "No, yes, I mean of
course I love her" (105). The seemingly confused short response contains a good deal more than a simple denial or affirmation: Jeanette
denies not her love for another woman, but the suggestion that it is a
love "reserved for man and wife." Thus she simultaneously refuses
patriarchal insistence to read her relationship as a pale imitation of
heterosexuality and affirms that it is something other than, perhaps
even more. She may be misunderstood by the pastor, her mother, and
others, but the misunderstanding is their flaw, their problem. However, because she is caught up in the binary logic of her mother's (and
the church's) version of the natural order, Jeanette never fully com-
prehends the political threat embedded in her actions; she can challenge those who question her right to love Melanie, but she cannot
break out of the binarism—she is, after all, her mother's daughter.

After Jeanette eventually comes to realize that there is no space for
her in the church, she has a final confrontation with Pastor Spratt during which she reveals an innate confidence in the rightness of her passion for women and dismisses as arbitrary and unfounded the rejection of her choice according to God's law. When Spratt asks, "Have
you no shame?" she replies "Not really" (157). Shame, Salman
Rushdie writes, is " a short word, but one containing encyclopedias of
nuance" (*Shame*, 39); one must recognize the cultural imperative
before shame can operate effectively. Thus, for Jeanette (and Winterson), lesbianism cannot be regulated, contained, or controlled by heterosexual hegemony because the lesbian, in refusing to acknowledge
its power, nullifies and renders it impotent. The simple transposition
of the binary in *Oranges* (lesbianism = natural and therefore good;
heterosexuality = unnatural, perhaps evil) paves the way for more
complex strategies with which Winterson will neutralize heteropatri-
archal authority and begin to map an alternative social order, one that
positions the lesbian at the center.

In Winterson's view, the homosexual is not an imitation of a heterosexual; the lesbian is not an inferior version of a man. When
Jeanette's mother, in referring to her daughter, mutters "with dis-
gust," "aping men," the narrator responds "Now if I was aping men

she'd have every reason to be disgusted. As far as I was concerned men were something you had around the place, not particularly interesting, but quite harmless. I had never shown the slightest feeling for them, and apart from my never wearing a skirt, saw nothing else in common between us" (127). Later, after two gay men enter the church holding hands and Jeanette's mother comments "Should have been a woman that one," the narrator observes: "This was clearly not true. At that point I had no notion of sexual politics, but I knew that a homosexual is further away from a woman than a rhinoceros. Now that I do have a number of notions about sexual politics, this early observation holds good. There are shades of meaning, but a man is a man, wherever you find it" (128). Homosexuals, male or female, with sexual politics or without, are not simply and unproblematically one gender trapped in the wrong (opposite) body. But what they are, even if they are separate, remains unclear, unspecified, as yet to be explored.

The representation of the lesbian in *Oranges* seems politically radical in the subversive affirmation of lesbian sexuality against a repressive and suspect heterosexual regime. That Winterson recognizes the relationship between sexuality and power is evident in Jeanette's eventual understanding that the rejection of heterosexuality calls for a concomitant rejection of authority, especially in the church and family, the two institutions most responsible for upholding heterosexual hegemony. However, the continued reliance on the terms of heterosexuality—indeed, the lesbian's inability to exist without it—is troubling because the lesbian is still positioned within binary logic itself. When Jeanette challenges the church's authority to label her love for Melanie as "unnatural," she shouts "To the pure all things are pure . . . It's you not us" (105). This social perception reveals that Jeanette is still her mother's daughter, absorbing, though modifying, the simple and restrictive binary terms ("you and us") of the struggle.

Winterson clearly presents lesbianism as the only viable and intelligible alternative for Jeanette; yet, on a fundamental level, Winterson remains (albeit unwittingly) in the realm of parody, of imitation, in the unproblematic reversal of binary terms—a strategy that privileges the status of the lesbian over that of the heterosexual but doesn't facilitate an ongoing critique of compulsory heterosexuality or patriarchal control. Winterson's own representation of the lesbian, now homosexist/heterophobic, continues to operate within the same cultural—and binary—opposition: natural and unnatural. Such a position is similar to the dependence that Butler discerns in Monique Wittig. In *Gender*

Trouble: Feminism and the Subversion of Identity, Butler argues that "Wittig's radical disjunction between straight and gay replicates the kind of disjunctive binarism that she herself characterizes as the divisive philosophical gesture of the straight mind" (121). Butler asserts that "the radical disjunction posited by Wittig between heterosexuality and homosexuality is simply not true, that there are structures of psychic homosexuality within heterosexual relations, and structures of psychic heterosexuality within gay and lesbian sexuality and relationships" (121). While lesbianism, for Wittig, is "a full-scale refusal of heterosexuality," Butler continues, "even that refusal constitutes an engagement and, ultimately, a radical dependence on the very terms that lesbianism purports to transcend" (124). Winterson's lesbian subject, though imbued with a voice and granted a threatening masculine power, still cannot transcend the condition of binarism, a predicament that interferes with the complete overthrow of heterosexual hegemony. In *Oranges* binaries are revealed at every turn, though never erased or eliminated. For the lesbian writer, the task, the political agenda if you will, is to displace and explode the binary.

Winterson's playful handling of the fruit metaphor, most frequently associated with female sexuality, holds the greatest promise in terms of displacing binarism in this early novel. Yet the orange (with a rough, thick, seemingly impenetrable exterior that contains a soft, delicately segmented inner fruit, at once sweet and tart) operates most simply as a metaphor for the self/world or self/other dichotomy (still other binaries, in other words), representing the separation between the inner and outer, unlike fruits with thin skins that allow easy access, such as apples or grapes. Fruit can also emblematize the disguise, deception, and disparity between the inner and outer: who would guess what hidden and juicy delights might be found inside a pineapple, for instance? It is only when the reader encounters the orange not in a natural state but as marmalade, a fruit conserve that calls for the slicing and combining of the outer and inner sections and for the removal of the seeds before cooking it, that the metaphor of fruit acquires more complexity. Marmalade embodies the orange's essence and, at the same time, no longer resembles an orange per se. Thus the opening epigraph, a literary device predictably announcing the theme to follow, collapses inner and outer. The epigraph, taken from Mrs. Beeton's cookbook, describes the process of making marmalade and states that "when thick rinds are used the top must be thoroughly skimmed, or a scum will form marring the final appearance." The thick rinds, evoking as they do the image of a thick skin, bring with them the danger of "scum" rising to the surface: an image that can only be seen as a kind of self-contained morality tale. But as Jeanette herself admits, while gazing at some oranges in a moment of crisis, "They were pretty, but not much help. I was going to need more than an icon to get me through this one" (132). Winterson's use of the fruit metaphor is more, much more, than an icon; it is her first tentative mechanism for imagining the fruition of a postmodern lesbian existence—though Winterson's somewhat evasive answer to interviewer Helen Barr's question "Why fruit?" would seem to suggest otherwise. Winterson replied that she's motivated by the extraordinary tactile nature of the world, "The things we can see, touch, smell, taste and hear delight me. . . . This is the awe and wonder of the *natural* world, which, largely now, we just close our eyes to" ("Face to Face," 32; emphasis mine). It is precisely the reproduction of that natural world—the scientific truth that from seeds comes new life—that Winterson's literary representations work to overturn and refute, in a word, to (re)conceive.

In *The Passion* (1987) Winterson shifts from the fruit metaphor to cross-dressing, a cultural performance that illustrates how perceptions of external "appearance" and internal "essence" interrelate in a problematic state of flux. Villanelle, the protagonist, dresses "as a woman in the afternoon and a young man in the evenings," because "that's what the visitors liked to see. It was part of the game, trying to decide which sex was hidden behind the tight breeches and extravagant face-paste" (62, 54). Cross-dressing thus maneuvers the dresser into a position of power, not only the power of knowledge and the ability to control perception but also, and more important, the power and freedom to choose and to play with choice. For Villanelle, this choice takes the form of whether or not she should declare herself as a woman when she meets and falls in love with a masked woman (a disguise that only partially obscures identity, though highlights seductiveness) at a Venetian gaming table one evening. Venice, the city of disguises, is a postmodern city par excellence in its mutability and is thus the ideal domain for Villanelle, now accoutered with a moustache and a man's shirt to hide her breasts. As with fruit, cross-dressing emphasizes the demarcation between various possible essences (hidden, secretive, delicious, and juicy) and appearances (which may or may not be a true indication of what resides beneath the surface). While debating on whether or not to reveal that she is in fact a woman, Villanelle herself

ponders how clothes are an unreliable and arbitrary source of information where sexuality is concerned: "What was myself? Was this
breeches and boots self any less real than my garters?" (66). By rais-
ing this question, Winterson moves beyond the inner/outer trope to
invest cross-dressing with what Butler claims for drag, namely, that it
"fully subverts the distinction between inner and outer psychic space
and effectively mocks both the expressive model of gender and the
notion of a true gender identity" (*Gender Trouble*, 137).

For Villanelle, this gender mocking is doubly inscribed both in her
choice of dress and in the fact that her body bears the marks of both
sexes, at least as far as Venetian culture is concerned. Villanelle, though
not a hermaphrodite, possesses the Venetian bodily equivalent through
her webbed feet, a prerequisite for male gondoliers; "there never was a
girl," we learn, "whose feet were webbed in the entire history of the
boatmen" (51). Just as Jeanette in *Oranges* usurps masculine power
through her "success in the pulpit" (134), Villanelle enters the male
domain because of a genetic inheritance. The oddity of webbed feet can
remain hidden for years beneath boots, but there's no mistaking the
implications: the search for clear-cut distinctions where gender is concerned is futile. In fact, the midwife who attempts to make a clear cut
between the male and female is repelled each time she attempts to insert
the knife between Villanelle's toes; the knife springs "from the skin
leaving no mark" (52). Such cultural insertions, Winterson suggests,
constitute a violation of nature—an apparent turnaround from
Oranges. In the first novel cultural authority over a socially constructed nature is available for the taking (not "is a lesbian natural?" but
"who is asking?"), whereas in *The Passion* it is the body or, more
specifically, the double gender encoding of Villanelle's body that
invites cultural confusion and unintelligibility (social [re]construction
cannot alter a genetic identity). The relationship between nature and
social construction is not a simple reversal from one novel to the next,
though. What the reader discovers in the natural upset Winterson
inscribes on Villanelle's female body (marking the masculine by the
slightest tissue of skin strategically situated between the toes) or in Villanelle's probing interrogation of the "self" and the "real" is not a
quest for a unified and coherent essentialized self but a consistent willingness to explore multiple and fragmented fictions of identity, that is,
to engage in endless speculation. Ultimately, the essential question has
far less to do with the nature of nature, for Winterson the novelist recognizes that, as Diana Fuss explains, "when [essentialism is] put into

practice by the dispossessed themselves . . . [it] can be powerfully displacing and disruptive" (*Essentially Speaking*, 32).

In *Sexing the Cherry* Winterson launches her most successful incursion to overturn the "natural" and collapse such distinctions as nature/culture or inner/outer, for what is imagined is nothing less than a wholly new genesis of gender. The writer returns to the fruit metaphor by inserting a visual series of fruit icons at the head of individual sections to announce different narrators and by aligning each character with a fruit against conventional expectations. Thus for the passages set in Restoration London, a pineapple heralds the voice of Jordan and a banana icon precedes his mother, Dog-Woman. In the contemporary sections, the pineapple split into two halves signals the voice of Nicholas Jordan, while the banana, now peeled and sliced in two, alerts the reader to a woman unnamed. This alignment might strike some readers as odd in light of our cultural immersion in Freudian symbolism—pineapple/male (Jordan) and banana/female (Dog-Woman)—but the reversal is intentional and important for it gestures toward Winterson's continued exploration of the ideology of gender, one only hinted at in Winterson's reference to "shades of meanings" in *Oranges* and one that confuses and fuses cultural expectations of constructions of masculinity and femininity.

Envisioning a social order that would permit the breakdown of oppositions, Winterson, in a frame break, tells the story of a princess and her woman lover. This feminist revision of a fairy tale enables Winterson to call appearances into question and, through the disruption of normative gender relations, reveal them as artificial and arbitrary constructions. In a highly erotic description of lesbian desire, one princess confides:

> I never wanted anyone but her. I wanted to run my finger from the cleft in her chin down the slope of her breasts and across the level plains of her stomach to where I knew she would be wet. I wanted to turn her over and ski the flats of my hands down the slope of her back. I wanted to pioneer the secret passage of her arse. . . . We kissed often, our mouths filling up with tongue and teeth and spit and blood when I bit her lower lip, and with my hands I held her against my hip bone. We made love often, especially in the afternoons with the blinds half pulled and the cold flag floor against our bodies. For eighteen years we lived alone in a windy castle and saw no one but each other. (*Sexing the Cherry*, 54)

Eventually the hatred and fear of heterosexual society invade, but before the lover can be taken away to be burned, the princess herself "saves" her from the mob and kills her "with a single blow to the head" (54). What I find most fascinating about this passage is the wording of the confession upon discovery: "Then someone found us and then it was too late. The *man* I had married was a woman" (54, emphasis mine). This reference to marriage, that privileged heterosexual institution, is curious even if the two women seem to have successfully fabricated a different sort of marriage through their isolation from society. The fact that their union ultimately culminates in death and destruction suggests that Winterson, in examining one possible solution—the possibility of parody or imitation as an effective way to undermine normative gender ideology—argues against it.

Winterson reaches a similar conclusion, it would seem, with gender blurring. Early in the narrative we learn that Jordan, a foundling scooped out of the river Thames by the enormous Dog-Woman, occasionally assumes female garb; he explains: "I have met a number of people who, anxious to be free of the burdens of their gender, have dressed themselves men as women and women as men" (31). Since cross-dressing works here as a liberatory strategy that relieves the "burden" of gender, which registers now as a weight, Jordan gains power and control over his body and the way in which he is perceived in the social order. Such a strategy is exceedingly advantageous for it permits a plethora of insights hitherto unavailable. He notices, for instance, that "women have a private language. A language not dependent on the constructions of men but structured by signs and expressions, that uses ordinary words as code-words meaning something other. In my petticoats I was a traveller in a foreign country" (31). As Butler points out, and as Winterson is well aware, cross-dressing, as well as drag and butch/femme, can effectively parody the "notion of an original or primary gender identity" (*Gender Trouble*, 137). But Winterson also realizes that cross-dressing—cultural perversion as cultural subversion—is only a temporary strategy to facilitate a break from imposed restrictions; it cannot enact permanent authentic social change.

What sort of radical transformative political strategy might unleash a more profound and complete disruption that would collapse restrictive gender boundaries and force the reconceptualization of alternative constructions? The task for Winterson is to create in fiction what Butler argues is "the more insidious and effective strategy"; that is, "a thoroughgoing appropriation and redeployment of the categories of identity themselves, not merely to contest 'sex,' but to articulate the convergence of multiple sexual discourses at the site of 'identity' in order to render that category, in whatever form, permanently problematic" (*Gender Trouble*, 128). This is, I would argue, precisely what Winterson attempts to inscribe in *Sexing the Cherry* through the practice of grafting, a replication process "whereby a plant, perhaps tender or uncertain, is fused into a hardier member of its strain, and so the two take advantage of each other and produce a third kind, without seed or parent" (78). This astonishing procedure, though simple enough to explain and understand, incurs both the wrath of churchmen (who declare it, like homosexuality, "unnatural" [78]) and the frustration of Jordan's mother (who asserts that "such things" have "no gender" and are "a confusion to themselves" [79]). Despite the disapproving objections of the perplexed, Jordan himself solemnly proclaims, in a phrase with scriptural resonances: "But the cherry grew, and we have sexed it and it is female" (79). With this statement, Winterson imagines that gender is socially constructed and enforced rather than inherent and, above all, that the hybrid—a third sex, a fusion of diverse strains, without seed and the strongest—illuminates the ways in which the dominant culture opts out of creatively and freely exploring boundless gender options and instead becomes mired in weary boundaries and binaries. Cultural authority (manifested here in the wariness of church fathers), it would seem, is quite correct in its suspicions because hybridization inevitably poses a dangerous challenge to the comfortable dualisms (nature/culture, natural/artificial, female/male) upon which patriarchal hegemony—and the hybrid itself—is based. The transnatural practice of grafting does not circumvent, eliminate, or destroy the original (gendered) biological matter that produces a hybrid, and as a result the process that makes an "other" ultimately registers the inceptive binarism as excess, as redundancy. The hybrid presupposes a biological precursor (as opposed to spontaneous regeneration), but cultural (in this case, scientific) intervention bears the responsibility for the act of creation. By becoming "something else" in a complex interplay of independence from and dependence on its biological precursors, the hybrid denatures dominant oppositional paradigms that set one against the other and subsequently accommodates more options. The fact that Jordan—himself adopted (like Jeanette and Winterson herself) and thus in a sense created without seed—chooses to experiment on the cherry, an emblem of virginity and a euphemism for the hymen, anticipates a solution well beyond the fruit metaphor or the superficial "peel" of cross-dressing; it is a solution that anticipates a different order to supplant the old. By imagining nascency emerging from virginity created and sustained outside binaries, outside of the seed, Winterson nips the old order in the bud before it even begins; a liberatory displacement that brims with new gender configurations and enacts a plausible "convergence of multiple sexual discourses," to borrow Butler's terms (*Gender Trouble*, 128).

Winterson recuperates the process of grafting, not as an artificial, scientific reproductive mechanism, but as sexual reproduction outside of (beyond) a heterosexual model and, in turn, spawning a third sex relatively free of binarisms. In effect, the introduction of the hybrid sets off a new chain of reproductive technologies whose progeny would further increase biological possibilities with each subsequent generation. The dizzying and chaotic recombinations generated by hybridization might seem an elusive and highly impractical solution on which to base an oppositional politics. After all, the notion of hybrid resonates with doing violence to "nature," which results (as any dictionary definition will remind us) in the scientific equivalent of freaks, mongrels, half-breeds and cross-breeds. Yet the concept of hybridization posits, however improbable, an alternative starting-point, working with different terms and conditions. Grafting can hardly constitute a grand strategy for lesbian feminists to undermine repressive hegemonies—but it can call certain conceptual underpinnings into question and thereby break down restrictive parameters of the unimaginable. Butler characterizes her own study as an attempt "to locate the political in the very signifying practices that establish, regulate and deregulate identity"; such an endeavor, she continues, "can only be accomplished through the introduction of a set of questions that extend the very notion of the political" (*Gender Trouble*, 147). In blasting away apparent cultural certainties, Winterson's grafting strategy disables hierarchical dualities and posits what is inconceivable to "extend the very notion of the political."

Winterson's project then, encapsulated in the act of grafting the cherry, envisions the contours and logic of a lesbian postmodern that collapses binarisms and creates a space not just for lesbians but for productive, dynamic, and fluid gender pluralities and sexual positionings. Such a project at the same time demonstrates clearly what lesbian theory and cultural practices might offer postmodernism. What Butler pioneers theoretically, Winterson enacts in her metafictional writing practices: a sexual politics of heterogeneity and a vision of hybridized gender constructions outside an either/or proposition, at once political and postmodern. Fiction, for Winterson, is the site to interrogate, trouble, subvert, and tamper with gender, identity, and sexuality; her fiction is a serious invitation to readers to imagine the emancipation of "normal" and "natural" from the exclusive and totalizing domain of patriarchal and heterosexual authority. The emergence of new paradigms throughout Winterson's work reverses, relativizes, and problematizes notions of normal and natural in order to "naturalize" cultural oddities, monstrosities, abnormalities, and conformities—from Jeanette's love of women, to Villanelle's masculine webbed feet, to Dog-Woman's enormous stature, or to Jordan's sartorial intuition and biological experimentation. The postmodern constructions of such innovative paradigms mobilize and animate a feminist political strategy of resistance, forcing and enforcing new mappings of the social and cultural order through feminist revision, reconsideration, and reconceptualization. Transformative feminist agendas, such a reading of Winterson's inventive literary representation suggests, need not be at odds with postmodernism. To be sure, the art of grafting—and the recombinations it engenders—is fraught with dangers precisely because it is threatening and profoundly destabilizing, just as the "intellectual and political incoherency of relativism" challenges "the feminist critique of patriarchy" (Felski, "Feminism," 36). But lesbian feminists must "sex" the postmodern, explore its powerful, unsettling, and rich multiplicity of potentialities, expand the political, and blur the repressive regime of heterosexual hegemony. Because lesbian feminist writers like Jeanette Winterson are already working in the postmodern realm, and because a lesbian postmodern is already shattering hierarchies and binaries, lesbian feminist critics and theorists have everything to gain from acknowledging the potential of a political postmodern.

Works Cited

Barr, Helen. "Face to Face: A Conversation between Jeanette Winterson and Helen Barr." *English Review* 2 (1991): 30–33.

Brown, Rosellen. "Fertile Imagination." *Women's Review of Books* 7 (1990): 9–10.

Brown, Wendy. "Feminist Hesitations, Postmodern Exposure." *differences* 3(1)

(1991): 63–84.

Butler, Judith. *Gender Trouble: Feminism and the Subversion of Identity*. New York: Routledge, 1990.

Di Stefano, Christine. "Dilemmas of Difference: Feminism, Modernity, and Post-modernism." In Linda J. Nicholson, ed., *Feminism/Postmodernism*, pp. 63–82. New York: Routledge, 1990.

Felski, Rita. "Feminism, Postmodernism, and the Critique of Modernity." *Cultural Critique* 13 (1989): 33–56.

Fuss, Diana. *Essentially Speaking: Feminism, Nature & Difference*. New York: Routledge, 1989.

Gerrard, Nicci. "The Prophet." *New Statesman and Society* (September 1, 1989): 13.

Gorra, Michael. "Gender Games in Restoration London." *New York Times Book Review* (April 29, 1990): 24.

Hutcheon, Linda. *The Politics of Postmodernism*. New York: Routledge, 1989.

Marvel, Mark. "Winterson: Trust Me. I'm Telling You Stories." *Interview* 20 (1990): 165–68.

Rushdie, Salman. *Shame*. London: Picador, 1984.

Winterson, Jeanette. *Oranges Are Not the Only Fruit*. London: Pandora, 1988.

——. *The Passion*. London: Penguin, 1988.

——. *Sexing the Cherry*. London: Vintage, 1990.

9 Inverts and Hybrids: Lesbian Rewritings of Sexual and Racial Identities

Judith Raiskin

Contemporary literary critics, anthropologists, and artists writing from and about "border zone" cultures have pushed the boundaries and the borders of modern identity on multiple fronts. The postmodern questioning of identity as something unified and coherent and of culture as authentic or pure can be most clearly seen at the site of the borders (national, sexual, racial) we have inherited from the last century. The fields of both postcolonial theory and lesbian and gay theory provide us with examples of the ways identities and cultures are invented, experienced, destabilized, and recreated through classification systems that change in relation to political and historical pressures. From their positions as "border intellectuals," lesbian writers Michelle Cliff and Gloria Anzaldúa each offer complex postmodern challenges to modern identity categories of sexuality, race, and nationhood, categories that are based on conceptions of biology and heredity from the nineteenth and the early twentieth centuries.[1]

Historians of science and cultural critics such as Nancy Stepan, Elaine Showalter, Sander Gilman, and Anita Levy describe these classifications as systems of analogy and metaphor. Their work shows the ways in which the categories and hierarchies of presumed racial difference that justified colonial exploitation were intricately related to ideas of class difference and sexual difference. Once science had constructed an elaborate model of racial hierarchies positing "Causasian" as the superior and "Negro" as the inferior races, nineteenth-century studies of sexual and gender differences found this template of racial inequalities (exemplified by brain weight, head and jaw shape, supposed aptitude for abstract and rational thought) remarkably helpful in explaining, or rather asserting, gender and class inequalities as well.[2] Categories of sexual behavior and identity created by nineteenth- and twentieth-century sexologists were also influenced by the classification systems of race, whereby people of color, particularly "mixed race" people, and homosexuals were conflated through the ideas of evolution and degeneration prevalent in the late nineteenth century. It is this conflation that Gloria Anzaldúa and Michelle Cliff rework in their own literary confrontations with the colonial legacy that defines them.

Whereas evolution was seen as a movement of slow progress, degeneration was imagined as a process threatening to reverse that progress with alarming speed. Not only were certain races considered to be "degenerate" in themselves, but those individuals who were the offspring of interracial sexual relations were, by the mid-nineteenth century, symbols of degeneration par excellence.[3] Degeneration was the result of any crossing of so-called natural boundaries: geographical, racial, sexual. The "mulatto," "half-caste," or "hybrid" became the symbol of all degeneration or deevolution. By the end of the nineteenth century, the metaphor of racial degeneration had become conflated with that of sexual degeneracy, perhaps because of the illicit sexuality exposed by "mixed-race" offspring or because of the European fascination with the sexual physiology and imagined sexual practices of Africans. The "mulatto," named after the sterile mule, was seen as a dyseugenic cross between separate *species* resulting in offspring both racially and sexually degenerate. As Eugene Talbot, whose book *Degeneracy: Its Causes, Signs, and Results* was edited by the sexologist Havelock Ellis in 1898, put it, "morbid proclivities and retrogressive tendencies are peculiarly rife among mulattos . . . the mulatto has factors of degeneracy which would be fatal to the establishment of an intermediate type on the environment of the white" (102). Nancy Stepan notes the extraordinary inclusiveness with which Talbot uses the term *degeneracy* to describe the darker "races," criminals, prostitutes and so-called sexual perverts who represented for him a "still blacker phase of biology." ("Biological Degeneration," 112–13). In fact, Talbot's taxonomy of degeneracy includes the category "ethical degeneracy" under which he includes crime, prostitution, sexual degeneracy, inebriety, pauperism, and moral insanity, all of which he describes as "buds of the same tree of degenerate heredity" (20). The sexual pervert, according to Talbot, "may be divided into precisely the same classes as other criminals" (323) who are all understood as revealing biological regressions in their behavior.

By the end of the nineteenth century, with the contribution of sexologists like Richard von Krafft-Ebing, homosexuality had replaced masturbation as the prime example of sexual degeneracy. For Krafft-Ebing, homosexuality, whether caused by psychological or physical abnormality, was a sign of degeneration, congenital and hereditary.[4] Drawing on the discourse of racial and medical science and evolution, in *Psychopathia Sexualis* Krafft-Ebing divided those who express the "antipathic sexual instinct" into categories of degeneration (varying in amenability to treatment and cure) based on physical characteristics. Those "inverts" who show the weakest sexual desire for their own sex are called "psychic hermaphrodites" (based on Ulrich's earlier terminology) although Krafft-Ebing persisted in seeking a "cerebral center" that, independent from other physical traits, determines sexual preference. Krafft-Ebing's slippage between the psychological and the physical is seen in his metaphor of the hermaphrodite (which he sometimes neglects to preface with the adjective "psychical" [i.e., 353]) and in his comparison of physical, mental, and stylistic attributes as masculine or feminine: "Gynandry represents the extreme grade of degenerative homosexuality. The woman of this type possesses of the feminine qualities only the genital organs; thought, sentiment, action, even external appearance are those of the man" (399).

It is no coincidence that the obsessive categorization of sexual acts and desires in Krafft-Ebing's work and in Havelock Ellis's *Studies in the Psychology of Sex* resembles the impossibly intricate racial categories of colonial discourse. The shift in the mid-nineteenth century, described by Michel Focault, in which sexual acts came to determine sexual identities, allowed sexologists of this period to use the models of anthropology and science to classify sexual "types."[5]

By engaging this conflation of racial and sexual type, Gloria Anzaldúa and Michelle Cliff critique the categories of identity along with the modernist nostalgia for an imagined lost innocence when everyone knew, or could know, her or his place. Stepan's claim that the discourse of racial biology is "a science of boundaries between groups and the degenerations that threatened when those boundaries were transgressed" ("Biological Degeneration," 98) is an apt definition for the discourse of sexology as well. Relying on a postmodern deconstruction of fixed identity and place, Cliff and Anzaldúa highlight and celebrate those very transgressions of racial and sexual boundaries. Their strategies are intriguingly different, each creating a different balance between constructionist and essentialist understandings of identity: Cliff reveals the myths of colonial classification systems to suggest possible alliances across difference; Anzaldúa envisions a collapse of the systems of categorization through the "mestiza" and "queer" consciousness created by them. The tension between postcolonial and postmodernist genres, with the former leaning on the political uses of identity that the latter denies, are seen in both Cliff and Anzaldúa's work.[6] While an identification with and recognition of particular individual and group "identities," (sexual, racial, ethnic) or postcolonial national statuses is implicit in current political rights movements, both Cliff and Anzaldúa address the limitations of these categories and their historically oppressive uses.

Gloria Anzaldúa allows homosexuality and mixed-race identity to reflect each other by using and reworking the language of nineteenth-century evolutionary theory. Her use is not a capitulation to the racism and heterosexism inherent in that discourse; rather, she forces a recognition of the metaphorical, even fantastic, elements of this language. In *Borderlands/La Frontera*, Anzaldúa claims that mestizas and homosexuals are the true inhabitants of the borderland:

> Borders are set up to define the places that are safe and unsafe, to distinguish *us* from *them*. A border is a dividing line, a narrow strip along a steep edge. A borderland is a vague and undetermined place created by the emotional residue of an unnatural boundary. It is in a constant state of transition. The prohibited and forbidden are its inhabitants. *Los atravesados* live here: the squint-eyed, the perverse, the queer, the troublesome, the mongrel, the mulatto, the half-breed, the half-dead; in short, those who cross over, pass over, or go through the confines of the "normal." (3)

Anzaldúa centers her arguments on a strain of essentialism that at first might seem dangerous. Rather than rejecting the Darwinian language of evolution outright, she quite easily refers to "blood" and "genetic streams" but turns that language on its head: "The mestizo and the queer exist at this time and point on the evolutionary continuum for a purpose. We are a blending that proves that all blood is intricately woven together, and that we are spawned out of similar souls" (77, 85). Not only are the poles of degeneration and evolution reversed, but the language of the physical blends with that of the metaphysical ("souls").

A similar strategy was used by Edward Carpenter, a turn-of-the-century homosexual intellectual and sexologist, to claim not only dignity but civil rights for homosexuals. In "The Intermediate Sex" (1908) and *Intermediate Types Among Primitive Folk* (1914) Carpenter postulates that homosexuals or "inverts," existing between the two sexes, represent an evolutionary step *forward*, not a degenerate state: "At the present time certain new types of human kind may be emerging, which will have an important part to play in the societies of the future—even though for the moment their appearance is attended by a good deal of confusion and misapprehension" ("Intermediate Sex," 186). This kind of strategic essentialism claims not only that inverts should not be punished for their "nature," but also asserts that they should be celebrated and recognized for their advanced development and for what they can offer civilization. In fact, one of the ironies Carpenter highlights is that among his so-called "primitive folk" the invert's special role is recognized while it is ignored in modern society.

Like Carpenter, Anzaldúa attributes spiritual and mystical properties to those who are "sexually different," who are *"mita' y mita'"*—half-and-half. In *Borderlands/La Frontera* she compares herself to a woman the people of her town called *"una de las otras*, 'of the Others' "* (19). The townspeople believed that for six months this person was a woman and for six months s/he was a man, a magical kind of hermaphrodite. Anzaldúa does not explicitly differentiate between this physical transformation of sexes and a psychic mixture of gender; both she and the magical hermaphrodite are half-and-halfs:

> There is something compelling about being both male and female, about having an entry into both worlds. Contrary to some psychiatric tenets, half-and-halfs are not suffering from a confusion of gender. What we are suffering from is an absolute despot duality

that says we are able to be only one or the other. It claims that human nature is limited and cannot evolve into something better. But I, like other queer people, am two in one body, both male and female. I am the embodiment of the *heiros gamos*: the coming together of opposite qualities within. (19)

By using this folktale of the hermaphrodite metaphorically, Anzaldúa does not merely create a new pathological "type" as does Krafft-Ebing; she describes a consciousness that can move from role to role, that can move across boundaries, even ones as material as our bodies.

Whereas Talbot argued that a racial "intermediate type" would be disastrous to civilization, Anzaldúa claims it is the mestiza consciousness that will save the world. The evolutionary development of the mestiza and the homosexual offers a synthesis of contradictory powers. The ability to live with ambiguity and contradictions allows the mestiza and the homosexual to serve as mediators and translators. As "supreme crossers of culture," homosexuals link people with each other (*Borderlands/La Frontera*, 84). For Carpenter, too, individuals who are members of the "intermediate sex" are valuable teachers and mediators: "These people have a special work to do as reconcilers and interpreters of the two sexes to each other" ("Intermediate Sex," 188). In Carpenter's analysis the "intermediate sex" is a position around which all racial difference collapses; he describes the varieties of roles for these "types" in a stunningly ahistorical and transcultural survey of cultures. From a description of ancient customs Carpenter slides effortlessly into his own time with practices of "primitive" peoples: "So far with regard to Syria and the Bible. But Dr. Fraser points out the curious likeness here to customs existing today among the Negroes of the Slave Coast of West Africa" (*Intermediate Type*, 32). Carpenter's collapse of antiquity, "primitive folk" (i.e., nonwhite) and lower-class people echoes the contemporaneous work of Caesar Lombroso and Havelock Ellis, both of whom describe what they call an "atavistic" origin of criminality, prostitution, and madness. This ahistorical and transcultural comparison seems not only naive today but dangerous in its obvious racism, sexism, and classism.

While Anzaldúa uses the essentialist language of Krafft-Ebing's "psychic hermaphrodite" and Carpenter's "intermediate sex," her use of this language relies on metaphor in a way theirs did not. This is perhaps most clear in her reworking of the modernist "mestizo" of Mexican nationalism. Anzaldúa bases her "New Mestiza" on the Mexican José Vasconcelos's rewritings of European understandings of race and heredity in the early twentieth century. For Vasconcelos, in 1925, the mestizo represented the inception of a "cosmic" race in which all races were blended, resulting not in degeneration but in the evolution of a new national identity. In her recent comparative study of eugenic movements in Latin America, Nancy Stepan reads Vasconcelos's work as both an inversion of European and North American racist ideas of white supremacy and as a statement of unity and nation-building at a time of social and political turbulence in Mexico. Unlike the developing eugenics policies during the 1920s and 1930s, which in Argentina promoted European immigration and in Brazil relied on wishful theses about the eventual "whitening" of the population, the concept Vasconcelos articulates of a "constructive miscegenation" grounds a unified Mexican identity in a racial mixture privileging neither the European nor the indigenous "races" of the country (Stepan, *Hour*, 145–53).[7]

As a "mestiza" (of Spanish, Indian, and Anglo background) and as a lesbian, Anzaldúa transforms the concept of the mestizo from this modern reevaluation of nineteenth-century racist classifications to a postmodern reinterpretation of the central terms of the debate. Although she opens her piece "La conciencia de la mestiza: Toward a New Consciousness," with Vasconcelos's vision of "la primera raza síntesis del globo . . . la raza cósmica," she quickly shifts the terms to her own vision of "a new *mestiza* consciousness, *una conciencia de mujer* . . . a consciousness of the Borderlands" (77). Anzaldúa's shift in focus allows her to use Vasconcelos's valuation of the mestizo without being tied to either his reliance on heterosexual reproduction (constructive miscegenation) or his conception of a unified national Mexican identity. The *mestiza* in Anzaldúa's writing is less a biological entity than a consciousness: "*la mestiza* is a product of the transfer of the cultural and spiritual values of one group to another" (78). This is not to say that Anzaldúa discounts the physical body, but for her the final product of the mixture of races and cultures can never be conceived of simply in physical terms, for the body has no meaning outside of culture. The body of the "mixed breed," rather than being the physical manifestation of an evolutionary step forward in Vasconcelos's terms, is for Anzaldúa a metaphor for the mixture of cultures, which is necessarily experienced through the body as a "struggle of flesh, a shock, at times a tearing apart." This mestiza Anzaldúa describes is also the lesbian body, described as intensely physical and female yet also outside the "natural" rhythm of sexual reproduction.

While Anzaldúa admires the inclusivity of Vasconcelos's cosmic race that embraces all races—"At the confluence of two or more genetic streams, with chromosomes constantly 'crossing over,' this mixture of races, rather than resulting in an inferior being, provides hybrid progeny, a mutable, more malleable species with a rich gene pool" (77)—her own vision challenges the modernist longing for unity and cohesiveness implicit in both his conception of the mestizo and his patriotic invention of the new Mexican identity. Anzaldúa not only accepts but celebrates the fragmented physical, national, and cultural experience of the mestiza consciousness. Her mestiza is not a reconciliation of difference and contradiction, but rather a tolerance for and even an active seeking out of ambiguity (79). It is through the conflict experienced by the "plural personality" of the mestiza that a synthesis can occur. While this synthesis does undermine the dualities of colonialism, racism, and sexism, for Anzaldúa the utopian vision is not a synthesis providing unity or stasis. Rather, it embodies a continual confrontation of difference, a "crossbreeding" that allows "for preservation under a variety of conditions" (81).

As a mestiza and a citizen of the "borderland," Anzaldúa also moves beyond the modern concept of national identity. The borderland, like the mestiza and the lesbian, is a "third country" (3, 11), an in-between entity. Her conception of political borders, like that of bodies is as much metaphorical as it is physical: "1,950 mile-long open wound / dividing a *pueblo*, a culture, / running down the length of my body, / staking fence rods in my flesh, / splits me splits me / *me raja me raja*" (2). It is not merely as a geopolitical space that she envisions Aztlán (where would its borders be?) but also as a psychological and cultural space that the dispossessed could reclaim as a homeland.

The impulse of Anzaldúa's challenge of racial, sexual, and national hierarchies is transcendent. While deconstructing these categories, her vision, like Carpenter's or Judy Grahn's in *Another Mother Tongue*, is ultimately utopian.[8] It is a vision that, while grounded in modernist longings for salvation, does not locate that salvation in a desire for coherence, simplicity, or stasis. Anzaldúa uses the tools of postmodern deconstruction to offer a new dream that in its slipperiness, its nonmateriality, can sustain us when the old fictions of identity or their dismantling threaten our psychological survival.

Michelle Cliff, a Jamaican-American lesbian writer, also reworks the conflation of race and sexuality in her novel *No Telephone to Heaven*. Unlike Anzaldúa, she does not claim a transcendence emerging from the collapse of the colonial discourses of race and sexuality. More than showing how we work through these discourses, she shows us how the discourses work through us. In *No Telephone to Heaven* Cliff creates two Jamaican characters—a light-skinned woman and a gay "mixed race" hermaphrodite—whose choices challenge the essentialist ideologies of both the Right and the Left, of both the racist legacies of colonialism and the revolutionary postures of identity politics. The central character of *No Telephone to Heaven* is Clare Savage whose racial ancestry is clearly mixed. Her father, "Boy" Savage, claims his English origins through his great-grandfather, Judge Savage, an owner of large plantations and of one hundred slaves whom he murdered on the eve of emancipation. Boy teaches Clare that regardless of her mother's more obviously "colored" background, as his daughter she is white. " 'You're white because you're a Savage,' " he tells her, ignoring not only the lack of logic in his claim, but the way his own name (Savage) betrays him by occupying the wrong side of the equation of colonial semantics. In the Caribbean context, Cliff identifies Clare as neither white nor black, but as "Creole" and mulatto. In Cliff's terminology, "Creole" is a shorthand expression covering a much more complex system of racial difference within the three-color system (white, Creole, black). At his Jesuit boarding school, Boy was taught the mathematical, and therefore natural, regularities of racial identity:

> A lesson from the third form on the history of Jamaica sprang to mind: mulatto, offspring of African and white; sambo, offspring of African and mulatto; quadroon, offspring of mulatto and white; mestee, offspring of quadroon and white; mestefeena, offspring of mestee and white. . . . These Aristotelian categories taught by a Jesuit determined they should know where they were—and fortunate at that. In the Spanish colonies there were 128 categories to be memorized. The class of multicolored boys rose and recited in unison. (56)

The weight of this history of supposed racial classifications determines, at least in her early life, Clare's highly specific placement, a placement based on both genealogy and color, thereby separating her from her darker mother and sister. Cliff describes the politics of what she calls "colorism" in her essay "If I Could Write This in Fire, I Would Write This in Fire":

> None of this is as simple as it may sound. We were colonists and we aspired to oppressor status. . . . Color was the symbol of our potential: color taking in hair "quality," skin tone, freckles, nose-width, eyes. We did not see that color symbolism was a method of keeping us apart: in the society, in the family, between friends. Those of us who were light-skinned, straight-haired, etc., were given to believe that we could actually attain whiteness—or at least those qualities of the colonizer which made him superior. We were convinced of white supremacy. If we failed, we were not really responsible for our failures: we had all the advantages—but it was that one persistent drop of blood, that single rogue gene that made us unable to conceptualize abstract ideas, made us love darkness rather than despise it, which was to be blamed for our failure. Our dark part had taken over: an inherited imbalance in which the doom of the creole was sealed.
>
> I am trying to write this as clearly as possible, but as I write I realize that what I say may sound fabulous, or even mythic. It is. It is insane. (72–73)

Cliff is much more leery and critical of the pseudoscientific language of heredity and genes than is Anzaldúa. It is the materiality of the language of genetics ("one rogue gene") that allows her to internalize a mythic tale of her own inferiority and the inferiority of others. On one level, the fine distinctions of complexion and hair texture are a tribute to the success of colonialist imaginings of racial difference. And yet Cliff shows how the wide spectrum of variation conceived of *within* the black-white dichotomy blurs the edges of that dichotomy to the point of confusion and distrust. As Booker T. Washington put it, "How difficult it sometimes is to know where the black begins and the white ends" (*Up From Slavery*, 85).[9] The white fear of racial fraud, of passing, is also an admission of the possibility of crossing boundaries conceived of as natural. Cliff stresses not only the historic weight of racial myth but also the insanity of such a system where family blood lines (if they are known) define one's racial place, and yet color divides parents from children and siblings from one another.

Racial identification in Cliff's work is relational, the constant evaluating of sameness and difference. The shifting terms of racial identification become a language in itself. In the novel, a "houseboy" for a light-skinned Creole family warns them at dinner that " 'when we get de power, de power fe de people, t'ings not gwan be easy fe de white smaddy of Jamaica dem.' " His warning, or threat, goes unheeded because the family ignores the economic and political meanings of "black" and "white": " 'We are not white, Joshua, so we are not worried.' The Mistress taking pity on the houseboy and deciding that his words come from benign concern. Flattered nonetheless that even this hignorant countrybwai did t'ink she white. Not understanding his use of metaphor" (20). The "houseboy's" metaphor acknowledges the way race is not an essential biological category but one intricately connected to class and political choice. This is the difficult terrain Clare travels in the novel as she negotiates between assigned place and political choice.

Throughout the novel Cliff reveals the fiction of racial systems by examining how they differ across time and space. As a child immigrant to the United States, Clare abruptly learns about race in a two-color system where "Creole" no longer defines her. She confronts the boundaries of racial identity and learns who has the power to assign racial position. When Clare enrolls in school in New York, for instance, Boy is quizzed on the racial status of his light-skinned daughter, and the principal sternly admonishes him, " 'I do not want to be cruel, Mr. Savage, but we have no room for lies in our system. No place for in-betweens' " (99).

Clare's in-between position is paralleled throughout the novel by the character Harry/Harriet, a gay mixed-race hermaphrodite who, rather than representing fragmentation or split consciousness, is the most whole and clear-sighted character in the book. Harry/Harriet is both the traditional Anansi trickster character and the revolutionary guerrilla fighting neocolonialist exploitation.[10] When Clare articulates the connection between them, " 'We are neither one thing nor the other,' " Harry/Harriet redefines the New York principal's words and gives Clare back the power of self-definition, " 'At the moment, darling, only at the moment . . . the time will come for both of us to choose. For we will have to make the choice. Cast our lot. Cyaan live split. Not in this world' " (131). At the end of the novel, both Clare and Harriet have made their choices: identifying with her darker roots, Clare has returned to her grandmother's land with a guerrilla group committed to fight against the white exploitation of Jamaica. Harry/Harriet has become a woman and goes among her people as a nurse, as both healer and warrior, "'the choice is mine, man, is made. Harriet live and Harry be no more.' "

It is significant that neither Clare nor Harriet makes a physical change; Clare is still light-skinned, and Harriet has not had a sex-change operation. By their own choices each has challenged the boundaries of racial and sexual classifications and stepped beyond the biological determinism of these positions. They not only challenge the hierarchies of race science and sexology but also complicate the meaning of "identity politics," a powerful political concept for feminists, gay men and lesbians, and people of color. These two characters are provocative because they challenge both the system of representation based on the visible and the idea of a true, if hidden, nature upon which a politics of resistance can be based. Despite her exploration of these positions that fall between the categories, Cliff sidesteps the danger of merely fine-tuning the system. Hers is not so much an argument that seeks recognition for another racial or sexual category misrepresented by a dominant discourse; rather, she allows her characters to reveal the fantasies of the dominant discourse itself, fantasies that locate subversion in biology rather than in culture. Cliff ensures that Clare's challenge to the racial system is not biological. Rendered sterile after a miscarriage, Clare is cut loose from the reproductive drama of racial "progress" or "degeneration."

Resisting the positions to which they have been assigned, Clare and Harriet do not take on new "truer" positions, but they choose roles that permit them to perform the political actions they believe in. This view of identity, at once shifting and strategic *and* psychically "real," approximates Judith Butler's theoretical articulation of postmodern identity as "performative."[11] Unlike Anzaldúa's, Cliff's vision is not utopian; the choices Clare and Harriet make are not those chosen freely nor do they guarantee freedom. While Clare and Harry/Harriet are able to transcend some of the boundaries that define them, Cliff does not offer a universalized vision of salvation. While the guerrilla group is international and interracial, Cliff makes no claims for a global "sisterhood" or "brotherhood." Deconstructing the boundaries of modern identity does not automatically privilege us with an effective politics. Where Anzaldúa spins for us a dream of cosmic interconnectedness, Cliff forces us to scrutinize not only the systems of representation we have inherited but also the new ones we create from within those systems as well.

For both these "postcolonial" lesbian writers, "place" is the metaphor that binds the deconstruction of race, sexuality, and the political state. At the center of each of their work is the desire for a metaphorical homeland, for a place outside of categories of racial, sexual, or national placement. Anzaldúa challenges all these borders at the same time: "As a *mestiza* I have no country, my homeland cast me out; yet all countries are mine because I am every woman's sister or potential lover. (As a lesbian I have no race, my own people disclaim me; but I am all races because there is the queer of me in all races)" (80).

Unwilling to make such claims, Cliff nonetheless allows Clare Savage to attempt to reclaim her "motherland" from the economics and political definitions of the nation Jamaica. This is a place to be fought for by an international group of revolutionaries whose dreams surpass their present abilities to throw off the places to which they have been assigned not only by what their bodies make visible but also by the mythologies of their families. As tempting as it might be, Cliff does not offer a utopian conclusion in which the diverse community—united across races, classes, and sexes—gloriously overcomes the neocolonial exploitation and reestablishes Jamaica, the homeland of the people. Although Clare has made her own choice to claim Jamaica and not England as her home, Cliff uses the ending of the novel to dramatize the way individual choices occur within historical paradigms. Clare and Harry/Harriet's choices, while they are important symbolic challenges to the hierarchical classification systems of race and sex, are no match for the force of these systems once set in motion. Betrayed by a member, the guerrilla group is ambushed, and Clare is killed at the end of *No Telephone to Heaven*. At her death, as she is literally burned into the land, the text of the novel becomes preverbal, "She remembered language. Then it was gone"; what is left are sounds of a land before or after meaning, language, or symbolic use. This is "place" prior or subsequent to the uses made of it by a logic of difference that assigns each of us a place—national, cultural, racial, sexual—determining our rights and the ways we come to know ourselves and to define our battles. The last words of the novel, "Day broke," disrupt the vision of a world outside of culture and deny even this Edenic escape, casting us back into history, meaning, and struggle.

Writing from the borderlands of racial, sexual, and national identities, Cliff and Anzaldúa expose the fictions that have framed both repressive and liberatory gestures over the last century. Neither of these writers describes the conflict created by the fictional categories as inherently tragic. Instead, conflict, shock, the "swamping of psychological borders," and experience that falls outside present definitions provide a source of creativity and new possibilities. Articulating a postmodern appreciation for the chaos that inevitably results from racist and sexist categories and from their dismantling, they envision new paradigms of consciousness and political strategy that surpass the limitations of identity as Euro-American philosophy and science have conceived it.

I would like to thank Marylynne Diggs, Steven Kruger, and Maurizia Boscagli for their helpful suggestions on an earlier draft of this essay.

Notes

1. The term *border intellectual* is borrowed from Abdul R. JanMohamed. This term creates a category encompassing a range of positions and experiences resulting from geographical relocation and/or changing political borders. Among the varieties of border intellectuals are immigrants, exiles, expatriates, intranational migrants, and those who live in national or cultural border zones. Despite the obvious differences in the colonial histories of the western United States and Jamaica, Anzaldúa and Cliff address similar aspects of a colonialist epistemology that continues to govern so-called postcolonial or neocolonial national imaginings.

2. Nancy Stepan summarizes the logic of scientific analogy as follows:

Through an intertwined and overlapping series of analogies, involving often quite complex comparisons, identifications, cross-references, and evoked associations, a variety of "differences"—physical and psychical, class and national—were brought together in a biosocial science of human variation. By analogy with the so-called lower races, women, the sexually deviate, the criminal, the urban poor, and the insane were in one way or another constructed as biological "races apart" whose differences from the white male, and likenesses to each other, "explained" their different and lower position in the social hierarchy. ("Race and Gender," 40–41)

3. Stepan cites Josiah Nott who in 1843 argued that the "mulatto," as a true hybrid, was "a degenerate, unnatural offspring, doomed by nature to work out its own destruction" (Stepan, "Biological Degeneration," 107). See also Sander L. Gilman, "Sexology, Psychoanalysis, and Degeneration: Theory of Race to a Race to Theory."

4. Krafft-Ebing writes in *Psychopathia Sexualis*: "I have designated this peculiar sexual feeling as a functional sign of degeneration, and as a partial manifes-

tation of a neuro- (psycho-) pathic state, in most cases hereditary. . . . By the side of the functional signs of degeneration attending antipathic sexual feeling are found other functional, and in many cases anatomical, evidences of degeneration" (338–39). Ulrich and later Hirschfeld used the congenital argument to stress that homosexuality was a normal, nonpathological variation and therefore should be decriminalized. For a history of sexology, see Gert Hekma's overview.

5. The pseudoscientific classifications of sexology are grounded in the equally pseudoscientific classifications of race. As Gert Hekma describes it, "Sexology functioned from the beginning as a social science with pretensions of being a natural science, a status to which it could only aspire through analogic thinking." Modeling itself on medical diagnostic categories and using the material of anthropological ethnographies, sexology from the beginning is grounded in a racist and sexist discourse and analysis ("A History of Sexology," 183).

6. For an excellent discussion of the tensions between postcolonial and postmodern theory and expression, see Annamaria Carusi.

7. As Stepan makes clear, centering Mexican nationality on the Europeanized mestizo also meant a depreciation of the "Indian" and the "Negro" and repeated much of the racism of European eugenics that Vasconselos and Mexican eugenics theorists presumably sought to reverse. The idealization of the "cosmic" race is grounded in the racist ideas of the period (Stepan, *Hour*, 150–51).

8. In claiming a gay and lesbian "culture" that has historical roots, Judy Grahn, like Carpenter and Anzaldúa, relies on apparent similarities across time and cultures. While the political and psychological need of gay men and lesbians for this kind of "evidence" of a history and culture is understandable, the research showing the variable meanings of sexual behavior historically and transculturally also offers us important understandings about the cultural and social construction of not only homosexual identity but heterosexual identity as well. For examples of the social construction theory of sexuality see Carol Vance and Jeffrey Weeks.

9. For two recent studies of the legal and social understandings of the ambiguities of racial definition in the United States, see Virginia R. Domínguez and F. James Davis.

10. In an interview Cliff described this representation of Harry/Harriet as particularly important, "I was determined in *No Telephone to Heaven* to make the most whole and sane character in the novel somebody who was homosexual, which is what Harry is. People may want to think of him as a transvestite, but he's not" (Raiskin, "The Art of History," 69).

11. Judith Butler describes this conception in terms of lesbian identity:

> To say that I "play" at being [a lesbian] is not to say that I am not one "really"; rather, how and where I play at being one is the way in which "being" gets established, instituted, circulated, and confirmed. This is not a performance from which I can take radical distance, for this is deep-seated play, psychically entrenched play, *and this "I" does not play its lesbianism as a role* ("Imitation and Gender Subordination," 18).

Works Cited

Anzaldúa, Gloria. *Borderlands/La Frontera: The New Mestiza*. San Francisco: Spinsters/Aunt Lute, 1987.

Butler, Judith. "Imitation and Gender Insubordination." In Diana Fuss, ed., *Inside/Out: Lesbian Theories, Gay Theories*, pp. 13–31. New York: Routledge, 1991.

Carpenter, Edward. *The Intermediate Type Among the Primitive Folk: A Study in Social Evolution*. London: Allen, 1914.

——. "The Intermediate Sex." In Noël Greig, ed., *Edward Carpenter: Selected Writings*, vol. 1: *Sex*, pp. 185–244. London: GMP Publishers, 1984.

Carusi, Annamaria. "Post, Post, and Post; or, Where is South African Literature in All This?" In Ian Adam and Helen Tiffin, eds., *Past the Last Post: Theorizing Post-Colonialism and Post- Modernism*, pp. 95–108. Calgary: University of Calgary Press, 1990.

Cliff, Michelle. "If I Could Write This in Fire, I Would Write This in Fire." In *The Land of Look Behind*, pp. 57–76. Ithaca, N.Y.: Firebrand Books, 1985.

——. *No Telephone to Heaven*. New York: Dutton, 1987.

Davis, F. James. *Who is Black?: One Nation's Definition*. University Park: Pennsylvania State University Press, 1991.

Domínguez, Virginia R. *White By Definition: Social Classification in Creole Louisiana*. New Brunswick, N.J.: Rutgers University Press, 1986.

Ellis, Havelock. *The Criminal*. London: Walter Scott, 1910.

——. *Studies in the Psychology of Sex*. New York: Random House, 1940.

Foucault, Michel. *The History of Sexuality*. Vol. 1. Translated by Robert Hurley. New York: Pantheon, 1978.

Gilman, Sander L. "Black Bodies, White Bodies: Toward an Iconography of Female Sexuality in Late Nineteenth-Century Art, Medicine, and Literature." *Critical Inquiry* 12(1) (Autumn 1985): 204–42.

——. "Sexology, Psychoanalysis, and Degeneration: Theory of Race to a Race to Theory." In J. Edward Chamberlin and Sander L. Gilman, eds., *Degeneration: The Dark Side of Progress*, pp. 72–96. New York: Columbia University Press, 1985.

Grahn, Judy. *Another Mother Tongue: Gay Words, Gay Worlds*. Boston: Beacon Press, 1984.

Hekma, Gert. "A History of Sexology: Social and Historical Aspects of Sexuality." In Jan Bremmer, ed., *From Sappho to De Sade: Moments in the History of Sexuality*, pp. 173–93. New York: Routledge, 1989.

JanMohamed, Abdul R.. "Worldliness-without-World, Homelessness-as-Home: Toward a Definition of the Specular Border Intellectual." In Michael Sprinker, ed., *Edward Said: A Critical Reader*. London: Basil Blackwell, 1993.

Krafft-Ebing, Richard von. *Psychopathia Sexualis with Especial Reference to the Antipathic Sexual Instinct*. Chicago: Login, 1929.

Levy, Anita. *Other Women: The Writing of Class, Race, and Gender, 1832–1898*. Princeton: Princeton University Press, 1991.

Lombroso, Caesar, and William Ferrero. *The Female Offender*. New York: Appleton, 1915.

Raiskin, Judith. "The Art of History: An Interview with Michelle Cliff." *Kenyon Review* 15(1) (Winter 1993): 57–71.

Showalter, Elaine. *Sexual Anarchy: Gender and Culture at the Fin de Siècle*. New York: Viking, 1990.

Stepan, Nancy. "Biological Degeneration: Races and Proper Places." In J. Edward Chamberlin and Sander L. Gilman, eds., *Degeneration: The Dark Side of Progress*, pp. 97–120. New York: Columbia University Press, 1985.

——. "Race and Gender: The Role of Analogy in Science." In David Theo Goldberg, ed., *Anatomy of Racism*, pp. 38–57. Minneapolis: University of Minnesota Press, 1990.

——. *"The Hour of Eugenics": Race, Gender and Nation in Latin America*. Ithaca: Cornell University Press, 1991.

Talbot, Eugene. *Degeneracy: Its Causes, Signs, and Results*. London: Walter Cott, 1898.

Vance, Carol. "Social Construction Theory: Problems in the History of Sexuality." In Theo van der Meer et al., eds., *Homosexuality, Which Homosexuality?*, pp. 13–34. Amsterdam: An Dekker/Schorer; London: GMP Publishers, 1989.

Washington, Booker T. *Up From Slavery*. In *Three Negro Classics* New York: Avon Books, 1965.

Weeks, Jeffrey. *Against Nature and Other Essays on History, Sexuality & Identity*. London: Rivers Oram, 1991.

10   Almost Blue: Policing Lesbian Desire in *Internal Affairs*

Dana A. Heller

Why *lesbian postmodern*? Why the formulation of this particular relation, an unlikely coupling that invites uncertainty as to which term is
actually doing the leading? Syntactically, are we avoiding the evocation of yet another problematic category of identity—a postmodern
lesbian—one more sitting duck for postmodernism's radical critique
of subjectivity? Or, on the contrary, is lesbian identity asserted in a
refusal to follow a term that has become a master signifier in its own
right, one with the potential power to eclipse the lesbian's visibility in
a volume giving her star billing while otherwise resisting any definition of her essence?

A more compelling possibility is suggested when Robyn Wiegman,
in her introduction to this volume, observes that the lesbian interruption of the postmodern (like the juxtaposition of terms in the title) "is
decidedly artificial, not because the lesbian's relation to the postmodern is in any sense inauthentic but rather because there is not, as yet,

a constituted object of inquiry known as the 'lesbian postmodern.' "
However, two serious questions arise from this proposition. How can
"the lesbian," or anyone for that matter, hold such a thing as an
authentic relation to postmodernism when the very terms of its debate
resist all notions of the genuine, the essential? And if indeed there is
no constituted object of inquiry known as the "lesbian postmodern,"
how certain can we be that there exists a constituted object of inquiry
known as a "lesbian?"

With regard to the second question, many of the contributors to
this volume would probably agree that we can be certain only to the
extent that there exist discursive contexts in which a lesbian identity
is theorized as a viable position to claim. However, what I want to
explore in this essay is a "constituted absence" of the object or of the
viable illusion of "real" sexual difference—lesbian difference—available at the level of mainstream Hollywood film. And I want to question the transfiguring contextualization of an ostensibly lesbian presence in popular film, for while Hollywood's acknowledgment of lesbians would seem at least to affirm their need for mainstream
representational space, the film industry's contradictory formulation
of images throws into question the progress presaged by the occasional appearance of cinematic characters who engage some manner
of lesbian identity, however ambiguous.

A prominent concern of much gay and lesbian criticism has been to
identify in various representational modes a kind of disaffected punitive supervision allegedly at work in the production and recognition
of sexual diversity. In order to illustrate just such a transvaluation,
Teresa de Lauretis has borrowed the phrase "sexual indifference"
from Luce Irigaray to stress the absence of any conceptual frame for
lesbian representation. Assuming the axiomatic position that there is
but *one* practice and representation of the sexual, de Lauretis differentiates between Irigaray's designation of hommo-sexuality, which is
the term of masculine heterosexuality (and a pun on the French word
for man), and its sound-alike term *homosexuality*, which is the discursive mark of gay or lesbian sexual desire ("Sexual Indifference,"
155–77). In conventional Hollywood narrative, the practice and representation of the sexual is understood to be determined by masculine
desire and by masculine desire *only*. Where they occur, homosexuality and its representation are always irretrievably bound to dominant
social codes by the indelible contract of heterosexual relations. Thus,
as Irigaray has claimed, there is but one sex capable of representa-

tion—the hommo-sexual, or masculine heterosexuality. Images of gay or lesbian subjectivity, when and where they appear at all, are marked essentially by "hommo-sexuality," the term of sexual/social indifference, a signifier that ultimately serves as a kind of heterosexual police force.

This argument is important for de Lauretis and for the critique I'm about to offer because of the deconstructive work it both reveals and invites. As a case in point, I want to discuss Mike Figges's *Internal Affairs* (1989), a film about the Internal Affairs Division of the Los Angeles Police Department. Of particular interest is a lesbian character, Detective Amy Wallace, played by Laurie Metcalf, the actress who plays Roseanne Arnold's sister on the television sitcom "Roseanne." The deployment of Metcalf's character in a police drama incorporating many of the narrative principles of traditional family romance illustrates how the trope of lesbianism itself is frequently contained—literally policed—by the ideological anxiety of the status quo—or the Hollywood film industry—whose explicit function in the gender-reactive decade of the 1980s was the preservation of patriarchal law and order.

When I say "in general," I mean, in the most provisional sense, that it's become possible to detect a pattern of lesbian or bisexual lawyers, police officers, detectives, or public figures in popular culture who represent the legal institution or who serve in the interest of enforcing a romanticized vision of the American justice system. *Internal Affairs* is part of what can only be described as an emergent trend in popular culture whereby lesbian identity is framed by conventional narratives involving legal process and law enforcement. These images may suggest the possibility of subversive signification within the matrix of the judiciary; however, by inscribing upon them the ineffaceable master terms of paternal-heterosexual privilege, these characters can be mobilized to sanction the very erasure of lesbianism their images ostensibly transcend. And while some may feel that co-opted lesbian images are better than none, I maintain that "the law" is a problematic site for lesbian intervention, particularly when that intervention in no way disrupts the technologies of gender or the guise of liberal tolerance beneath which the psychosocial oppression of lesbianism is reinforced.

Admittedly, the judiciary domain has long been a favored forum for Hollywood's representation of the "straight" butch-femme fatal. Take Kathleen Turner's *V. I. Warshawski*, and the promotional copy's fetishistic solicitation, "Killer Smile, Killer Legs, Killer Instincts." The self-conscious reification of the instinctual and the peculiar conflation of desire with a public license to kill typically defines the conflictive position of the female law enforcer in Hollywood police drama. Lorraine Gamman articulates the signifying work of such popular narratives and opens a door to understanding the paradoxical nature of the text when an inversion of sexed identity occurs: "As an entertainment genre, cop [films] function ideologically to reproduce notions of male social authority and to legitimate contradictory aspects of police work by securing consent for the most brutal components of the repressive state apparatus" (*The Female Gaze*, 8). Consequently, police dramas featuring female law officers depend on individual attributes generally repressed in the conventional narrative construction of woman—action, movement, psychic if not physical strength, and knowledge. "Such scenarios permit focus on female *activity* rather than on female *sexuality*," Gamman argues in support of the genre's feminist contributions(19). However, she also highlights the categorical separation of activity and sexuality, the incongruence of female desire and male law, an incongruence that corresponds to the social division of internal (domestic) and external (market) spheres. When women are represented as the agents of the law, the result may be an inversion of spatial metaphors that holds structural oppositions firmly in place while still allowing for greater female mobility and the exploration of new cultural themes. However, when the agent of the law is a lesbian, a figure who stands uncompromised by the definition of woman as property of the law, the result is not simply a co-option of feminist ideology nor a deconstruction of a phallogocentric legal system but a reconceptualization of gender possibility that undermines the ideology of separate spheres, a division long held as the structural foundation of modern social institutions.

A primary feature of poststructuralism's break with structuralism is a turbulent rejection of binary metaphysics and with that a rejection of one of the most basic assumptions of Western logic. Assuming that postmodern theory appropriates and, to some extent, expands on poststructuralism's attack against Western metaphysics, the "postmodern turn" presages a disruption or transgression of structural boundaries in its production of new models of aesthetic and social experience. And arguably it is here that "the lesbian" and "the postmodern" meet. In other words, it is perhaps at this point—the point where the structural division of private and public spheres collapses—

that the disruptive presence of a lesbian agent within a heterosexual framework can be viewed as an indicator of postmodernism's radicalizing potential. Like Monique Wittig's metaphorical lesbian, postmodern discourse interrogates social and sexual boundaries, thus suggesting radical cultural upheaval. By "outing," so to speak, the full range of sexual possibility, by revealing woman-to-woman desire as a public as well as private issue, the representation of lesbianism within traditional narrative forms holds the potential to enact similar narrative disturbances that may have equally powerful social implications.

In *Internal Affairs* this potential is nervously held in check although the contradictory premise of a lesbian police officer whose job it is to protect and defend the patriarchal family holds revolutionary possibility. These possibilities are restrained by the Internal Affairs Division, whose operations *effect* the appearance of order and unity. Newly employed by the I.A.D staff is Detective Ramon Avilla, the main character, played by Andy Garcia. His partner, Amy Wallace, is a highly competent, mildly sarcastic career woman whose supposed lesbianism is a thinly veiled secret among the I.A.D. staff. It is significant, however, that at no point in the film does Wallace ever identify *herself* as a lesbian. Only the male characters in the film name her, and when they do so, she is randomly dismissed as "the dyke." The epithet is thrown about as an instrument of desexualization; it renders Wallace useless, harmless, an object of ridicule who provides no currency in the matrix of fraternal competitions and devotions that hold the police force together. After his first day of work, Avilla's wife, Kathy, asks if his female partner is pretty. "She's pretty smart. She's a good cop," he answers, ostensibly indicating his lack of interest in Wallace's private life, but more likely suggesting that Wallace's lesbianism is information far more threatening to his marriage than an assessment of her professional qualifications. Later, when Kathy rationalizes her husband's lack of sexual interest by accusing him of having an affair with Wallace, he shouts, "I'm not fucking my partner, my partner's a dyke!" Suddenly, Wallace's private life is given public voice, but only because her lesbianism serves as a defense when masculine virility is called into question.

Of course, Wallace's reputation as "a good cop" indicates that she has earned a certain amount of respect from her colleagues. She is grudgingly acknowledged as a member of the tribe. However, Wallace can not be treated exactly like "family," nor can she be treated exactly like a woman. Her blue uniform marks her as different from other women. Her sex marks her as different from other cops, much like Avilla's ethnicity marks him as different, a Latino whose name none of the white officers can correctly pronounce. However, while Avilla's ethnicity increases his heroic potential by making it possible for him to participate in both the street life of East Los Angeles and the life of the police precinct, Wallace's lesbianism in no way enables her to break down social barriers or better serve the law. If anything, she is an outlaw, an agent of chaos rather than an agent of order.[1] So how then—and why—is Amy Wallace molded to fit this uniform?

According to Judith Butler, if we are to understand the reproduction of heterosexual desire through the compulsory function of the law, we need to see how "the law might be understood to produce or generate the desire it is said to repress. . . . In other words, desire and its repression are an occasion for the consolidation of juridical structures: desire is manufactured and forbidden as a ritual symbolic gesture whereby the juridical model exercises and consolidates its own power" (*Gender Trouble*, 75–76). Consequently, when lesbian identity is manufactured within this framework, agonizing conflicts result. In many contemporary images of lesbians, the structural contradictions of what Gayle Rubin calls the "sex/gender system" become mapped against a discourse of liberal tolerance. And it is at this juncture that we discover the deceptive "ideology of pluralism, where social difference is also, at the same time, social indifference" (de Lauretis, "Sexual Indifference," 155). The representation of lesbian identity thus works systematically to assure the erasure of lesbian identity, the rendering of her desire as benign. From this perspective, I would argue that Amy Wallace does not, as appearances might otherwise suggest, represent an alternative lifestyle among the deteriorating heterosexual relations depicted in *Internal Affairs*. Nor is she an exception to the Hollywood film industry's relentless reproduction of patriarchal family images. Rather, she is co-opted in the name of "sensitive" gay discourse to reinstate the power of a repressive social agenda whose inconsistencies, we are led to believe, are the inevitable outgrowths of liberal pluralism.

Wallace's place within the I.A.D. system—a system specifically organized to penetrate the private lives of police officers—appears to challenge the authority of the sex/gender system with every move she makes "in the name of the law." As I.A.D. staff, Wallace represents a kind of metaauthority. She is the cop of the cops; it is her job to keep the force clean, and this proves to be no easy assignment. However, the performative effects of this reversal and of the gay/female straight/male collision work to condense categories of sexual identity rather than to disseminate them across the wide discursive field of erotic possibilities. Wallace's inscription serves essentially to center a patriarchal, heterosexist regime by maintaining a strict binary division of sexual definitions. By establishing supposedly symmetrical oppositions of meaning within the boundaries of the department, *Internal Affairs* keeps "female" subordinate to "male" and "gay" subordinate to "straight." In other words, Wallace is offered up as a kind of semiotic martyr whose main task is not to clean up the force but to reinforce the compulsory devaluation and ultimate exclusion of women, homosexuality, and homosexual women. In this way, the viewers' identification with heterosexual norms is what is ultimately being policed in *Internal Affairs*. The film suggests that social deviants may become functional when placed within the boundaries, devices, and rituals of the law enforcement nexus. Certainly, we may speak of Wallace as a potentially disruptive signifier, but she remains a latent signifier throughout.

Another way of examining the problem Wallace presents is to posit her character within what Eve Kosofsky Sedgwick calls an "open-secret structure" (*Epistemology of the Closet*, 22). Lesbianism is constructed in the film as a site of self-silencing and obedient patterning on heterosexual (male) expressions of desire. Thus, arguably, *Internal Affairs* participates in the construction of an "epistemology of the closet" that, according to Sedgwick, requires "the deconstructive understanding that particular insights generate, are lined with, and at the same time are structured by particular opacities" (8). As a woman, a lesbian, and a cop, Wallace doesn't so much defy typical representation as much as she helps define a new category of identity, a reification of silences that constitute lesbian identity by forcing it to conform with the heterosexist opinion that homosexuality is purely a private, "internal" matter. Granted, Wallace is presented neither in a voyeuristic manner "as spectacle," nor is she set up for heterosexual conversion. It is clear that we, as viewers, are being asked to sympathize with her. However, our sympathies are carefully filtered through our primary identification with Avilla and his indifference to what makes Wallace "different" from the other cops and the other women portrayed in the film.

How does *Internal Affairs* command the effects of silence to enforce the closeting of lesbian sexuality? In the film, Wallace's dedication to her investigative function, her honest belief in the system, is set against the corrupt, violent, and dishonest organization of the street cops, the worst of whom are arrogant, abusive, racist, sexist, drug-addicted, and willing to turn a blind eye to acts of blatant injustice and exploitation of the judiciary system. Richard Gere plays Officer Dennis Peck, a raging and malicious psychopath who becomes the object of Avilla's and Wallace's investigation when they begin to suspect that Peck has supplementary business interests outside the force. He controls 40 percent of the force by providing second incomes to the rookie cops struggling to support their young families. In return, Peck exacts their submission to his public authority within the force and to his private authority within the domestic and sexual lives of the officers.

Peck, as it turns out, is a hit man for a local crime boss. He launders cash through his numerous ex-wives to cover up his income. By the time the narrative reveals that Peck has connections with local organized crime, we understand him to be utterly ruthless, sexually menacing, and erotically ubiquitous. Interestingly enough, Peck is also a father figure to the rookie cops whom he manipulates in his quest for complete punitive power. He is also an exemplary cop, one of the most productive cops on the staff. His productivity extends outside the force as well: he is the father of eight children, a ninth is on the way. Dennis Peck, whose very name connotes crude phallic authority, embodies an excess of "hommo-sexuality," ironically perceived as reproductive heterosexuality. The inscription of violent heterosexual excess and the counterimages of homoerotic intimacy between Peck and his partner, Van Stretch, problematize gender representation almost to the point of collapsing it. Peck's sexual claim on his partner's wife enacts the exchange of women whereby men consolidate bonds of trust and community; however, the abuse of women as sexual currency can also be seen as a channeling of homoerotic desire repressed to the point of violence. Peck's excessive hommo-sexuality threatens to collapse heterosexuality into gay sexuality; however, at the same time homoerotic possibility is kept anchored to images of extreme psychological dysfunction and sadistic exploitation, as the dynamic between Peck and Stretch suggests in both their names and actions.

In other words, Peck is an embodiment of a vicious sexual economy in which only those subjectivities marginalized by the paradigm of the positive oedipus complex are explainable in terms of excesses or lacks. Hence, "too much" paternal authority indicates transcendent possibilities. In a society where gay sexual practice is historically and legally framed in terms of secrets, private preference, and closed doors, the heterosexual social contract, in excess of its own laws, inverts its own internal value system and becomes an affair of the closet. A sexual fascist, Peck is the incarnation of a homophobic vision of uncontainable polymorphous masculinity, a masculinity fully invested with the authority of the law. "Don't worry," says Peck when a man who wants his parents murdered warns him to keep quiet about the hit, "I'm a cop." Thus, Peck *is* the law, and he redefines "law" to signify an excess of paternal-heterosexual privilege that ultimately results in self-parody, the policeman's ball as camp. Thus, Peck persistently reveals himself as pecker-less. This structural inversion, however, remains a potential repressed within the narrative; the police department itself becomes a repository for the secret of masculine lack, a closet where hypermasculine sexuality "tells us more about the fantasies that a fearful heterosexual culture produces to defend against its own homosexual possibilities" than about gay experience itself (Butler, *Gender Trouble*, 87). Wallace's lesbianism, in this context, is reduced to a reification of difference that is consequently regarded with total indifference.

In part this indifference—and the dismissal of lesbianism as a legitimate category of identity—comes about as a result of the presumed incongruence of lesbianism and patriarchal family relations, which remain, in the world of the film, the foundation of culture. Kinship and the potential dissolution of the patriarchal kinship unit constitute the organizing metaphor of the film, and it operates simultaneously at a number of interrelated levels. The film rallies encouragement for the preservation of the modern marriage contract, dramatized in the subplot depicting Avilla's troubled relationship with his wife, who, although immersed in her own career, feels that his obsessive commitment to the force is draining their relationship of its intimacy and passion. In Van Stretch's abusive relationship to Penny Stretch we see the dark side of a marriage torn apart by drugs, deceit, violence, and greed. And in Dennis Peck's extended family of ex-wives and children from various marriages we see not so much the possibilities for redefining kinship structures, but a vision of the post–nuclear family as harem. It is here that Peck dictates his extremist interpretation of the essential function of the heterosexual social contract: reproduce, reproduce, reproduce.

Parallel to the private family there is the male society of the police force, a tribe also concerned with the reproduction of its own social authority, a familial order bound by the rights of exchange and the intensity of the dangers they daily face together. Ironically, it is Van Stretch's reported use of "excessive force" on the job that initially alerts Wallace and Avilla to the illegal activities being conducted by Peck. When Stretch begins to break under I.A.D. questioning, Peck arranges an "accidental" shooting during a routine assignment. When Stretch doesn't die immediately from the shot fired into his chest, Peck crouches down besides him, cradles his partner's head in his arms, and strangles him to death.

As the white male hierarchy begins to self-destruct under the intense scrutiny of Avilla and Wallace—a Latino and a lesbian—a utopian vision of social pluralism—a global family, so to speak—is superficially suggested by the need for unity among the different individuals who make up the police force and the world outside the force. As Internal Affairs investigators, Detectives Avilla and Wallace share the task of negotiating and monitoring these levels of social relationships. Thus, the social margins move to occupy the presumed center of power, but still our heroes remain marginalized because of the fact that they are distrusted and resented by the street cops who see them as promotion-greedy informers and traitors to the familial structure of the department.

The more Wallace and Avilla attempt to find out about the private affairs of Dennis Peck and the more they threaten to expose him, the more seriously Peck threatens to seduce Avilla's wife and exploit his knowledge of Avilla's private sexual matters. In this way, *Internal Affairs* seems to hint at the unavoiable blurring of private and public, and the inevitable gender confusions that result from the cross-mapping of family and work. However, the film ultimately rejects this notion in favor of developing what D. A. Miller calls an "undeclared defense of the status quo" (quoted in Caserio, 268). Taking issue with Miller's suspicion of the novel as police, or more specifically with his argument that "privacy and domesticity, supposed to be a refuge from power's oppressions, mime their opponent, and make the 'outside' of power the twin of power," Robert Caserio argues that while indeed some gay narratives collaborate in the construction of a homophobic discourse by cultivating an ideal of the private family, there is no "compelling reason to . . . see family structure as necessarily—and in every possible form—the ally of supervisory and disciplinary constraint" ("Supreme Court Discourse vs. Homosexual Fiction," 268–70).

What's so confusing about the film *Internal Affairs* is that it appears to argue Caserio's point from both sides of the fence, on the one hand positioning a lesbian character as a defender of patriarchy while on the other hand implying that she is free to lead her own life as she pleases. Ultimately, however, the film unravels its own liberal intentions in much the same way that Miller unravels Dickens's efforts to outsmart the police. Almost in spite of itself, *Internal Affairs* offers the assurance that no lesbian agent, no matter how good a cop she may be, can disrupt or deter the enforcement of compulsory heterosexuality and the survival of the private family. There is no avoiding the gradual recognition that while Avilla's life outside the force has public consequences, Wallace's does not. Or in other words, her inclusion within the film requires that she be excluded from playing any meaningful part in the self-reflexive critique that makes her role within the all-male, all-straight police force so crucial.

Wallace's lesbian difference becomes social indifference at the point where the film appears to construct an interesting diacritical pattern that could potentially decenter the notions of public authority and private freedom. Intervention, that is, interaction between the private and public, between the inside and the outside of the law, is shown to be a fundamental concern of the state apparatus even while the ideology of "family" assures a safe haven beyond the control of the external world. While *Internal Affairs* focuses on the dialectic dimensions of such structural oppositions as private/public, male/female, homosexual/heterosexual, Wallace is given no identity outside the force whatsoever. She appears to have no home, no private life, no lover, not even a friend, and this absence becomes more and more obvious as the narrative progresses.

Why is it that Wallace is the only character to be placed in this familial void? Indeed, the film shows almost every significant character in a domestic context. Does Wallace's credibility as a reliable servant of the law depend on her having no attachments in her life other than to her work? "Go home to your wife," she advises Avilla as they work late into the night. But if there's anyone waiting for her at home, we'll never know about it. Wallace is relieved of a place in the world beyond the precinct, and Avilla is relieved of having to care about it. Wallace's complete lack of a life outside the force reveals the film narrative's own homophobic pitfalls. The portrayal of Wallace suggests that lesbianism will be tolerated as long as its kept under cover. To represent a woman who is known as a lesbian is acceptable, but to represent a woman who knows and defines *herself* as a lesbian is unacceptable. By denying her self-knowledge, or an internal affair of her own, *Internal Affairs* exposes its own "undeclared defense of the status quo." And although I don't want to imply that the credibility of female characters—lesbian or otherwise—depends on their depiction within a romantic, domestic, or familial framework, I would suggest that there is a very thin line between the granting of visibility to lesbians in popular representational forms and their control through the imposition of a supposedly nonhomophobic system of surveillance.

Interestingly, the assertion of patriarchal authority through surveillance and its replication through the metaphor of the gaze is briefly examined during one of the more humorous scenes of *Internal Affairs*. Avilla and Wallace sit side by side in the front seat of the patrol car. They are following Van Stretch's wife, whom they suspect is involved with Peck's money-laundering scheme, and they are preoccupied with fast food. Suddenly, without saying a word, they are simultaneously alerted to the approach of a tall, long-legged woman in a tight, white dress. Both officers gawk at her, then turn to watch her as she passes by. Avilla loses interest first and turns back around just in time to observe Wallace still staring at the woman's back. In the next beat, Wallace and Avilla look directly at one another. Wallace meets his inquisitive expression head-on, grins, and coyly sips from her straw. Avilla remains silent as new knowledge registers on his face. In the following instant the "serious" action of the film resumes as Penny Stretch appears.

In this sequence Wallace comes dangerously close to naming her desire through the active gesture of looking, and she very nearly becomes the sexually subversive agent who remains otherwise conspicuously repressed throughout the film. Wallace's "look" is a risky moment in the film, a co-option of masculine authority that functions simultaneously as a tease to the audience involved in its own voyeuristic pleasure. However, what we see is the replication of a nonheterosexual construct within a heterosexual setting. Thus, Wallace's look parodies heterosexual naturalness and therefore the imperative of heterosexual production that obsesses Dennis Peck. Wallace's gaze is anything but a reproductive gaze.

However, at the same time, her look is recorded by Avilla, and it is his gaze that ultimately frames the moment. Lesbian desire thus becomes constituted in the gaze that is decidedly a masculine privilege. The camera interprets the object of desire as a projection of hetero- sexual narrative, the conventional narrative of Hollywood film. The steamy nondiegetic music, the hyperfemme articulations of the woman's hips as she walks, and her tight dress all declare that there is but one desire capable of representation, a unified sexuality constitut- ed through the institutional markings of sexual (in)difference. Desire is not exchanged between two women—presumably the female passerby is not aware that she is being watched. Rather, desire remains in the sphere of male authority. The "conventions of seeing, and the relations of desire and meaning . . . remain[ed] partially anchored or contained by a frame of visibility that is still heterosexu- al" (de Lauretis, "Sexual Indifference and Lesbian Representation," 173). Through the male-monitored construction of lesbian meaning, lesbian homosexuality, or the possibility of its representation, is appropriated by the fraternal elite.

Consequently, Wallace's gaze works to constitute Avilla's authori- ty over the erotic rather than to constitute her own lesbian subjectivi- ty. Through this double cross, the possibility of lesbian representation remains caught in the tropism of heterosexuality. Immersed in the world of macho cops, Detective Wallace may flirtatiously arrest the masculine gaze, but no one is looking back at her except the male police. Lesbian desire and identity is thus carefully contained in a glance that reconstitutes the police as author and woman as muse. Wallace's position as a cop allows her recreational access to the men's locker room, which functions in this case as a kind of structural alter- native to the closet.

Internal Affairs boasts of challenging the boundaries of private and public, gender, and erotic possibility through the inclusion of a character whom everyone else knows to be a "dyke." But this is merely paying lip service to the notion of liberal gay discourse. In every conceivable way, the film's strategies of representing sexual dif- ference are shot through with homophobia and prejudice. At the con- clusion of the narrative, internal affairs, both public and private, are set straight, so to speak. Dennis Peck seriously wounds Wallace in the final manhunt scene, and we observe the ambulance ride to the hos- pital as Avilla stoutheartedly spurs her on to "hang in there." We never find out whether or not she survives; all we are left with is Avil- la's assurance that she is "a fighter." Once again, as John Leo argues, the gay presence provides an opportunity for straight characters to become liberalized. The "dramatic problem" is not to resolve the dilemma of the lesbian character but to reaffirm the conventional hierarchy by representing "a properly liberal reaction within the 'normality' of social pluralism and consensus." ("The Familialism of 'Man,' " 36).

From this point on, Detective Wallace remains outside the primary dramatic focus. Avilla finally "gets his man," in a manner of speaking, and kills Dennis Peck when he finds him holding Kathy hostage in their own bedroom. Thus, the destruction of megalomaniacal sexual desire within the police department's kin-based social organization reestablishes the primacy of an egalitarian heterosexual contract. Avilla and his wife are presumably reconciled; the maintenance of sexual desire within the home is proven to be a matter of public importance. Corruption is shown to exist along a continuum of kinship systems that become unstable only when they dare to move beyond the limits of the law.

Kate Adams has demonstrated how in post–World War II literature the discourse of psychoanalysis acted as the lesbian's chaperon "whenever she comes out into the mainstream of popular culture" ("Making the World Safe for the Missionary Position," 269). What I have attempted to show is that images of lesbians may also be chaperoned and held in place by a judiciary system's reactionary response to a breakdown in the ideology of separate spheres. Indeed, perhaps we are no longer concerned with the psychic origins of a "disorder" but rather with the legislative effects of a politics of identity that threatens familial ideology and patriarchal law. If so, the representation of lesbian identity will require containment and framing within ideological structures that police the referent and undermine sexual difference. Along these lines, it is important that when Avilla finally introduces Wallace to his wife, they are at an officer's funeral and Wallace is dressed in full uniform. The convention of dress constitutes a legally "produced and approved identity" ("Making the World Safe for the Missionary Position," 269). Again, lesbian identity is co-opted to dramatize the agency of heterosexual heroes who transform the law and represent our most valued constructs of truth and knowledge. However, the film cannot repress the lesbian's potential to reveal that the *law* as an origin for social order is nothing more than a parody of the desire for order and absolute authority.

In conclusion, the formulation of an authentic lesbian image in Hollywood film, like the formulation of an "authentic" lesbian relation to the postmodern, "depends on separating out the two contrary undertows that constitute the paradox of sexual (in)difference" (de Lauretis, "Sexual Indifference and Lesbian Representation," 159). In its desperate defense of the status quo, *Internal Affairs* is an example of one contemporary film that registers social anxiety at the postmodern prospect of "isolating but maintaining" the sexual and the political, the private and the public, the police and the policed, the internal and external affairs of the lesbian body. For even when she appears as an identity reconstituted for the purpose of consolidating the institutional power of the patriarchal family, the lesbian character in mainstream Hollywood cinema assists postmodern critique by revealing the extent to which no internal affair exists undetermined by public consequences, just as no public affair exists undetermined by lesbian desire.

Notes

1. A substantial body of scholarship exists that addresses the image of the lesbian as outlaw. See, for example, Andrea Weiss, "Lesbian as Outlaw: New Forms and Fantasies in Women's Independent Cinema," *Conditions* 12 (1985): 117–31.

Works Cited

Adams, Kate. "Making the World Safe for the Missionary Position: Images of the Lesbian in Post–World War II America." In Karla Jay and Joanne Glasgow, eds., *Lesbian Texts and Contexts: Radical Revisions*, pp. 255–74. New York: New York University Press, 1990.

Butler, Judith. *Gender Trouble: Feminism and the Subversion of Identity*. New York: Routledge, 1990.

Caserio, Robert L. "Supreme Court Discourse vs. Homosexual Fiction." *South Atlantic Quarterly*, special issue, *Displacing Homophobia*, edited by Ronald B. Butters, 88(1) (1989): 267–300.

de Lauretis, Teresa. "Sexual Indifference and Lesbian Representation." *Theater Journal* 40(2) (1988): 155–77.

Gamman, Lorraine. "Watching the Detectives: The Enigma of the Female Gaze." In Lorraine Gamman and Margaret Marshment, eds., *The Female Gaze: Women as Viewers of Popular Culture*. Seattle: The Real Comet Press, 1989.

Leo, John R. "The Familialism of 'Man' in American Television Melodrama." *South Atlantic Quarterly*, special issue, *Displacing Homophobia*, edited by Ronald B. Butters, 88(1) (1989): 31–52.

Rubin, Gayle. "The Traffic in Women: Notes on the 'Political Economy' of Sex." In Rayna R. Reiter, ed., *Toward An Anthropology of Women*, pp. 157–210. New York: Monthly Review Press, 1975.

Sedgwick, Eve Kosofsky. *Epistemology of the Closet*. Berkeley: University of California Press, 1991.

11 We Girls Can Do Anything, Right Barbie? Lesbian Consumption in Postmodern Circulation

Erica Rand

This essay originated from my attempt to teach a 1989 *On Our Backs* photo essay called "Gals and Dolls" in an art history/women's studies class.[1] When I first encountered "Gals and Dolls," which features a woman inserting a Barbie doll (feet first) into her vagina, I immediately wanted to teach it. The photographs seemed a refreshingly direct response to an often asked postmodern lesbian query: how can pop culture be subversively refunctioned for women's pleasure? Compared to the typical feminist product of thinking about women's pleasure—opaque theoretical discourse—the image of the Barbie dildo seemed a more interesting and more accessible "teaching tool." Barbie play also seemed like a great takeoff point for considering cultural appropriation in general and lesbian appropriation in particular. Surely Barbie was a cultural icon to whom virtually all my students, who varied widely in age and social background, could relate. After all, Barbie has been ubiquitous now for three decades; most of us (especially women) who grew up or raised children during the past thirty years remember having had to position ourselves somehow in relation to Barbie. And Barbie has some features particularly conducive to lesbian reappropriation: the nifty Barbie-of-the-eighties slogan "We girls can do anything" (or "Go Girl" as Queer Nation Barbie might put it) and a series of wardrobe-crafted identities to pull out of her closet. Like Madonna, already established in lesbian subculture, Barbie suggests that roles are only as fixed as costumes.

Yet the difficulties of inserting a Barbie dildo, like other images of lesbian sexual and gender play, into heterosexist contexts, such as university classrooms, are obviously many. Is it possible, I worried, to frame the "Gals and Dolls" images discursively so as to be more than scandalous, so as to avoid merely reinforcing stereotypes about lesbian perversity? Besides, is it really possible to liberate Barbie from Mattel anyway? One potential limit to Lesbian Barbie obsessed me: Barbie's closet may be diversely stocked, assuming one can make what one can't buy, but her body, with its permanently pointed breasts and feet, seems unalterably femme. Might Barbie, firmly premolded by Mattel, actually figure the limits more than the potential of the lesbian postmodern?

In this essay, I follow the low-theory, experience-oriented approach of "Gals and Dolls" to explore issues of consumption raised by the Barbie-dildo images. There are, admittedly, other worthwhile approaches. Barbie offers opportunities for content analyses and theoretical refinements that would make many a cultural critic ecstatic. One might, for example, discuss "Gals and Dolls" in terms of how the configuration of woman-and-Barbie-dildo subverts the predominant and heterosexist available theoretical models that are posited on binary sexual figurations, which distort and render invisible lesbian sexuality by overlaying a male/female model onto two female partners. Not only does woman-and-Barbie-dildo figure the difference between penetration and phallic penetration, given Barbie's bendable legs; more important, the image cannot be resolved into a masculine fucker and a feminine fuckee, since a decisively feminine figure rears her lovely head precisely where one would expect to see the penis. The Barbie dildo, which calls up while simultaneously warding off the penis, is thus interestingly apotropaic in the manner of that favorite of many a theorist, the Medusa's head, although much more subversively than the more-penis-like snakes. In addition, if we view the Barbie-dildo as Lesbian Barbie, her femmy appearance here represents another antibinarist feature of the image since, while one could (regressively and inaccurately) theorize the butch according to a heterosexual model as a masculine person who desires a feminine object, this logic can never explain why the fem, who would thus have a complementary desire for a masculine object, does not just choose a man. As both female (non)phallus and fem, Barbie-as-dildo doubly disarticulates heterosexist theoretical models.

While the implications of this observation are important, I choose not to follow here the approach that led me to it for several reasons. The first reason is political. I question the political value of sophisticated postmodern readings when their liberatory message cannot adhere in circulation. As the discussion of my classroom experience with "Gals and Dolls" will suggest, such is the case with the woman-with-Barbie-dildo picture: the students in my introductory course did not have the training to engage difficult theoretical issues of binary sexual figuration, and, regardless of that, it was impossible to keep in view even the less opaque postmodern concept of sticking it to regressive icons of the pop culture, given the predominant picture of lesbian perversity with which many of my students came to class. My motivating concern in this essay is thus less about how we can appropriate the postmodern for lesbians than whether such a project is worth our political efforts.

The second reason, paradoxically, is both critical and theoretical. I do not believe that approaches to Barbie such as the analysis I performed above actually tell us much about how Barbie signifies—except perhaps to postmodern critics—once practices of consumption come under scrutiny. In the four years since I came across "Gals and Dolls," I learned more about consumption from conversations about how people actually used and perceived Barbie than from available theoretical models of visual pleasure, sexual/gender identification, and cultural reception. My findings also belied what one might expect from the more typical critical approach of content analysis. On the one hand, I found that subversive Barbie play usually occurred far to the side of postmodern theorizing—that it was presumptuous of me to expect that Subversive Barbie was Postmodern Barbie. On the other hand, I found that the liberatory and oppressive features revealed by consumer stories did not match what postmodern analyses would suggest them to be.

Given that some of my concerns here are indeed theoretical, I should indicate more precisely what I mean when I identify my approach as "low-theory." I do not mean that I am not "doing theo-ry"; I mean that I am not doing theory for the sake of theoretical refinement itself but as part of a political project to use, understand, and subvert popular culture in ways that abet the liberation struggles of oppressed peoples, including lesbians. This political concern also informs my writing strategy: because I believe that postmodern theo-ries and practices deserve lesbian appropriation only if they can circu-late beyond academia, I have chosen to "do theory" not in the ver-nacular of postmodern theory but, one might say, in Barbie vernacu-lar—that is, in language accessible to more Barbie consumers than those who haunt MLA conventions.[2] In this essay, then, I share my experience with Barbie and with Barbie consumers in order to suggest here some critical political and intellectual issues that need to be addressed for productive lesbian cultural intervention.

The Classroom Story Continues

When I first thought about teaching "Gals and Dolls," my primary worry had to do with maintaining spin control, both before and dur-ing class. If I followed the ordinary procedure for having slides made, I would give *On Our Backs* to the curator of the slide library who would attach a work order marked "instructor's personal copy" and send it to the technicians generally referred to as "the guys in dupli-cating." Issues of gossip, homophobia, and safety arose since the word would undoubtedly be "out," and so did the matter of job security. Even if my job situation had not been as precarious as it in fact was, I would have wondered what my colleagues would think about me teaching, let alone owning, lesbian porn. I had greater concern about spin control in the classroom. Assuming that most of my students had a quite limited mental stockpile of lesbian images, could any discur-sive framework prevent them from thinking that these photographs typified lesbian practice? I didn't want them to think that all lesbians lived in pairs with two children, many Birkenstocks, and a sex life characterized by nurturing sweetness, but I didn't necessarily want them to think of woman-with-Barbie-dildo as normative either.

I also worried about the ethics and politics of circulating lesbian erotica among nonlesbians. I knew I wouldn't be violating the wishes of the images' publishers; *On Our Backs*, which advertises in straight if "alternative" publications, such as the Chicago *Reader*, is hardly a separatist publication.[3] Nor did I ordinarily balk at showing images that generated discomfort, but I wondered how the dykes in the class would react. Would flashing our subcultural sex products on the screen or the predictable derisive class comments make any of them feel uncomfortable, unsafe, or violated?

I wanted to ask them. But I didn't know exactly who they were. And most of the women I knew were dykes had come out to me, as often happens in the classroom and elsewhere, only through subtly revealed coded gestures offered up on the tacit condition that nothing would ever be explicitly articulated. To approach them on the subject might be more violating than showing the images without their input. Clearly, no collective classroom-dykes decision was possible.

So I consulted friends and colleagues, whose responses can be loosely coded by gender and sexual orientation. Liberal straight men (I encountered no gay men in my casual survey) said "Show them— and I'd be happy to look at them first if you're unsure." Straight women immediately got this sick, trapped look in their eyes; they thought it might be a bad idea but feared giving the impression that they wanted to censure either the images or the acts depicted. The dykes first said, "Don't show them," but after further discussion advised me semiseriously to have the slides made, read my horoscope on the day of class, and go for it if the signs were favorable.

What eventually happened confirmed both my hopes and my apprehensions about using the photo of the Barbie dildo as a teaching tool. I had decided on a compromise designed to sidestep "the guys in duplicating," to protect myself somewhat, and to semi-forestall lesbian discomfort: I presented the discursive frame without the pictures. With an (honest) introduction about having received the photographs from a friend in San Francisco who knew I was interested in pop culture—thus distancing myself a bit from the images—I described both the images and my struggle over whether to show them, using the incident to introduce a paper topic on how the meanings of images change in circulation. Initially, my strategy seemed to work. From the limited discussion that followed, I thought that the move had been pedagogically successful, and I left class with the little thrill that calculated risk and the illusion of discursive control can bring. This euphoria lasted until a student raised her hand in the next class and said: "I don't understand the point of that story. What is it that you like to do with Barbie dolls?"

My assessment of Barbie appropriation at this point, unsurprisingly, was mixed. Clearly, when using a Barbie dildo to stick it to Mattel, I could not guarantee that I was not actually sticking it to myself. Does this apply to other Barbie appropriations as well, or do postmodern Barbie appropriations exist that can be circulated with their liberatory postmodern readings more firmly attached? In the following sections, I discuss my preliminary findings on this issue from several perspectives: what Mattel says about what Barbie can do, and about what we can do with Barbie; what children have, in fact, done with Barbie; and what Barbie offers to grown-up players and critics.

We Girls Can't Do Everything, Can We, Mattel?

From the doll's first appearance in 1959, Mattel has worked to situate Barbie in carefully crafted, if vexed, relations to both fantasy and reality. Since Mattel markets the doll to children five to fifteen years younger than Barbie appears to be and encourages the child to fantasize about being Barbie—as opposed to being Barbie's dorky eight-year-old sister or the mother of a baby doll whose milieu is just like the child's own—she is clearly meant to inhabit a fantasy future for the 95 percent of American girls aged three to eleven who Mattel estimates own a Barbie doll.[4] In the words of Ruth Handler, who, as the story goes, invented Barbie when she saw how much her own daughter, named Barbie, loved to play with paper fashion dolls: "These dolls become an extension of the girls. Through the dolls, each child dreams of what she would like to be."[5]

Contributing to the child's identification with Barbie and to the scope of imaginative play is the vagueness of Barbie's biography. Unlike a human teenager, Barbie is apparently unburdened by restrictions of specific origin.[6] Although the 1962 novel *Barbie's New York Summer* (in which Barbie gets to go to New York as a modeling intern for a teen magazine, lose ten pounds for the camera, and have a summer flirtation with a world-weary young man from Buenos Aires named Pablo)[7] reveals that Barbie has parents named Margaret and George Roberts and small-town, middle-class roots, Barbie ordinarily appears to be parentless, leaving her with neither history nor authority figures to restrict her future actions. To borrow Eve Kosofsky Sedgwick's characterization of the Romantic rediscovery of ancient Greece, Mattel has "cleared out—as much as created—a prestigious, historically underfurnished imaginative space in which relations to and among human bodies might be newly a subject of utopian speculation."[8]

Barbie's imaginative space, however, is obviously as heavily over-accessorized as it is historically underfurnished. She has always, of course, come with an allowance for clothing and accessories far beyond what the characterization of the Robertses as "ordinary people" in *Barbie's New York Summer* would appear to support.[9] William K. Zinsser, writing from the perspective of a bemused father, recorded in 1964 that Barbie and her friends not only had travel costumes that enabled them to dress "like natives" in Japan, Switzerland, Mexico, and Holland—"Pity the father who comes home to learn that Barbie and Ken have decided to take the Grand Tour"—but also had purchase options that give new meaning to the concept of providing for one's child's future: "Should [Barbie] want to go to college, she can buy a 'campus,' which consists of a dormitory room, soda shop (with phone booth), football stadium and drive-in movie. Should she flunk out, which seems likely, she has her own fashion shop with modeling stage, display corner, and model's dressing room."[10] A perusal of Barbie literature reveals many other options given to Barbie and her friends over the years. One finds Candy-Striper Barbie, Malibu Barbie, Student Teacher Barbie, Doctor Barbie, Ken-A-Go-Go, and Growing-Up Skipper (1975) who, as Marilyn Ferris Motz describes, "grew taller and developed small breasts when her arms were rotated."[11] Of special interest, perhaps, to lesbian Barbie pals is the short-lived series of friends sold in pairs, holding hands, in 1970.[12]

As some of these titles suggest, Barbie's appearance, friends, and career options have changed with the times, thus attaching Barbie fantasy, with Mattel's characteristically weak linkage, to her contemporary historical context. Particularly in the 1980s Mattel picked up on the somewhat feminist re-vision of the American dream. This is not to say that Barbie had not shown previous signs of being a liberated female; she had been an astronaut as early as 1965.[13] And as Don Richard Cox noted in 1977, Barbie's huge collection of habitats, clothing, and recreational gear, combined with her apparent lack of adult supervision, rendered her perpetually liberated in a way that made him fear for the future of her living playmates. After commenting that Barbie was "apparently free to embark unescorted on all kinds of outings with Ken, including camping overnight" and to have Ken visit her plush domiciles at any hour, he writes:

Will [young girls], like Barbie, resist the responsibility of having children, or, following Barbie's lead more completely, resist the responsibility of marriage and family altogether? There is also the question of the sexual mores of today's Barbie owners. Barbie is a physically attractive woman with no visible permanent attachments. Will she produce a generation of sexually liberated playmates intent on jetting from resort to resort?[14]

Cox worried primarily that girls of the Barbie generation might eschew family for pleasure; ten years later, he might have been more worried about their career aspirations. By this time, Barbie had acquired a rock band and a military rank, among other roles. In 1985 Mattel executive Jill Barad—who also invented She-Ra, Princess of Power and L'il Miss Makeup—created Day-to-Night Barbie, an executive whose pink suit can be transformed into evening wear by reversing the skirt and removing the jacket; 1989 and 1990 career updates include Doctor Barbie and Flight Time Barbie, "who doubles as a pilot and a flight attendant—with a sparkly after-hours outfit."[15]

In addition to picking up on feminism according to *Cosmo*, Mattel has also been following the discourse and the marketing potential of "diversity." The company, which gave Barbie a black friend in 1968, introduced "black and Hispanic" Barbies in 1980, although it was not until 1990 that Mattel decided to create ad campaigns targeted to consumers of like ethnicity.[16] In 1991, after "black" Barbie sales rose 20 percent as a result of targeted advertising,[17] Mattel introduced a new line of "African-American Fashion Dolls," Shani, Asha, and Nichelle, who each come with a different skin tone, although all have long hair, a feature Mattel considers regrettably unauthentic but necessary for a totally fulfilling play experience.[18] The promotional material is worth excerpting at length here, for it epitomizes Mattel's ability to pull the glitz out of liberation discourse and liberation discourse out of the conditions that require it:

> Shani is tomorrow's African-American woman. She's young, strong, beautiful, and fresh. . . . Shani knows what she wants and has the self-confidence to go after it by being the best she can be. . . . Shani is fun, but she is also serious. Not "just a pretty face," she has high aspirations for her future. She's also very conscious of her culture, which she views as a rich tapestry of history, custom, and family values. . . .
>
> With a look that moves easily across the terrains of West Africa to the sunny horizons of the Caribbean and on to the cosmopolitan metropolises of America, Shani is equally at home in *kente* cloth or

glittering glamour. . . . Shani is many things. She is light and darkness. Sweetness and courage. Committed, sincere, and inquisitive. . . . Shani is what we want our little girls to be—the best of all worlds, a hope for the future which will make us proud.[19]

Mattel has clearly mastered the discourse of infinite possibility.

Yet, as both critics and fans have long noted, Barbie's accessories have always worked to predetermine her choices in the world of infinite possibility she purportedly inhabits. Barbie never could do anything or wear anything. Her career must be glamorous: "Barbie would never be a waitress," commented Kitty Black-Perkins, one of her fashion designers, in 1989.[20] And her look must be antisubversive. In 1964 Ruth Handler noted proudly that Barbie got girls out of jeans and into a dress.[21] Barbie deliberately scorned the leather-jacket look although she, like James Dean, was and remains a teenager without a cause. Despite a controversy in 1990 in which a logging organization complained that Mattel was abetting leftist eco-values through its promotion of Barbie's nature-lovin' characteristics, Barbie is clearly meant to have no politics beyond a mild fondness for "world peace."[22] Mattel accessories include no pro-choice buttons, no ANC T-shirts, no Silence=Death stickers. Nor did Mattel rush to pick up Laura Philips's (1984) idea for "Michigan Barbie," accessorized with menstrual sponge, Barbie's new name, and Barbie's healing herbs 'n' stuff.[23]

Mattel won't send Barbie to the Michigan Women's Music Festival, but they wont marry her off either. Unsurprisingly, it is Mattel's position on Barbie's marriage that reveals the extent and the brilliance of Mattel's attempt at Barbie image control. Mattel sells more wedding dresses than any other costume, with five million sold,[24] and in 1991 featured Barbie as a bridesmaid for her friend Midge. Yet Barbie herself has not been sold into matrimony since 1965. Explanations by Mattel spokespersons vary from "Little girls find marriage too confining" to "Little girls are marrying and unmarrying Barbie all the time. If we were to officially set it, it would cut off the fantasy."[25] Whence, then, the wedding dresses? Mattel markets new Barbie bridal gowns every year; there was Wedding Fantasy Barbie in 1991 and Dream Wedding Barbie in 1992. But the text on the box explains that Barbie is merely fantasizing about what her wedding will be like. Here, Mattel offers one of Barbie's most true-to-life social-context accessories: compulsory heterosexuality. Mattel doesn't force Barbie to get married or even to date Ken, but it clothes her in garments and ideology that make marriage seem like her natural, her most desirable, and her freely chosen destiny. As important, to girls who have read the box, marrying Barbie to white-bread Ken may even appear to be transgressive play, since the law of the corporate father dictates that Barbie's marriage is not supposed to occur now. In a classic hegemonic move, Mattel has managed to carve out a permitted space for subversive play in which the subvertors actually abet dominant discourse.

Mattel also carefully allots such a space to adults. The most blatant signs of Mattel's desire to circumscribe Barbie's options are its lawsuits against those who would besmirch Barbie's reputation. In the past few years, for instance, Mattel forced a stripper duo to stop using the stage names Barbie and Ken. Apparently Barbie, who is constantly taking off her clothes, cannot do so for money. Nor, it seems, must she ever be associated with the excessive dieting her unnaturally thin figure (36–18–33 in human terms) must encourage; Mattel also tried to prevent the showing of Todd Haynes's film *Superstar*, which used disfigured Barbie dolls to portray the life and death from bulimia of Karen Carpenter (a censorship successfully pursued by Karen's brother Richard).[26] Mattel did, however, authorize the use of Barbie in the American Postcard Company's 1990 series called "Nostalgic Barbie," which gently pokes fun at her plastic world through captions like "Every morning I wake up and thank God for my unique ability to accessorize" and "I recommend no-fuss, machine-washable, plastic children."[27] Again, the law makes the regime appear liberatory.

As Mattel's ideological and legal strategies make clear, the slogan "We girls can do anything, right Barbie?" is a question as pseudorhetorical as Barbie's body is pseudoproportional. According to Mattel, Barbie can't do everything, and neither can we girls (and boys). Or can we?

We Girls Have Done Everything, Haven't We Barbie?

One reason that I loved the *On Our Backs* Barbie dildo, aside from its potential as a teaching tool, was that it gave me an opportunity to extract Barbie from a context of painful childhood memories. My mother disapproved of Barbie and did not want me to have one. Like many mothers, she considered the pointy-breasted teenager, who literally couldn't stand on her own two feet, a bimbo; she also disdained the military-glamorizing G.I. Joe. But after my father died when I was six, the influx of toys for the children included a Barbie doll and a Barbie Queen-of-the-Prom game for me and a G.I. Joe for my three-year-old brother. While my brother adored his G.I. Joe—failing, as I noted with some sibling-rivalry satisfaction, to understand its political retroness—I followed my mother's lead and determined to show little interest in my bad doll. I remember my junior feminist analysis of Barbie's dubious value as a role model and my childlike socioeconomic analysis of future Barbie play. I reasoned that my collection of Barbie costumes would not expand beyond the outfit she had come with, observing that only girls with rich mothers or with mothers who sewed had lots of clothes to play with. Mostly, however, I remember reciting to myself over and over a peculiarly telling explanation of my mother's reluctance to separate my brother from his G.I. Joe: "Mom can't take it away from him because *he's* already lost too much." This construction of myself as a rational yet emotionally attuned grown-up caregiver for those I labeled more bereaved than myself established a habit of dislocating my own grief that took several decades to unknot. For years, I thought this was primarily a story about Barbie, since it was she upon whom I most consciously expended my emotional and intellectual labor; only recently did I realize that this was fundamentally a story about something else.

My story is relatively unique, I believe, in that it is a story about gender identity and death instead of gender identity and sex, but my understanding of a remembered childhood relation to Barbie as a revelatory feature of my psychological development seems fairly typical. Many people with whom I discussed Barbie and many people who have published accounts of Barbie play either saw their childhood disinterest in Barbie as an early herald of their adult status as a gender-role outlaw or had some similarly intense story to tell about Barbie play that seemed as self-illuminating to them as my Barbie story seems to me. A few interesting examples of Barbie reaction follow.

Some women consider their Barbie poses predictive of their future dykehood, reporting that they just "didn't get it" or got it but just didn't want it: "I hated Barbie; you couldn't spread her legs." Some found a different doll from the Barbie "family" with which to identify. "I didn't want to be Barbie; I wanted to be Ken. He had better clothes, and I cross-dressed as a child—anyway, he didn't have a penis," said Julien Murphy. Theresa Ortega, who spent lots of childhood time playing with Barbies, nonetheless shunned her as a role model: "I wanted to be Skipper; she had a teenager look, flat feet, and could do sports." Ortega also relates that when she got into the Los Angeles punk scene at age fifteen, she retrieved Skipper from the discard pile and punked her out with tattoos and other unauthorized accessories. She notes, too, that of the women in her office now, the dykes remember thinking G.I. Joe was too big to date Barbie while the straight women made him Barbie's dream date.

Penny Pollard remembers being aided in turning Barbie into the girl of her dreams:

> I had a crush on my babysitter, Janet (who was also the only person who could get me into a dress). Her mother had turned two Barbies into "Janet" and "Carol" dolls, named after her and her sister, dressing girls and dolls in matching clothes. I got the dolls when they were too old for them, and used my "Janet" doll to act out what I wanted to do with the real Janet.

This anecdote underscores Barbie's ability to move between the realms of cause and effect, reality and representation, a mobility recently foregrounded by Mattel's lawsuit against makers of the "Miss America" doll, which, Mattel claims, infringes on Barbie's copyrighted look. As many have noted, if Miss America wannabees craft themselves after Barbie, shouldn't a Barbie rip-off be considered an instance of truth rather than deception in marketing—besides being the ultimate homage to Barbie?

A frequent feature in Barbie stories is violence. Several women report destroying their Barbies—for example, by decapitating her and throwing her head into the fireplace—as the only violent action of their childhoods. For some women, these acts are part of the "I was destined to be a dyke because" narratives. For some, they indicate how other issues, such as those of race, inflect or subordinate matters of gender construction. Lisa Jones, who posits that every black journalist gets around to recording their doll story, remembers what she did in an era when there were not yet black Barbies or black Barbie friends. After buying two blond Barbies from girls at school with her Christmas money, she cut off their hair, dressed them in African-print fabric, and set them up to live with a black G.I. Joe she had bartered from neighbor boys until a racist incident made her sever her Barbie ties:

> After an "incident" at school (where all of the girls looked like Barbie and none of them looked like me), I galloped down the stairs

with one Barbie, her blond head hitting each spoke of the banister, thud, thud, thud. And galloped up the stairs, thud, thud, thud, until her head popped off, lost to the graveyard behind the stairwell. Then I tore off each limb, and sat on the stairs for a long time, twirling the torso like a baton.[28]

These are stories of anti-Barbie violence. But, crucially, violence against Barbie does not always signal (conscious) hostility to Barbie. Many beloved Barbies have lain around dismembered. While Mattel would shudder to promote this feature, Barbie's "dismemberability" appears to be one of her biggest attractions. Are we really always acting out some devastating departure from the mirror phase, from fantasies of originary wholeness? Barbie has also experienced other violations. One woman remembers imagining Barbie being raped by G.I. Joe. Ana R. Kissed details a particularly inventive game: "My sister (a future longtime rugby player) used to play 'Man from U.N.C.L.E.' with her friends. They took off Barbie's clothes, tied a rope around her neck, and flushed her down the toilet, hoping she would emerge in the toilet bowl downstairs to spy on family activity." This tale brings up another important feature of Barbie play. As Theresa Ortega queries, "If Barbie had so many clothes, why was she always naked?"

These adult memories suggest both Mattel's stunning success at creating a doll who could stand for ideals of U.S. teenagehood and an equally stunning inability to control Barbie consumption. Barbie's apparent conformity to socially acceptable ideals rendered her an object of hatred to those who refused or weren't permitted to embrace this identity as their own. Owning one Barbie did not lead them to scrub their faces and put on "nice clothes," as Handler claimed, nor to acquire more products from the Barbie line, as Mattel obviously desires. Other girls found themselves an unauthorized place in the Barbie world by identifying with different dolls or by using and abusing Barbie in ways that would never appear on a Barbie ad or in *Barbie* magazine. Mattel might have sold us Malibu Barbie to date Malibu Ken; we probably turned her on to Malibu Midge—if, that is, we let her live.

Yet when I witness contemporary Barbie play by children, I wonder if this collective adult memory of sticking it to Mattel is not a memory distorted to fit lesbian (or other subcultural) postmodern fantasy and if our vivid memories of rejecting Barbie/Mattel obscure the strength of less subversive positionalities that preceded them. It's not that I don't see naked and dismembered Barbies strewn around, Barbies fucking other Barbies, and Barbies trying to cross-dress. But I also see a huge reverence for Barbie and what she stands for. Many friends have recently and reluctantly bought Barbies for their four-year-old children, a purchase often preceded by the following conversation:

"Why do you want Barbie?"
"Because she's the most beautiful."
"Avi's beautiful, and she doesn't look like Barbie; Paula's beautiful, and she doesn't look like Barbie. Aren't they beautiful?"
"Yes."
"Then why do you want Barbie?"
"I want Barbie; she's so beautiful."

Even if the children are not merely assenting about the beauty of their friends' moms for strategic reasons, they have clearly bought some of Mattel's ideological line, despite, or alongside with, heavy counter-programing. When they look back, will they, too, primarily remember sticking it to Mattel?

And to what extent do our outlaw memories and postmodern critical stances prevent us from seeing instances of Barbie play that *Barbie* magazine would gladly report? A 1988 set of photographs by Rose Marasco of a ten-year-old girl in upstate New York made me rethink my own preconceptions.[29] When Marasco asked "Jessica" if she could photograph her, the girl set up four dolls from the Barbie and the Rockers series on the base ledge of her family's trailer, positioned herself in front of them with plastic keyboards, and assumed a sequence of classic rock-musician poses. I first saw the photographs as testimonies to the validity of postmodern theories of gender and identity. They seemed to document the child's early sense that gender identities are matters of costume, performance, and posing as well as the importance of cultural products in identity construction. And since Jessica did not actually reproduce the Rockers' poses, the photographs also seemed to invite an optimistic conclusion about the inability of hegemonic culture to inscribe the restrictive models of gender-appropriate behavior it usually propagates.

Marasco, however, has a different interpretation. She posited that Jessica deliberately declined to replicate the Rockers because she considered them her back-up band; other poses, naturally, were appropriate for a lead singer. This assessment, which now seems totally obvious to me, does not by itself undermine my preliminary interpretation. Indeed, since Jessica probably gleaned these lead-musician poses from images of male rock stars—one photograph shows her rendition of the classic my-instrument-is-an-extension-of-my-penis posture—her resistance to given models of gender appropriation seems doubly articulated and the postmodernist insights suggested by the photographs doubly confirmed. But Marasco suggests, rightly, I believe, that Jessica was primarily constructing herself in resistance not to dominant gender ideology but to her own economic circumstances. With dolls who signified an economic status far above her own, Jessica turned her dingy surroundings into a stage on which she outshone the glamorous Rockers—a fantasy, Marasco sensed, that Jessica enacted often: "I felt that she had been doing this on her own for a long time; she knew exactly where the dolls should go."[30]

What is striking to me about Jessica's Barbie game, seen from this angle, is how much it conforms to Mattel's promotional material about what Barbie can do for girls. According to Mattel, Barbie gives girls outlets for fantasy, enabling them to expand their sense of possibilities by envisioning themselves in glamorous futures and careers for which they might not otherwise find models in their own environment. In Jessica's case, the Rockers helped her to transport herself imaginatively out of her trailer park. Moreover, the ability to do so was clearly an important part of her self-identity; as Marasco emphasizes, "this was her own idea for a portrait."

Jessica is unlike many girls I've discussed, although like many I presume to exist, in that she found her fantasy escape by following Mattel's directions. My preliminary study of consumer practices suggests that Barbie engenders subversion far more frequently than the fruits of content analysis would cause one to expect; girls often do use Barbie to construct themselves not in her image, but against it. My study also suggests, however, that borrowing the oppositions we often use to map cultural production—imitation versus subversion, dominant versus emergent, hegemonic versus counterhegemonic—will not suffice to map cultural consumption since seemingly divergent products often serve similar ends. I produced Discard-Pile Barbie and Jessica produced Madison-Square-Garden Barbie. But for both of us, I imagine, crafting a place for ourselves in relation to Barbie was part of a strategy designed to make our own situations livable, perhaps by letting us play at the ultimate fantasy: the fantasy of being able to control one's place in relation to the circumstances, cast of characters, and accessories one is given. After all, a child can buy a Barbie with her

Christmas money (if she has it) or choose to spend it elsewhere; she can disrobe her and dismember her or dress her in official Barbie out-fits; she can play the games that Mattel invites her to play or invent her own. But she can't buy back dead parents or get a real-life Brady-bunch house at the toy store.

Our two stories also suggest that postmodern theorizing often fails to point accurately toward either liberating or oppressive features of acts of cultural construction. Jessica and I were decentered subjects trying to center ourselves, to borrow authority for our positions, to make ourselves authors, and to fit into dominant culture. Postmodern theories locate pleasure, survival, and self-awareness precisely in refusing such centerings and authorizings. The postmodern prescription is here, I believe, contraindicated. Is the postmodern project con-traindicated as well?

We Girls Can Be Postmodern, Right Barbie?

The examples of Barbie play discussed above suggest that the world of Barbie has always been, to recall a formerly fashionable phrase, "always already" postmodern. Barbie is what she wears. She performs her gender. Her dismemberability gives the lie to fantasies of whole-ness; one swift twist of a limb decenters the subject. She betokens the "law of the father" yet constantly signals his inability to rule absolute-ly. She is constructed by discourses issuing forth from macro- and microregimes of power, alternately serving hegemonic and counter-hegemonic aims. While she is visibly a product of her socio-historical-political-economic-cultural context, she constantly demonstrates the insufficiency of mere reflection theories, calling to mind words like "refraction" and "disarticulation" instead.

For all these reasons pointy-breasted Barbie is ripe for postmodern appropriation and particularly for lesbian postmodern appropriation, given the current fashion for fashion play and genderfuck among (especially young and urban) actively subcultural lesbians. I am hard-ly the only person to notice this. Since I began studying Barbie, anti-Mattel Barbie has become as popular as Malibu Barbie, and lesbo-Barbie has become the rage. I offer here only one example, the lesbo-Barbie piece in my collection, *Barbie's Dream Loft*, a "we-are-the-world" diversity scenario in which a standing Chicana Barbie top (a.k.a. Western Fun Nia)[31] fucks a white blond Barbie bottom, bent over a chair, in a setting replete with radical-chic furniture, a Barbara Kruger poster, an official Barbie p.c., and, of course, a makeup mirror (environment by Nadine McGann; additional dolls, outfits, objects, and reposings provided by the following female accessories: Susan Hill, Karen Corrie, Laurence Kucinkas, Cheryl Daly, Erica Rand). Finally, I can say: "I love my Barbie."

But not without reservations. I struggled with how to assign roles to my two Barbies. Putting Chicana Barbie on top reinforces racial stereotypes of the dark brute overpowering the less animalistic white girl; the hair contrast alone places my dream loft firmly within the het-ero-generated tradition of lesbian representation, which often features an aggressive, dark-haired vixen seducing a blond innocent. Putting blond Barbie on top would have subverted these stereotypes but per-formed white supremacy. In terms of race, there was no way out of dominant discourse.

I turned over blond Barbie because it seemed like the lesser of two evils. I also rationalized, according to currently popular lesbian ideol-ogy, that since power play "in bed" needn't reflect nor determine power relations "out of bed," I was not destining Bottom Barbie to political "bottomness"; besides, Top Barbie was probably about to be flipped anyway. Following the example of Theresa Ortega—who told me that when viewing the Barbie scenes in *On Our Backs*, it is impor-tant to understand that Barbie is not merely a tool of sexual pleasure but "a woman in her own right"—I constructed a discursive frame-work to redeem the Barbie bottom. Through this framework, Bottom Barbie could be construed to fit the requirements stipulated by the writer of a personal ad I recently read. The writer was looking for someone "Fem But Functional." What more could you want to find or to be?

A lot. You could want to find the ability to inscribe your careful-ly crafted discursive framework in the minds of every potential view-er of your piece; I doubt that I would have more success circulating the dream loft than I had in teaching "Gals and Dolls." You could want Mattel to manufacture Queer-Nation Barbie, so that girls like Jessica who look for their fantasy escape in Mattel's scripts would have more from which to choose. You could want Mattel to manu-facture fat Barbie, flat-chested Barbie, and trailer-park Barbie, so that girls who buy the line that Barbie is beautiful will also recognize Barbie's beauty in themselves and in other non-Barbie-esque females. Most of all, you could want to live in a world where putting Chicana Barbie on top does not always represent a subversion of predominant distributions of power, where human Barbie can date human Midge without fear of losing her job, her children, her home, or her life, and where everyone or no one can afford each coveted accessory.

Until Barbie's real-life context gets reaccessorized for justice, lesbo-Barbie cannot help figuring the limits of postmodern strategies, lesbian or otherwise, and of our ability to wrest from Mattel more than a temporary illusion of infinite possibility—although I still love my Barbie for its value as a teaching tool and as an unwitting agent of politicization. When I consider the disparity between Jessica's (self-)portraits and Barbie ads, I wonder how long Mattel continued to serve her needs, and I suspect that Jessica's Barbies may have suffered a fate akin to Jones's. Barbie ads are never set in trailer parks; they feature traditionally beautiful little girls in affluent settings. Neither making Barbie look more like you, as Jones did with her African fabrics, nor making yourself look more like Barbie, as Jessica did with her toy keyboards, will get you those little girls' privileges if the skin or the home you inhabit dictates otherwise, just as a strap-on can never do what a penis can do to protect you from sex discrimination. For better and for worse, the game stops here.

Notes

1. *On Our Backs* 5 (March/April 1989): 32–34. The credit line states "photos and models: Evans, Brill, Smith." While I remember no childhood Barbie pals, playing with Barbie as an adult has been quite a social process, with many insights interactively gained from people who have shared with me stories, sources, and, of course, accessories. Thanks to players Paula Matthews, Ana R. Kissed, Ken Wissoker, Theresa Ortega, Susan Hill, Jean Walton, and Nadine McGann, among many others, and to my student assistants at Bates College, Elise Greven and Kelly McCullough. I also owe special acknowledgments to three people: to Joanne Kalogeras, for sending me "Gals and Dolls" when she thought I was basically a good girl at heart, to Kelly Hensen, for reminding me to put the "play" back into "power play" when she thought that I wasn't, and to Annette Dragon, for being so very good and so very bad when I was writing this essay.

2. Thanks to Andrew Parker for helping me to articulate this point.

3. In contrast, for instance, to a publication like *Lesbian Connection*, whose editors and contributors repeatedly admonish readers not to share it with nonlesbians.

4. *New York Times*, February 8, 1991, section D. Mattel also estimates that it

has produced 500,000,000 Barbie dolls (including dolls of Barbie's friends and relatives), which, placed head to toe, would circle the earth three and a half times, and that today a Barbie is sold every two seconds. Michael Forrest, "Wow! Barbie is Thirty!," *Antiques and Collecting Hobbies* 94 (September 1989): 25. On the difference between typical baby-doll play and typical Barbie play, see Marilyn Fetz Motz, " 'I Want to Be a Barbie Doll When I Grow Up': The Cultural Significance of the Barbie Doll," in Christopher D. Geist and Jack Nechber, eds., *The Popular Culture Reader*, 3d. ed. (Bowling Green: Bowling Green State University Press, 1983), 127.

5. William K. Zinsser, "Barbie Is a Million-Dollar Doll," *Saturday Evening Post*, December 12, 1964, 73.

6. Barbie's origins as a consumer product are also vague, with competing legends of origin that well befit the empire that the world of Barbie has become. The most popular story attributes Barbie to the inspiration of Ruth Handler (sometimes described as co-creator with her husband Elliot, whose contribution remains vague and unspecified). Occasionally, the invention of Barbie is attributed to Jack Ryan, who also helped design Chatty Cathy and the Sparrow and Hawk missiles and attained additional fame by marrying Zsa Zsa Gabor. (See, for instance, "Jack Ryan and Zsa Zsa: A Millionaire Inventor and his Living Doll," *People*, July 14, 1975, 60–63). These stories, each with delectable features, can be reconciled by according different meanings to the word "invent" in each case; presumably Ruth Handler had the idea, and Jack Ryan designed the actual object. What both stories obscure, however, is that Handler's inspiration came partly from seeing a German sex-symbol doll, Lili, primarily marketed to adult men; Mattel bought the rights to this doll and turned her into Barbie. (See Cy Schneider, *Children's Television* [Lincolnwood, Ill.: NTC Business Books, 1987], 26.)

7. By Cynthia Laurence (New York: Random House, 1962).

8. *Epistomology of the Closet* (Berkeley: University of California Press, 1990), 136.

9. The novel does, however, offer some rationale for the contradiction between Barbie's middle-class "cultural capital," to borrow Pierre Bordieu's term for class-based training for cultural consumption, and her high-class fashion knowledge: Barbie, unschooled in these matters at home, learns about fashion and elegance in New York, acquiring through her internship an insider's knowledge that few girls of her background are privileged to obtain.

10. Zinsser, "Barbie," 72–73.

11. Motz, "Cultural Significance," 127. Two great guides for Barbie's various manifestations are the collectors' guide, written and periodically updated by Paris and Susan Manos, *The World of Barbie Dolls: An Illustrated Value Guide* (Paducah, Ohio: Collector Books, 1983), and a history called *Barbie: Her Life and Times* (New York: Crown Books, 1987), written by Barbie fan Billy Boy, a fashion designer who has worked for Mattel.

12. *Moneysworth* 10 (January 1980): 3.

13. William E. Geist, "At 25, Barbie is Healthy, Wealthy, and Celebrated,"

New York Times, February 25, 1984, section B.

14. "Barbie and Her Playmates, *Journal of Popular Culture* 2 (Fall 1977): 305–6.

15. Kim Masters, "It's How You Play the Game," and Leah Rosch, "The Brains Behind Barbie" (article inset), *Working Woman* 15 (May 1990): 90. Barad, previously a cosmetics executive, got her start at Mattel by pitching to them the idea of marketing cosmetics for children; although Mattel didn't buy the idea, they acquired her and let her market a doll who wears makeup in 1988 (Masters, "It's How You Play the Game," 89).

16. Kim Foltz, "Mattel's Shift on Barbie Ads," *New York Times*, July 17 1990, section D.

17. Lisa Jones, "A Doll is Born," *Village Voice*, March 26, 1991, 36.

18. On the hair and color of these dolls see Lisa Jones, "Skin Trade, *Village Voice*, March 26, 1991, 36.

19. Quoted in "Barbie's Other," *Harper's* 283 (August 1991): 17.

20. Denise Gellene, "Forever Young: After Thirty Years Barbie has More Clothes, Friends, and Fans than Ever," *Los Angeles Times*, January 29, 1989, section 4, 4.

21. Zinsser, "Barbie," 73.

22. The Oregon Loggers Group, which lobbies against much pro environment legislation, was protesting ads for Mattel's Barbie Children's Summit—in which forty children from twenty-seven nations chose "world peace" as the cause to receive $500,000 from Mattel. In the ads children sing, "The world would be a better place if we could save the trees and the eagles," and "We can save our world together . . . we can stop the trees from falling" (Martha Groves, "Loggers Want Barbie to Play a Different Tune," *Los Angeles Times*, December 19, 1990, section D, 4).

23. Cartoon in *Lesbian Contradiction: A Journal of Irreverent Feminism* 9 (Winter 1984–85): 5.

24. Beverly Beyette, "A Dress-up Job: Barbie's Principal Designer Scales Down Glamour and Plays Up Fantasy," *Los Angeles Times*, February 6, 1991, section E, 5.

25. Candace Irving in Geist, "Barbie," 3; Jill Barad in Rosch, "Brains," 90.

26. Peter Bowen, "A New Toxic Avenger," *Outweek*, April 17, 1991, 56. Mattel's habit of suing people deemed to besmirch Barbie's name is behind my decision not to reproduce either the *On Our Backs* images or *Barbie's Dream Loft* (discussed below); in conjunction with the editor, I decided that since the objects could be described relatively well, the risk of legal action was not worth taking in this case.

27. The cards, which are sold individually and in a postcard book, each have on the back "Barbie is a trademark owned by and used under license from Mattel, Inc."

28. Jones, "A Doll Is Born," 36.

29. Unfortunately, Marasco could not secure permission from the child's parents to reproduce the images in this book.

30. Conversation with the artist, December 22, 1991.

31. My understanding of Nia as Chicana was based on the general perception of friends about what Mattel was trying to signify with the odd color of her plastic skin; I learned later, however, that Mattel identifies her on its fact sheets, but not on the box, as "American Indian."

12 F2M: The Making of Female Masculinity

Judith Halberstam

The postmodern lesbian body as visualized by recent film and video, as theorized by queer theory, and as constructed by state of the art cosmetic technology breaks with a homo-hetero sexual binary and remakes gender as not simply performance but also as fiction. Gender fictions are fictions of a body taking its own shape, a cut-up genre that mixes and matches body parts, sexual acts, and postmodern articulations of the impossibility of identity. Such fictions demand readers attuned to the variegated contours of desire. The end of identity in this gender fiction does not mean a limitless and boundless shifting of positions and forms, rather it indicates the futility of stretching terms like *lesbian* or *gay* or *straight* or *male* or *female* across vast fields of experience, behavior, and self-understanding. It further hints at the inevitable exclusivity of any claim for identity and refuses the respectability of being named, identified, known. This essay will call for new sexual vocabularies that acknowledge sexualities and genders as styles rather than life-styles, as fictions rather than facts of life, and as potentialities rather than as fixed identities.

Axiom 1 of Eve Kosofsky Sedgwick's *Epistemology of the Closet*: "People Are Different From Each Other." Sedgwick's genealogy of the unknown suggests the vast range of identities and events that remain unaccounted for by the "coarse axes of categorization" that we have come to see as indispensable. Sedgwick claims that to attend to the "reader relations" of texts can potentially access the "nonce tax-onomies" or "the making and unmaking and remaking and redissolu-tion of hundreds of old and new categorical meanings concerning all the kinds it may take to make up a world."[1] All kinds of people, all kinds of identities, in other words, are simply not accounted for in the taxonomies we live with. Nonce taxonomies indicate a not-knowing already embedded in recognition.

We live with difference even though we do not always have the con-ceptual tools to recognize it. One recent film, Jenny Livingston's *Paris Is Burning*, shocked white gay and straight audiences with its repre-sentations of an underexposed subculture of the African-American and Latino gay world of New York. The shock value of the film lay in its ability to confront audiences with subcultural practices that the audience thought they knew already. People knew of voguing through Madonna, of drag shows through gay popular culture, but they did not know, in general, about Houses, about walking the Balls, about Realness. Livingston's film, which has been criticized in some circles for adopting a kind of pedagogical approach, was in fact quite sensi-tive to the fact that there were lessons to be learned from the Balls and the Houses, lessons about how to read gender and race, for example, as not only artificial but highly elaborate and ritualistic significations. *Paris Is Burning* focused questions of race, class, and gender and their intersections with the drag performances of poor, gay men of color.

How and in what ways does the disintegration and reconstitution of gender identities focus upon the postmodern lesbian body? What is postmodern about lesbian identity? In the 1990s lesbian communities have witnessed an unprecedented proliferation of sexual practices or at least of the open discussion of lesbian practices. Magazines like *Outlook* and *On Our Backs* have documented ongoing debates about gender, sexuality, and venues for sexual play, and even mainstream cinema has picked up on a new visibility of lesbian identities (*Basic Instinct* [1992], for example). Lesbians are particularly invested in proliferating their identities and practices because, as the sex debates of the 1980s demonstrated, policing activity within the community and commitment to a unitary conception of lesbianism has had some very negative and problematic repercussions.[2]

Some queer identities have appeared recently in lesbian zines and elsewhere: guys with pussies, dykes with dicks, queer butches, aggressive femmes, F2Ms, lesbians who like men, daddy boys, gender queens, drag kings, pomo afro homos, bulldaggers, women who fuck boys, women who fuck like boys, dyke mommies, transsexual lesbians, male lesbians. As the list suggests, gay/lesbian/straight simply cannot account for the range of sexual experience available. In this essay, I home in on the transsexual lesbian, in particular, the female to male transsexual or F2M, and I argue that within a more general fragmentation of the concept of sexual identity, the specificity of the transsexual disappears. In a way, I claim, we are all transsexuals.

We are all transsexuals except that the referent of the *trans* becomes less and less clear (and more and more queer). We are all cross-dressers but where are we crossing from and to what? There is no "other" side, no "opposite" sex, no natural divide to be spanned by surgery, by disguise, by passing. We all pass or we don't, we all wear our drag, and we all derive a different degree of pleasure—sexual or otherwise—from our costumes. It is just that for some of us our costumes are made of fabric or material, while for others they are made of skin; for some an outfit can be changed; for others skin must be resewn. There are no transsexuals.

Desire has a terrifying precision. Pleasure might be sex with a woman who looks like a boy; pleasure might be a woman going in disguise as a man to a gay bar in order to pick up a gay man. Pleasure might be two naked women; pleasure might be masturbation watched by a stranger; pleasure might be a man and a woman; but pleasure seems to be precise. In an interview with a pre-op female-to-male transsexual called Danny, Chris Martin asks Danny about his very particular desire to have sex with men as a man. "What's the difference," she asks, "between having sex with men now and having sex with men before?" Danny responds: "I didn't really. If I did it was oral sex . . . it was already gay sex . . . umm . . . that was a new area. It depends upon your partner's perception. If a man thought I was a woman, we didn't do it."[3] Danny requires that his partners recognize that he is a man before he has "gay" sex with them. He demands that they read his gender accurately according to his desire, in other words, though, he admits, there is room for the occasional misreading. On one occasion, for example, he recalls that a trick he had picked up discovered that Danny did not have a penis. Danny allowed his partner to penetrate him vaginally because, "it was what he had been looking for all his life only he hadn't realized it. When he saw me it was like 'Wow. I want a man with a vagina.' "

Wanting a man with a vagina or wanting to be a woman transformed into a man having sex with other men are fairly precise and readable desires—precise and yet not at all represented by the categories for sexual identity we have settled for. And, as another pre-op female-to-male transsexual, Vern, makes clear, the so-called gender community is often excluded by or vilified by the gay community. Vern calls it genderphobia: "*Genderphobia* is my term. I made it up because there is a clone movement in the non-heterosexual community to make everybody look just like heterosexuals who sleep with each other. The fact is that there is a whole large section of the gay community who is going to vote Republican."[4]

Genderphobia, as Vern suggests, indicates all kinds of gender trouble in the mainstream gay and lesbian community. Furthermore, the increasing numbers of female-to-male transsexuals (f to m's) appearing particularly in metropolitan or urban lesbian communities has given rise to interesting and sometimes volatile debates among lesbians about f to m's.[5]

Genderbending among lesbians is not limited to sex change operations. In New York, sex queen Annie Sprinkle has been running "Drag King For A Day" workshops with pre-op f to m Jack Armstrong, a longtime gender activist. The workshops instruct women in the art of passing and culminate in a night out on the town as men. Alisa Solomon wrote about her experience in the workshop for *The Village Voice*, reporting how eleven women flattened their breasts, donned strips of stage makeup facial hair, "loosened our belts a notch to make our waistlines fall, pulled back hair, put on vests."[6] Solomon felt inclined, however, to draw the line at putting a sock in her Jockeys because she "was interested in gender, not sex. A penis has nothing to do with it." She also notes in response to Jack Armstrong's discussion of his transsexuality: "I could have done without his photo-aided descriptions of phalloplasties and other surgical procedures. After all I had no interest in how to *be* a man; I only wanted, for the day, to be *like* one."

Solomon's problematic response to the issue of transsexualism is indicative of the way that many lesbians embrace the idea of gender performance, but they reduce it to just that, an act with no relation to biology, real or imagined. Solomon disavows the penis here as if that alone is the mark of gender—she is comfortable with the clothes and the false facial hair, but the suggestion of a constructed penis leads her to make an essential difference between feigning maleness for a day and being a man. In fact, as she wanders off into the Village in her drag, Alisa Solomon, inasmuch as she passes successfully, *is* a man, is male, is a man for a day. The insistence here that the penis alone signifies maleness, corresponds to a tendency within academic discussion of gender to continue to equate masculinity solely with men. Recent studies on masculinity[7] persist in making masculinity an extension or discursive effect of maleness. But what about female masculinity or lesbian masculinity?

In the introduction to her groundbreaking new study of transvestism, *Vested Interests*, Marjorie Garber discusses the ways in which transvestism and transsexualism provoke a "category crisis."[8] Garber elaborates this term suggesting that often the crisis occurs elsewhere but is displaced onto the ambiguity of gender. Solomon obviously confronts a "category crisis" as she ponders the politics of stuffing her Jockeys, and presumably such a crisis is one of the intended byproducts of Sprinkle/Armstrong's workshop. Solomon attempts to resolve her category crisis by assuring herself that she wants to look *like* a man, not *be* a man, and that therefore her desire has nothing to do with possession of the penis. But, in fact, what Solomon misunderstands is that penises as well as masculinity become artificial and constructible when we challenge the naturalness of gender. Socks in genetic girls' jockeys are part and parcel of creating fictitious genders; they are not reducible to sex.

But what then is the significance of the surgically constructed penis in this masquerade of sex and gender? In a chapter of her study called "Spare Parts: The Surgical Construction of Gender," Garber discusses the way in which the phenomenon of transsexuality "demonstrates that essentialism *is* cultural construction."[9] She suggests that f to m surgery has been less common and less studied than male-to-female transsexual operations, partly because medical technology has not been able to construct a functional penis but also on account of "a sneaking feeling that it should not be so easy to "construct" a "man"—which is to say, a male body" (102). Garber is absolutely right, I think, to draw attention to a kind of conscious or unconscious unwillingness within the medical establishment to explore the options for f to m surgery. After all, the construction of a functional penis for f to m transsexuals could alter inestimably the most cherished fictions of gender in the Western world.

If penises were purchasable, in other words—functional penises, that is—who exactly might want one? What might the effect of surgically produced penises be upon notions like "penis envy," "castration complex," "size queens"? If anyone could have one, who would want one? How would the power relations of gender be altered by a market for the penis? Who might want a bigger one? Who might want an artificial one rather than the "natural" one they were born with? What if surgically constructed models "work" better? Can the penis be improved upon? Certainly the folks at *Good Vibrations*, who have been in the business of selling silicone dildos for years now, could tell you about many models as good as, if not better than, the "real" thing.

Obviously, the potential of medical technology to alter bodies makes natural gender and biological sex merely antiquated categories in the history of sexuality, that is, part of the inventedness of sex. Are we then, as Jan Morris claims in her autobiography *Conundrum: An Extraordinary Narrative of Transsexualism*, possibly entering a post-transsexual era?[10] I believe we are occupying the transition here and now, that we are experiencing a boundary change, a shifting of focus, that may have begun with the invention of homosexuality at the end of the nineteenth century but that will end with the invention of the sexual body at the end of the twentieth century. This does not mean that we will all in some way surgically alter our bodies; it means that we will begin to acknowledge the ways in which we have already surgically, technologically, and ideologically altered our bodies, our identities, ourselves.

One might expect, then, in these postmodern times that as we posit the artificiality of gender and sex with increasing awareness of how and why our bodies have been policed into gender identities, there might be a decrease in the incidence of such things as sex-change operations. On the contrary, however, especially in lesbian circles (and it is female to male transsexualism that I am concerned with here) there has been, as I suggested, a rise in discussions of, depictions of, and requests for f to m sex change operations. In a video documenting the first experience of sexual intercourse by a new f to m transsexual, Annie Sprinkle introduces the viewers to the world of f to m sex changes. The video, *Linda/Les and Annie*, is remarkable as a kind of post-op, postporn, postmodern artifact of what Sprinkle calls "gender flexibility." It is archaic, however, in its tendency to fundamentally realign sex and gender. In the video, Les Nichols, a post-op f to m transsexual sexually experiments with his new surgically constructed penis. The video records the failure of Les's first attempt at intercourse as a "man," and yet it celebrates the success of his gender flexibility.

By reading *Linda/Les and Annie* alongside a film about female transvestism, Sergio Toledo's *Vera*, I hope to be able to articulate some of the issues that may be at stake as we come to terms with a postmodern lesbian body, a body produced within and between cinematic representation and medical technology. Gender's technology, I will argue, is its very artificiality although it is increasingly allied with a cosmetic industry of sex change. Furthermore, reading these two films together opens up a space in which to argue that gender is a fiction requiring readers; in *Vera*, I will explore the costs of misreading or of refusing to read another person's gender.

Before I approach these fictions of gender, it is worth examining the so-called facts of gender—the facticities at least—that are perhaps best revealed by the medical discourse surrounding transsexual operations. While I want to avoid the inevitable binarism of a debate about whether transsexual operations are redundant, I do think that the terms we have inherited from medicine to think through transsexualism, sex changes and sexual surgery must change. Just as the idea of cross-dressing presumes an immutable line between two opposite sexes, so transsexualism, as a term, as an ideology, presumes that if you are not one you are the other. I propose that we call all elective body alterations for whatever reason (postcancer or postaccident reconstruction, physical disabilities, or gender dysphoria) *cosmetic* surgery and that we drop altogether the constrictive terminology of crossing.[11]

An example from a recent series on plastic surgery in the *Los Angeles Times* may illustrate my point. The series by Robert Scheer, entitled "The Revolution in Cosmetic Surgery," covers the pros and cons of the plastic surgery industry. By way of making a point about the interdependence of the business of cosmetic surgery and the fashion industry, the writer states the obvious, namely, that very often media standards for beauty impose a "world-wide standard of beauty" that leads non-Western, nonwhite women to desire the "eyes, cheekbones or breasts of their favorite North American television star."[12] By way of illustrating his point, Scheer suggests that "turning a Japanese housewife . . . into a typical product of the dominant white American genetic mix—for whatever that is worth—is now eminently doable." He quotes from an Asian woman who says she wants to be like an American, "You know. Big eyes. Everybody, all my girlfriends did their eyes deeper, so I did." Scheer asks her what is next on her cosmetic surgery agenda: "Nose and chin this time around." Scheer comments:

> Eyelids are often redone too. Asian women don't have a crease in the middle. Why does one need an extra fold like two tracks running horizontally across the eyelid? Why is the smooth expanse of eyelid skin not perfect enough? The answer is that the desirable eye, the one extolled in the massive cosmetic industry blitz campaigns, is the Western eye, and the two lines provide the border for eye shadow and other make-up applications.

Scheer's rhetorical question as to why "the smooth expanse of eyelid skin" is not acceptable is supposed to ironize the relationship between body politics and market demands. His answer to his own question is to resolve that the dictates of the marketplace govern seemingly aesthetic considerations. And, we might add, the racially marked face is not only marginalized by a kind of economy of beauty, it is also quite obviously the product of imperialist, sexist, and racist ideologies. The cosmetic production of occidental beauty in this scene of cosmetic intervention, then, certainly ups the ante on racist and imperialist notions of aesthetics, but it also has the possibly unforeseen effect of making race obviously artificial, another fiction of culture.

Cosmetic surgery, then, can, in a sometimes contradictory way, both bolster dominant ideologies of beauty and power, and it can undermine completely the fixedness of race, class, and gender by making each one surgically or sartorially reproducible. By commenting only upon the racist implications of such surgery in his article, Scheer has sidestepped the constructedness of race altogether. To all intents and purposes, if we are to employ the same rhetoric that pertains to transsexualism, the Japanese woman paying for the face job has had a race change (and here we might also think of the surgical contortions of Michael Jackson). She has altered her appearance until she appears to be white.

Why then do we not mark surgery that focuses on racial features in the same way that we positively pathologize surgery that alters the genitals? In "Spare Parts," Marjorie Garber makes a similar point. She writes:

> Why does a "nose job" or "breast job" or "eye job" pass as mere self-improvement, all—as the word "job" implies—in a day's work for a surgeon (or an actress), while a sex change (could we imagine it called a "penis job"?) represents the dislocation of everything we conventionally "know" or believe about gender identities and gender roles, "male" and "female" subjectivities?[13]

The rhetoric of cosmetic surgery, in other words, reveals that identity is nowhere more obviously bound to gender and sexuality than in the case of transsexual surgery. And gender and sexuality are nowhere more obviously hemmed in by binary options.

Transsexual surgery, in other words, unlike any other kind of body-altering operations, requires that the medically produced body be resituated ontologically. All that was known about this body has now to be relearned; all that was recognizable about this body has to be renamed. But oppositions break down rather quickly in the area of body-altering surgery. Transsexual lesbian playwright Kate Bornstein perhaps phrases it best in her latest theater piece called "The Opposite Sex Is Neither." Describing herself as a "gender outlaw," Bornstein writes: "See, I'm told I must be a man or a woman. One or the other. Oh, it's OK to be a transsexual, say some—just don't talk about it. Don't question your gender any more, just be a woman now—you went to so much trouble—just be satisfied. I am not so satisfied."[14] As a gender outlaw, Bornstein gives gender a new context, a new definition. She demands that her audience read her not as man or woman, or lesbian or heterosexual, but as some combination of presumably incompatible terms.

In *Linda/Les and Annie*, Les Nichols talks about *his* new gender identity not in terms of being an outlaw but in a rather simple series of reversals. Where once Les was a radical lesbian feminist who attacked a system built around male privilege, now Les claims that one of the most pleasurable experiences he has had in his new body is the automatic and immediate respect he receives simply because people perceive him as a man. The video alternates between three modes of representation: a sentimentalized fiction of new love between Les and Annie, a graphic depiction of sex between Les and Annie, and, finally, a pseudodocumentary interview with Les. It is in this last mode that Les is almost offensive in his glorification of the male mystique.

By apparently understanding his gender performance as no performance at all and his gender fiction as the straight-up truth, Les Nichols takes the *trans* out of transsexualism. There is no movement, or only a very limited and fleeting movement, in crossing from a stable female identity to a stable male identity, and Les seems not to challenge notions of natural gender at all. Indeed his self-presentation simply employs the reductive rhetoric of inversion that suggests that one true identity hides within an other waiting for an opportunity to emerge.

However, what I have called the postpornographic scenes of the video do undermine a little Les's totalized and seamless self-presentation. The sex scenes are "postpornographic" in that not only do they show everything, they show more than everything. Not only do we see the phallus, but we see its constructedness; not only do we witness the sex act, but we see its failure and then its simulation and ad-libbed imperfection. The sex between Les and Annie, much more than Les's discussion of his new gender, makes sexuality into an elaborate and convoluted ritual that strives to match body parts and make complementarity out of sometimes unwilling flesh.

Les's body is scarred and tattooed, a patchwork of stitching and ink. This is the Frankenstein effect, a suturing of identity and flesh, the grafting of skin onto fantasy. Les's imperfect penis is a skin sack formed from skin taken from his forearm and his abdomen. Heavy scars below his navel culminate in the less than intimidating phallus, and below the phallus Les retains his clitoris. Les's breasts have been removed and the testosterone has given him facial and chest hair. In order to make his made-to-order penis erect, Les must insert a rod into the sac—unfortunately, half-way into Annie Sprinkle the rod works its way through the end of the penis, and Les is forced to insert his thumb into the penile skin to give it tumescence.

Apart from its appeal to a kind of freakish voyeurism, the sex scene between Les and Annie manages to accomplish what the more factual and explanatory parts of the video could not—it shows the degree of difficulty involved in the sex act, a difficulty that can enhance or diminish pleasure as the case may be, and it oddly but interestingly refocuses the gaze away from Les's transitivity and toward Annie Sprinkle's. It is Annie's body as much as Les's that represents a postmodern lesbian desire in this video for it is she who most obviously gets off on the spectacle of the female body becoming male. Annie's desire, her ability to be a reader of gender, her titillation and pleasure, are all stimulated by the ambiguity of Les's body parts, by his hermaphroditic genitals, by his sewn and painted skin. Her fantasy, her sexuality, is a part of the enactment of "trans-sex" rather than its object or incidental partner.

Much of the literature on transsexualism pays little or no attention to the desire directed toward the transsexual. While Judith Butler's dictum from *Gender Trouble* that some girls like "their boys to be girls"[15] has been understood widely in terms of a butch-femme aesthetic, it can also apply quite literally to those girls who like their boys to have been genetic girls. As in the earlier example of the man who had been looking all his life for a guy with a pussy, there are some women who have always been searching for a woman with a dick or a dyke with a dick. Annie Sprinkle says that Les is perfect for her because of her own "bisexuality"; somehow Les's imperfect masculinity and his possession of penis and clitoris appeal to some very specific phantasmatic projection. While some girls are content with boys who retain genetically female bodies, others desire the transgendered or cosmetically altered body.

Contexts, then, and what I am calling readers of gender fiction, as much as bodies, create sexuality and gender and their transitivities. In many situations gender or gendering takes at least two. While obviously the binary code of gender and the binary homo/hetero code of sexuality are inadequate to the task of delineating desire, occupying a gender or fictionalizing a gender for some people requires an other, or others, witnesses or readers who will (like Annie Sprinkle in the video and like Danny's male tricks) confirm the gender performance, who will read the gender fiction. Danny, we may recall, spoke of not wanting to have sex with men who perceived him as a woman. Danny requires that his sex partner participate in or read accurately the fiction of gender that he subscribes to. By turning to another representation of gender fiction, the film *Vera*, I want to give an example of transsexual desire that does not involve cosmetic body alterations. In so doing we might ask questions like what is the difference between cross-sexing and cross-dressing in terms of the representation and the reading of gender? Or, to what degree is the postmodernity of the lesbian body determined by its will to be gendered? What happens when the gender reader refuses to read? What happens to a gender fiction that is misunderstood? We can also return here to the question of to what extent we live in a posttranssexual era.

Sergio Toledo's film *Vera* explores the intricate story of Vera

Bauer's negotiation of her sex and gender contradictions. Vera changes her name to Bauer and begins to dress in drag as she successfully (if temporarily) becomes a man. Bauer, up until the end of the film, seems satisfied with her creation of a gender fiction—by dressing up in a suit and tie and appearing in public as a man, she lives and owns the particular fiction of her gender. This film, by centering upon a young woman's desire to be a man but avoiding a direct discussion of transsexualism, directs our attention to the complex negotiations that take place between body, sex, and gender to create an experience of dysphoria.

But dysphoria does not always and in every case require surgical intervention in order to be resolved; in fact, dysphoria does not necessarily need to be resolved at all. Indeed, gender dysphoria within lesbian circles is often embraced and channeled within sex play as a libidinal force. In the Los Angeles lesbian zine *Scream Box*, for example, Cathie Opie, a photographer whose work depicts gender ambiguity, challenges readers with a photograph of herself in butch drag. The caption reads: "Your parents should be happy that you have such a man for a girlfriend."[16]

This photograph resonates with a moment from *Vera* when Bauer passes herself off as a very respectable young man to her girlfriend's parents. The parents do not see through Bauer's act even for a moment; there is no double-take, no vertiginous refocusing of their expectations. Bauer *is* a man and Opie *is* a man, and as each artificially takes on her manhood, they both become more adept at masculinity than most men could hope to be.

Vera poses the question of dress and identity in a fascinating way; Vera Bauer is a young woman who refuses to be female. She wraps her breasts and dresses in a man's suit, and she tells her guardian that she has the wrong body. In a relationship that develops between Bauer (as she insists on being called) and another woman, Bauer's lesbianism promises to solve her gender dysphoria. However, in a crucial scene between Bauer and her lover, Bauer discovers that she can no more be a woman for a woman than she could be a woman for a man.

The question posed by this film is whether and how dressing and cross-dressing stabilize or destabilize sexual identity. In *Vera*, Bauer dresses up in a costume in order to hide some supposedly "true" identity, but in fact as the film progresses the costume becomes equivalent to self. The disguise, in other words, reveals the artificiality of the sexual dress code, and at the same time it seems to produce another sexuality, a set of desires previously inaccessible. The cross-dressing sexuality is worn outside the body like another skin, it replaces anatomy in the chain of signifiers that eventually stabilizes into something like a sexual identity: sexuality in this model is a surface that hides and is hidden, an outfit that covers and lays bare.

Vera Bauer cross-dresses because, as she tells her girlfriend Clara, "I am a man, you know." Bauer and Clara sit across from each other in a dark restaurant, Bauer lip-syncs "I'm Your Man" and defies Clara to contradict her. The lip-sync act replicates perfectly Bauer's gender act, her cross-dressing, transgendered identity, but it also makes a point about Bauer's implicit belief that she is stuck in the wrong body. Lip-syncing is an act of simulation but no less real for that; the match between mouthed words and recorded voice, taped music and "live" silence, symbolizes the intricate meanings of Bauer's speech act. When Bauer says "I am a man" to her girlfriend, she lip-syncs the masculinity that she both wears and owns.

The tragedy of this film lies not in Bauer's gender confusion however, but in her girlfriend's inability or unwillingness to read the code of Bauer's desire from her cross-dressed performance. In a poignant sex scene between Bauer and Clara, Clara lies naked on the bed and asks Bauer to also remove her clothes because it is "not fair" unless they are both naked and by implication vulnerable. Bauer slowly removes her clothes in front of a mirror. The camera focuses on the mirror as if to suggest that in the act of disrobing, Bauer's identity

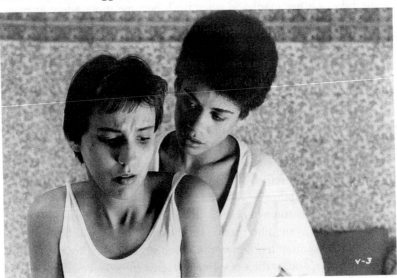

splinters and can no longer reflect her sexual desire. Clara coaxes Bauer to continue until Bauer sits in front of the mirror in an undershirt, not vulnerable now but totally lost in the image that confronts her in the mirror. As Clara tries to touch her breasts, Bauer panics, grabs her clothes, and runs from the room.

In a review of *Vera* in 1987 in the *Village Voice* B. Ruby Rich described this bedroom scene as evidence that Bauer has rejected lesbianism for "transsexual aspiration." Rich writes:

> *Vera* is a tough film to read. As a lesbian tale, it's problematic. Sure we know about the stone butches of the 50's, the girls who wouldn't let their femme lovers touch them, wouldn't take off their clothes in bed . . . but they knew they were dykes. Vera doesn't have a clue.[17]

This film is indeed "tough to read," but it is not exactly a case of Vera Bauer misreading her own lesbian desire. Bauer needs another woman to validate her gender fiction so that she can be the man she needs to be. Bauer must fuck in her clothes because her clothes represent her gender in a way that her anatomy cannot; as long as anatomy is not destiny and as long as gender can perform a sexuality that appears to be at odds with biological sex, there is no reason why Bauer should undress. Indeed, the very act of dressing for Bauer is making herself vulnerable; she has bared her desire, she has revealed her sexuality, and she makes explicit the gender performance that produces and is produced by her costume.

Bauer may not know she is a dyke, but she knows that she is not a woman. In a series of flashbacks to scenes from Bauer's childhood in the girls' reformatory, Toledo establishes a homosocial tension between the girls who divide up into butches and femmes. The director of the institution lines the butches up one day and warns, "I'm concerned about this butch-girl business." He looks them all up and down and then yells at them, "Okay, you're so butch, let's see your pricks." Of course, butch does not require penile proof, a fleshly monument to "real" masculinity. Butch is a belief, a performance, a swagger in the walk; butch is an attitude, a tough line, a fiction, a way of dressing. But Bauer has no support for her butch performance, she is surrounded by people who must see her dick if they are to approve her masculinity, or her breasts if they are to prove her masculinity is simply a facade.

But facades are never simple, and they are often more convincing than the real thing. In the scene already mentioned with Clara's parents, the latter, ironically, accept Bauer as a man when she introduces herself to them as Clara's boyfriend. Clara's mother and father have no problem with Bauer's performance, but Clara insists that performance be sublimated to reality. Bauer must be out as a woman for Clara, but in as a dyke. When Bauer publishes a love poem to Clara in the library newsletter, Clara is furious. Clara insists upon a public performance of platonic friendship, but in private she demands naked truth. Bauer, however, makes no distinction between public and private; she dresses in drag in public, and she refuses to undress in private.

Clothes maketh the man, and clothes make Bauer into a perfect icon of masculinity. Freud suggests that women cannot have fetishes since the fetish is what allows the little boy to sustain his belief in the mother's penis.[18] Bauer's cross-dressing sexuality, however, makes her a fetishist in that she is simultaneously the boy who refuses to acknowledge castration and the mother who both is and is not phallic. Clara refuses Bauer her act of fetishism. The name Clara, of course, means "clear" or "truthful"; Clara is the one who sees through the act. And yet, seeing through an act is to see that there is nothing underneath, nothing to be revealed, no truth, no certainty, only the disconcerting image of gender dysphoria. Clara clearly sees, but she sees Vera not Bauer. Vera means truth and, interestingly enough, Bauer comes from the German *Bau*, "construction." *Bau-er* makes construction active, and she builds her identity by refusing "truth." Bauer needs her clothes, she needs her gender, she needs her fetish, just as Clara needs to be naked and female. There is, in fact, nothing naked about nakedness; it is simply another costume, a skin costume that may or may not fit.

This film, like *Linda/Les and Annie*, explicitly stages the theatricality or fictionality of gender and makes of it a script we often fail to follow. The ad lib and the lip-sync are both improvisational techniques designed to remake the gendered body. Bauer makes dress into the complicated machinery that both produces and reflects desire, while Les makes her sutured skin her costume and responds therefore to Annie Sprinkle's desire for a bisexual body. While Clara refuses to read Bauer's gender, Annie Sprinkle embraces the ambiguity and constructedness of Les's gender. If *Vera* is a tragedy, then, it is a tragedy of misreading, not of gender dysphoria. Bauer needs a reader, needs an other to reflect her masculinity back to her in the form of desire. Without it she is reduced to the seemingly debased status of "stone butch," a kind of castrated lesbian for all intents and purposes. But the "stone" in stone butch does not have to be a problem of inversion that requires surgery; as I have suggested throughout, masculinity or femininity *may* be simulated by surgery, but they can also find other fictional forms like clothing or fantasy. Surgery is only one of many possibilities for remaking the gendered body.

Vera concludes with an ambiguous scene that marks the dangers of gender rigidity. Bauer, rejected by her coworkers, her girlfriend, and now also her foster family, sits crouched on a toilet and draws her hand out from between her legs, and there is blood on it. It is not clear whether Bauer has mutilated herself or whether she is menstruating, and the two possibilities lead the film in very different directions. If Bauer has mutilated her genitals, then the closing shots of the body huddled in the bathroom mark the film as tragedy—the conclusion to gender dysphoria, in other words, is a lonely attack upon the immutability of the flesh itself. If the blood is menstrual blood, however, then the film concludes by confronting Bauer with her biology and allows an essentialist symbolism to creep into the picture. Either way, of course, the body loses, and the conventions of gender win.

Bauer's masculinity, her desire to be a man who has sex with women, is no more or less precise or fixated than that of a genetic man who desires women, or a genetic woman who wants to be with a f to m, or a lesbian who wants to be naked with another lesbian, or a genetic female who wants to be a gay man having sex with two other genetic men, etc. The term *stone butch* itself suggests that even (or especially) among lesbians there has been historically some inflexibility about the genders we have authorized. Lesbians are also gendered, and the virtual explosion of information about and depictions of sexuality in recent times in lesbian sex magazines and zines attests to the ways in which what we have known as "lesbian sex" (sex between two genetic females acting as women) may be a marginal practice among many other sexual practices in the lesbian community. Discussions of butch-femme and s/m over the years have indicated that lesbians are also turned on by gendered sexual practices and restricted by the limiting of gender to bio-binarism.

We are all transsexuals, I wrote earlier in this essay, and there are no transsexuals. I want both claims to stand and find a place in relation to the postmodern lesbian body, the body dressed up in its gender or surgically constructed in the image of its gender. What is the relationship between the transsexual body and the postmodern lesbian body? Both threaten the binarism of homo/hetero sexuality by performing and fictionalizing gender. The postmodern lesbian body is a body fragmented by representation and theory, overexposed and yet inarticulate, finding a voice finally in the underground culture of zines and sex clubs.

Creating gender as fiction demands that we learn how to read it. In order to find our way into a posttranssexual era, we must educate ourselves as readers of gender fiction, we must learn how to take pleasure in gender and how to become an audience for the multiple performances of gender we witness everyday. In a "Posttranssexual Manifesto" entitled "The Empire Strikes Back," Sandy Stone also emphasizes the fictionality or readability of gender. She proposes that we constitute transsexuals as a "genre—a set of embodied texts whose potential for *productive* disruption of structured sexualities and spectra of desire has yet to be explored."[19] The *post* in posttranssexual demands, however, that we examine the strangeness of all gendered bodies, not only the transsexualized ones and that we rewrite the cultural fiction that divides a sex from a transsex, a gender from a transgender. All gender should be transgender, all desire is transgendered, movement is all.

The reinvention of lesbian sex, indeed of sex in general, is an ongoing project, and it coincides, as I have tried to show, with the formation of, or surfacing of, many other sexualities. The transgender community, for example, people in various stages of gender transition, have perhaps revealed the extent to which lesbians and gay men are merely the tip of the iceberg when it comes to identifying sexualities that defy heterosexual definition or the label straight. The breakdown of genders and sexualities into identities is in many ways, therefore, an endless project, and it is perhaps preferable therefore to acknowledge that gender is defined by its transitivity, that sexuality manifests as multiple sexualities, and that therefore we are all transsexuals. There are no transsexuals.

Notes

1. See Sedgwick, *Epistemology of the Closet*, 23.
2. See Alice Echols, "The New Feminism of Yin Yang," in Snitow, Stansell, and Thompson, eds., *Powers of Desire*, 439–59; and "The Taming of the Id: Feminist Sexual Politics, 1968–1983," in Vance, ed., *Pleasure and Danger: Exploring Female Sexuality*, 50–72.
3. Interview, "Guys With Pussies" by Chris Martin with "Vern and Danny."

Part of this interview was published in *Movement Research Performance Journal* 3 (Fall 1991): 6–7.

4. Interview with Chris Martin, "World's Greatest Cocksucker," in *Movement Research Journal* 3 (Fall 1991): 6.

5. See, for example, Marcie Sheiner, "Some Girls Will Be Boys," in *On Our Backs* (March/April 1991): 20.

6. Alisa Solomon, "Drag Race: Rites of Passing," *Village Voice* (November 15, 1991): 46.

7. For example, see Kaja Silverman, *Masculinity in the Margins* (New York: Routledge, 1992) or Victor Seidler, *Rediscovering Masculinity: Reason, Language, and Sexuality* (London and New York: Routledge, 1989).

8. Garber, *Vested Interests*, 16.

9. Ibid., 109.

10. Morris, *Conundrum*.

11. As I was writing this piece, I read in a copy of *Seattle Gay News* (January 1992) that a transsexual group in Seattle was meeting to discuss how to maintain the definition of transsexual operations as medical rather than cosmetic, because if they are termed "cosmetic," then insurance companies can refuse to pay for them. As always, discursive effects are altered by capitalist relations in ways that are unforeseeable. I do not think we should give up on the cosmeticization of trans-sexualism in order to appease insurance companies. Rather, we should argue that cosmetics are never separate from "health," and insurance companies should not be the ones making such distinctions, anyway.

12. Robert Scheer, "The Cosmetic Surgery Revolution: Risks and Rewards," *Los Angeles Times* (December 22, 1991): A1, A24, A42.

13. Garber, *Vested Interests*, 117.

14. Bornstein's play, *The Opposite Sex is Neither*, played in San Diego at the Sushi Performance Gallery, December 13–14, 1991. The quotation is from "Transsexual Lesbian Playwright Tells All" in Scholder and Silverberg, eds., *High Risk*, 261.

15. Butler, *Gender Trouble*, 123. The sentence reads: "As one lesbian femme explained, she likes her boys to be girls, meaning that 'being a girl' contextualizes and resignifies 'masculinity' in a butch identity."

16. Cathy Opie, *Scream Box* 1 (November, 1990): 11.

17. B. Ruby Rich, "Vera," *Village Voice* (October 20, 1987).

18. See Sigmund Freud, "Fetishism" (1927) in *Sexuality and the Psychology of Love*, edited by Philip Rieff (New York: Collier, 1963), 214–19.

19. Sandy Stone, "The Empire Strikes Back: A Posttranssexual Manifesto," in Epstein and Straub, eds., *Body Guards*, 296.

Works Cited

Butler, Judith. *Gender Trouble: Feminism and the Subversion of Identity*. New York: Routledge, 1990.

Epstein, Julia, and Kristina Straub, eds. *Body Guards: The Cultural Politics of Gender Ambiguity*. New York: Routledge, 1991.

Garber, Marjorie. *Vested Interests: Cross-Dressing and Cultural Anxiety*. New York: Routledge, 1992.

Morris, Jan. *Conundrum*. New York: Harcourt, Brace, Jovanovich, 1974.

Scholder, Amy, and Ira Silverberg, eds. *High Risk*. New York: Penguin, 1991.

Sedgwick, Eve Kosofsky. *Epistemology of the Closet*. Berkeley and Los Angeles: University of California Press, 1990.

Snitow, Ann, Christine Stansell, and Sharon Thompson, eds. *Powers of Desire: The Politics of Sexuality*. New York: Monthly Review Press, 1983.

Vance, Carole, ed. *Pleasure and Danger: Exploring Female Sexuality*. Boston and London: Routledge, Kegan Paul, 1984.

13   The Butch Femme Fatale

Terry Brown

*Jody, I'm asking you to please look into your heart and at least
give me the chance with this historic deed to gain your respect and
love.*

I love you forever.   —John Hinckley

Why me?   —Jodie Foster

John Hinckley's 1981 attempt to assassinate President Ronald Reagan
in order to gain Jodie Foster's "respect and love" may be the ultimate
gesture of the postmodern movie fan who so perfectly sutures with the
film that he extends the fantasy beyond the cinema and plays it out in
"real life." The word *fan*, short for *fanatic*, comes from the Latin
fanaticus, suggesting possession by a "demon or deity." Insofar as the
celebrity "possesses" the fan, then the celebrity becomes both demon
and deity to the fan, as Jodie Foster became for John Hinckley. While
John Hinckley's fanaticism may be considered pathological, psychotic in fact, it is nonetheless a playing out in the extreme of the relation
between *any* fan and *any* celebrity. In other words, the relationship
between John Hinckley and Jodie Foster—a relationship that she
would say was "no relation"—enacts the psychic structure of fan and
celebrity, in which the celebrity makes the fan's desire both possible
and impossible, structures as it castrates. While John Hinckley may be

the consummate fan, Jodie Foster may be the consummate movie star, having been more or less raised in the movies. Jodie Foster's public image may be taken as a study in postmodern celebrity; it is an image that is most perfect when most vacant, presenting itself as a screen onto which any fan's fantasies may be projected.

Jodie Foster began her career at the age of three as the Coppertone baby, then played in Martin Scorcese and Disney films as well as in TV sitcoms of the 1970s, such as "The Partridge Family" and "Mayberry R.F.D." By the time she graduated from college, she had achieved a kind of cult status. She appears on the cover of the September 1987 issue of *Interview* magazine sitting with her arms around her knees, wearing only a simple black turtleneck and loosely holding a jeans jacket. She looks directly at the camera and does not smile, appearing contemplative and vaguely androgynous, an image of the quiet and serious cult figure that she was becoming for fans who saw something different, something campy and queer, in her film career. Attesting to Jodie Foster's cult status, a skateboard punk band took perverse delight in the fact that she was the one John Hinckley was trying to impress when he shot Ronald Reagan and named themselves Jody Foster's Army (following Hinckley's misspelling of her name), sym-bolically appointing themselves her protectors.

Jodie Foster was considered cool even among the contemporary art crowd who liked her for her willingness to play weird parts in weird movies, like the part of Franny in Tony Richardson's *Hotel New Hampshire* (1984) or the part of Nancy in Mary Lambert's *Siesta* (1987). In February 1991 the Walker Arts Center in Minneapolis pre-sented a month-long retrospective of her films, entitled "Jodie Foster: Growing Up On-Screen," which culminated in a three-hour live dia-logue between Jodie Foster and the lesbian feminist film critic B. Ruby Rich. At the reception for Foster afterward, lesbian fans who had grown up identifying with the tomboy actress in the seventies only to fall in love with her in the eighties and nineties, circled Foster, attest-ing to her status among another devoted subculture.

Her performance in *The Silence of the Lambs* (1991), the most suc-cessful film she has appeared in, placed her once and for all in the mainstream, which may explain why her image in the popular media has changed. Following the release of *The Silence of the Lambs*, Jodie Foster appeared on the cover of just about every major popular mag-azine, smiling and looking very feminine, hardly the brooding butch of the 1987 *Interview* cover. Jodie Foster is now so popular, so beloved by the mainstream press, that *Time* magazine would call the disappointing and mediocre *Little Man Tate* (1991), which she directed, "a damned fine" film. If her popularity now disqualifies her as a cult figure (Jody Foster's Army recently disbanded, coincidentally), she remains an unqualified heroine for some fans, particularly for feminists who see her as representing what mainstream cinema has never given women—a subjectivity of their own.

This feminist view of Jodie Foster has been articulated best by B. Ruby Rich, who has said that Jodie Foster represents a new subjectivity for women in cinema, one that refuses to be objectified by "the male gaze." In order to illustrate the fact that Foster represents "a different kind of woman," Rich points to Foster's roles in films such as Jonathan Kaplan's *The Accused* (1988), in which Foster plays a woman who is gang raped, and in Jonathan Demme's *The Silence of the Lambs*, in which she plays an FBI agent. Rich argues, "However often she may be victimized, though, she never plays the victim. She brings bravado to her performances and prevents the demolition of her characters' subjectivity" ("Nobody's Handmaid," 8). Rich attributes the feminist revolutionary nature of Foster's screen presence to her sexuality, which she characterizes in hyperbolically abstract terms:

> The very fact of her sexuality (one that appeals to audiences across all kinds of generational, gender, and national boundaries, unifying her publics in a commonality of desire) is fused to her obvious personal authority, to create a fascinating tension, one that says as much about gender definition in late twentieth-century America as about her own career. (8)

Rich abstracts Foster's sexuality to the point of meaninglessness, leaving unnamed "the fact" of Foster's sexuality, romanticizing it instead as a utopian moment in the cinematic representation of female sexuality. Such a reading of Jodie Foster represents a tendency among some feminist cultural critics to seek out and find in any female pop icon who appeals to women more than men (Madonna is another one, for instance) the "elsewhere" of female subjectivity that Teresa de Lauretis has theorized so convincingly.[1] The effect of such unqualified celebration is that it simplifies the complicated knot of desire, identification, and *aggression* in the relationship between fan and celebrity. I disagree with Rich's reading of Jodie Foster, and I would argue instead that far from unifying her audiences in a "commonality of desire," Jodie Foster's desire to be the object of no one's and everyone's desire at once is precisely the reason that all fantasies organized around her image are fractured and fail. That is, I see Jodie Foster as an opportunity to talk about a discursive space in which fantasies—lesbian feminist, mainstream, straight, psychotic, and gay—write themselves and fail, collapsing such categories as gay/straight, public/private, queer/normal, inside/outside, secrecy/revelation, butch/femme, fantasy/reality. The impossibility of knowing the difference in any of these categories marks a moment in what might be called the lesbian postmodern. The postmodern (lesbian) subject, then, becomes the one about whom we cannot say anything for sure, and what we can and cannot say about Jodie Foster is what we can and cannot say about any (lesbian) subject.

"Jodie Foster . . . Looks Like a Boy and Talks Like a Man."—Kathleen Carrol, *New York Daily News*, January 30, 1975

What has been said about Jodie Foster publicly from the start of her career has been characterized by a peculiar code. Although reviewers never name it as such, Foster's performances as a child actor are marked by a tomboyish excess, an excess that is safe as long as she's a child. Foster's mother describes her tomboy child: "[Jodie] was never a traditional-looking little girl. And I think that has a lot to do with her success. It was just at the beginning of women's liberation, and she kind of personified that in a child. She had a strength and uncoquettishness. Maybe it comes from being raised without a father to say, 'Turn around and show Daddy how pretty you look'" (quoted in Rich, "Jodie Foster," 9). Reviewers of Foster's performances as a child actor recognized the tomboy but called it something else. One reviewer of *Taxi Driver* (1976) called Foster "an unusually physical actress," while a reviewer of *Alice Doesn't Live Here Anymore* (1974) said she "looks like a boy and talks like a man." In a recent cover story about Jodie Foster, *Time* magazine quotes a few remarks that she made as a teenager: "I never had the gift of looking cute," she said. "I hate dresses and jewelry, and the only doll I played with was a G.I. Joe. And I've got this deep voice. That's why they call me Froggy at school" (Corliss, "A Screen Gem Turns Director," 68). *Time*, of course, does not comment on the fact that Jodie Foster was a tomboy—the fact is too obvious, too meaningful, too suggestive that the tomboy may have grown up into something other than the smiling femme that the mainstream media has gone to lengths to construct.[2]

The tomboy's innocent dream of sexual indeterminacy is impossible to maintain once the tomboy grows up, and the signifier *tomboy* gathers a meaning in adulthood that exceeds itself and suggests too much. It is interesting to note that the fate of the tomboy who is shamed out of her fantasy parallels the fate of the term etymologically: according to the *Oxford English Dictionary*, the term originated innocently enough denoting a "frolicsome" girl, but by the late nineteenth century, at a moment that coincides with the creation of the category of lesbian, the usage suggests perversion.[3] Consequently, with respect to the child that Jodie Foster says she was, the tomboy is never named, disappears, and is forgotten but rematerializes safely in the body of the eight-year-old boy in *Little Man Tate*, a movie about a boy genius, which may be read figuratively as a movie about growing up queer. Foster admits that *Little Man Tate* may have a "biographical parallel" to her own childhood insofar as she was "different" as a child because she was an actor. But in another sense Foster has projected her tomboy fantasy onto the boy in the movie while playing his tomboy mother, oddly desexualized and childishly playful.

In order for Jodie Foster to have achieved the celebrity status she now has, that tomboy excess had to be forgotten or at least translated into something that could be comprehended within the heterosexual economy of mainstream cinema. Thus, Foster plays desexualized roles that safely contain what I have until now been calling a tomboy excess, roles such as that of the FBI agent Clarice Starling in *Silence of the Lambs*, a movie in which she runs, climbs, wields a gun, and deflects the romantic interests of men. It is this "gutsy" quality that a feminist critic like B. Ruby Rich rightly applauds but describes in heavily coded language: "Foster presents us with characters who are strong-willed, not weak; active, not passive; direct, not coy; openly sexual, not repressed or puritanical" ("Nobody's Handmaid," 9). The quality that Rich describes but does not name ("strong-willed," "active," "direct"), goes by the name of "butch" in the lesbian vernacular that Rich knows well. Far from being "openly sexual," however, the characters Foster plays carry a butch edge at the expense of sexuality. When Hannibal Lecter asks Clarice if her boss "dreams of fucking" her, she answers, "That doesn't interest me, doctor," although we cannot tell whether she is referring to sex with her boss or sex in general. There is a way in which Clarice's response is emblematic of the desexualization of Jodie Foster's screen presence that began with her part in *The Accused* in 1988.

After Foster graduated from Yale in 1984, it appears that Hollywood was not certain whether or not it could accommodate the tomboy once she had grown up. An anecdote illustrates my point. When Foster was suggested for the lead in *The Accused*, director Jonathan Kaplan hesitated. There are various stories about why Kaplan hesitated to put Foster in the part. Foster herself says that it was because Kaplan did not think she was pretty enough. In one version of the story, Kaplan said that he would have to see her before he cast her, implying that she may have gained too much weight. Kaplan may have been less concerned with whether Foster looked too "fat" than he was with her looking too "butch," a different kind of excess. Reviewers of *The Accused* described her Oscar-winning performance with words such as "blunt," "tough," and "from the gut." "Butch," in other words, is translated into something else (in this case, the toughness of a working-class woman) while the part that Foster plays is desexualized. After she is gang raped, Sarah Tobias cuts her hair, kicks her boyfriend out, and makes no sexual connection (she rarely even makes eye contact) with any character in the film—particularly not with the prosecuting attorney played by Kelly McGillis.[4] The desexualization of Sarah Tobias in *The Accused*, I would argue, parallels Jodie Foster's own cinematic desexualization, which became inevitable after her years at Yale when her sexuality became a liability, having provoked a fan to such a point that he would try to kill the president simply to get her attention.

"Dear Jody"—John Hinckley

In March 1981, during Jodie Foster's freshman year at Yale, John W. Hinckley, Jr., shot President Ronald Reagan in order "to impress" her. Five years earlier, in 1976, Hinckley had watched Martin Scorsese's film *Taxi Driver* fifteen times. Hinckley apparently identified with Travis Bickle, the taxi driver who grows more and more alienated and disgusted with "the scum" of New York City. In the film, Bickle attempts to assassinate a political candidate apparently to get the attention of a woman (Cybil Shepherd) who has scorned him. When he fails, he instead "rescues" Iris, a teenaged prostitute played by Foster, by executing her pimp and john, only to be publicly recognized in the end as a hero.

Conventional explanations of Hinckley's behavior characterize him as an acutely isolated and alienated young man (Hinckley was twenty-five when he shot Reagan), unable to hold a job or stay in college. In and out of Texas Tech, Hinckley dreamed of fame either through music or politics. He had lived in Hollywood briefly, hoping to be discovered as a rock musician and songwriter, then joined the Nazi party, only to quit because it was not militant enough for him. After reading in *People* magazine that Jodie Foster had begun her freshman year at Yale, Hinckley decided to "court" her and followed her to New Haven, sending her flowers and letters. When Foster did not respond, he decided to do the one thing that would guarantee her attention: shoot the president of the United States (Caplan, *The Insanity Defense*, 77). He wrote to Foster hours before shooting Reagan: "I'm asking you to please look into your heart and at least give me the chance with this historic deed to gain your respect and love" (*The Insanity Defense*, 11–12).

Psychiatrists at Hinckley's sanity trial described him as suffering from "an identity disturbance manifested by uncertainty about several issues relating to identity, namely, self-image and career choice" (quoted in Caplan, *The Insanity Defense*, 70). Hinckley, according to the psychiatrists, had no clear sense of his identity, so he tried to fashion one himself by incorporating bits and pieces of cultural artifacts as his own reality. Hinckley seemed to represent a new monstrosity in American life—the man who, lacking a clear sense of self ("a nonentity even in crime," *Newsweek* said ["Profile of a Gunman," 41]), takes his cues from a "dangerous" movie like *Taxi Driver*, which, according to the prosecuting attorney who missed the irony in the film, boiled down to the message: " 'Violence, horrible as it is, was rewarded' " (*The Insanity Defense*, 77).[5] While explanations of Hinckley's identification with Travis Bickle seem at least plausible, explanations of his obsession with Jodie Foster are not as convincing.

Yet there is nothing new in Hinckley's obsession with Jodie Foster; in fact, it is as ancient as the figure of the femme fatale. Hinckley, like Travis Bickle a heterosexual failure, projected his fears about his own sexual inadequacy onto a woman who becomes his ideal ego, the very thing he is not—much the way Buffalo Bill in *Silence of the Lambs* covets and collects skins of women in order to construct an ideal female self. Both Hinckley and Buffalo Bill lose their sense of self in a frenzied and dangerous fantasy of identification with the very object whose unattainability structures their desire: Jodie Foster represented not so much the power to fulfill Hinckley's desire as the guaranteeing of his desire by making fulfillment impossible. Mary Ann Doane has argued that the femme fatale

> is an articulation of fears surrounding the loss of stability and centrality of the self, the "I," the ego. These anxieties appear quite explicitly in the process of her representation as castration anxiety. Virginia Allen has associated the femme fatale with "that moment of abandonment in the sex act" and the ensuing "loss of self-awareness." The power accorded to the femme fatale is a function of fears linked to the notions of uncontrollable drives, the fading of subjectivity, and the loss of conscious agency. (*Femme Fatales*, 2)

Jodie Foster was John Hinckley's symptom, the beyond of his own sexuality, the possibility and impossibility of a subjectivity of his own. The "Jody" that Hinckley, misspelling her name, addresses in love letters to Foster is an appropriate signifier for the ideal ego that Jody embodied for Hinckley.

Like the femme fatale who is often punished or destroyed, Jodie Foster was both idealized and despised by Hinckley, who threatened to kill her during his trial (*The Insanity Defense*, 16). As Doane explains, the femme fatale's

> power is of a peculiar sort insofar as it is usually not subject to her conscious will, hence appearing to blur the opposition between passivity and activity. She is an ambivalent carrier. . . . Indeed, if the femme fatale overrepresents the body, it is because she is attributed with a body which is itself given agency independently of consciousness. In a sense, she has power despite herself. (*Femme Fatales*, 2)

Or, in Foster's own words after the shooting, "It's not myself that's involved. . . . I'm not involved in any of this" ("Profile of a Gunman," 42).

In spite of her effort to dissociate herself from Hinckley, Jodie Foster, like the femme fatale, carries a meaning that resonates beyond her conscious control. After making *The Accused*, in yet another version of the story about how Foster got the part in the film, director Jonathan Kaplan explained that he had hesitated about giving Foster the role because he was worried "about the baggage she would bring to the role. Like the fact that she'd been through the whole Hinckley thing might be distracting for the audience" (Johnson, *Maclean's*).

Since Yale, however, Jodie Foster has tried very hard to unload the baggage she picked up there by choosing desexualized roles that are neither heterosexual nor homosexual and by refusing to speak publicly either about her sexuality or about John Hinckley. Foster's secrecy, her "stonewalling" on the subject of her sexuality and on John Hinckley, ironically organizes an erotics of silence around her image. The effect is to endorse rather than negate her role as the femme fatale who is allied with "deception, secretiveness, a kind of anti-knowledge" (Doane, *Femme Fatales*, 3). The will to know the "truth" about Jodie Foster has become more urgent as she has become more secretive.[6] In interviews, Foster speaks with an enticing, sometimes infuriating, vagueness about sex, which simply leaves the audience wondering. For instance, when Foster says in an interview with *Redbook* that she wants "to explore female sexuality in a way that people don't get to see on screen," the interviewer seems baffled by her vagueness: "What things? What people?" (Segell, "What's Driving Miss Jodie," 79). As the fans close in on Foster, who is now thirty, the parallel with Rock Hudson seems inevitable. In 1955 a tabloid wrote: "Fans are urging twenty-nine-year-old Hudson to get married—or explain why not" (Meyer, "Rock Hudson's Body," 272). Hudson married the next year, an effort to verify the heterosexual fantasies of his fans. There is a point at which, lacking verification, heterosexual fantasies about Jodie Foster no longer make sense, but that is not to say that homosexual fantasies work any better.

"Et tu, Jodie"—John Hinckley

Since *The Silence of the Lambs* was released in 1991, some members of the gay press, Michaelangelo Signorile, in particular, have tried to "out" Jodie Foster, as if punishing her for her participation in the homophobic depiction of yet another homosexual psycho killer. Douglas Crimp has commented on the rift between lesbians who defend the film and gay men who condemn it:

> What makes the debate about *Silence of the Lambs* troubling, however, is its polarization along gender lines. Women, including lesbians, tend to defend the film, while gay men usually decry it. And Jodie Foster gets caught in the middle. As B. Ruby Rich, an "out" lesbian, put it in the *Village Voice*, "Male and female desires, fears, and pleasures in the cinema have rarely coincided, so it should come

as no surprise that dyke and faggot reactions to this movie are likely to diverge as well." For gay men, Foster lends her prestige to the film's homophobic portrayal; for women, including lesbians, she lends her skill to a feminist one. For gay men, Foster is a closeted oppressor; for lesbians, she's a role model. ("Right On, Girlfriend," 18)

If lesbians have tended to defend Foster's role in *The Silence of the Lambs* and have refused to out her, they have simply used a more subtle strategy to talk about Foster's sexuality. B. Ruby Rich, for instance, condemns efforts to out Jodie Foster. But when she wants to make the point that Foster has reached a new level of achievement with her directorial debut of *Little Man Tate*, she describes a photograph of Foster directing the film "in a pose that couldn't help but recall certain Dorothy Arzner poses" ("Nobody's Handmaid," 10). On the surface, the comparison is innocent enough—a simple comparison of two women directors. But on another level, the comparison is deliberately suggestive, particularly for those who know that Dorothy Arzner was a cross-dressing, butch director. Judith Mayne has commented on the overdetermined nature of photographs of Arzner and the way photographs are used to say what is left unsaid about Arzner:

> For all the attention that has been given to Arzner's work, one striking aspect of her persona—and of her films—has been largely ignored. Although the photographs of Arzner that have accompanied feminist analyses of her work depict a woman who favored a look and a style connoting lesbian identity, discussions of her work always stop short of any recognition that sexual identity might have something to do with how her films function. . . . One begins to suspect that the simultaneous evocation and dispelling of an erotic bond between women in Arzner's work is a structuring absence in feminist film theory. (*The Woman at the Keyhole*, 104, 107)

That "absence" is perpetuated in B. Ruby Rich's comparison of Foster and Arzner, a comparison that evokes lesbianism while negating it since we cannot say for certain that Arzner (or Foster for that matter) was (or is) a lesbian.[7]

The critical issue here is, as it always is with questions of sexual difference and the cinema, one of visibility and invisibility. The answer to Michaelangelo Signorile's question "Jodie, are you a dyke?" demands a verification that is just as impossible to verify as John

Hinckley's question to her, "You are a virgin, aren't you?" (*The Insanity Defense*, 43). Rock Hudson attempted to verify his heterosexuality with photographs of him and his bride on their wedding night, images that were read like a virgin bride's bloodstained sheets but would signify nothing in the end ("Rock Hudson's Body," 272). What would it mean if Jodie Foster stated publicly what a lot of people think they already know about her? As Judith Butler asks: "Is the 'subject' who is 'out' freer of its subjection and finally in the clear? . . . What or who is it that is 'out,' made manifest and fully disclosed, when and if I reveal myself as lesbian? What is it that is known, anything? . . . For it is always finally unclear what is meant by invoking the lesbian-signifier, since its signification is always to some degree out of one's control" ("Imitation and Gender Insubordination," 15).

Jodie Foster's revelation, her coming out as either heterosexual or homosexual, would only set up expectations that would exceed the sign under which she had placed herself. That is, the revelation would subject her and make her vulnerable to a set of fantasies that would be out of her control. "Outness can only produce a new opacity," Judith Butler says, "and the closet produces the promise of a disclosure that can, by definition, never come" (16). I think of the climactic scene in *The Silence of the Lambs* as a metaphor for the problem of coming out, as Judith Butler describes it, where the disclosure amounts to stepping blindly into an even darker closet where the killer can see you, but you can't see him. No one knows better than Jodie Foster, having played the femme fatale on-screen and off, what it feels like to step blindly into another's fantasy, the inevitable failure of that fantasy, and the potentially violent consequences of that failure: as Iris, Travis Bickle's fantasy of innocence sullied by a perverted world, provoking him to a violent bloodbath, as Hinckley's fantasy of perfect innocence provoking him to attempt to assassinate the president of the United States.

I have been arguing that any fantasies of Jodie Foster are bound to miss their mark, and I have suggested that Travis Bickle and John Hinckley represent in the extreme the allegorical playing out of the failure of such fantasies. What she couldn't be for Travis Bickle or John Hinckley, she cannot be for any fan. Now if my aligning the fantasies of two psychotics with the fantasies of "healthy" fans seems unreasonable, consider a remarkable letter to the editor of *Outweek*, a now-defunct gay publication out of New York. The letter appeared in response to one of Michaelangelo Signorile's columns condemning

Jodie Foster for starring in *Silence of the Lambs* and for not coming out. The letter is from a man who says that he met Jodie Foster some years ago at a gathering of "Yalesbians" (or Yale lesbians), which he attended with a classmate of hers. He describes her "amorously colorful behavior with a striking woman in the corner of the room," and he remembers feeling very hopeful that this lesbian movie star would go on to mean great things for the gay community. He says that a few years after that meeting he was serving his internship in clinical psychology at St. Elizabeth's Mental Hospital, Criminal Division, in Washington, D.C., and happened to be assigned to John Hinckley. The intern describes the way Hinckley ranted for a while about the AIDS epidemic being "entirely artificially produced and manufactured" by George Bush and then turned to the subject of Jodie Foster, whom he has despised ever since his trial. The intern says that he couldn't resist the temptation to tell Hinckley what he thinks he knows about Jodie Foster:

> "You know, John," I provide, "that Jodie Foster is a lesbian. I've met her myself. She very much prefers the company of women." He looks at me for a moment, his head tilted and his eyes slightly askew, sizing me up to determine what part *I* play in this conspiracy entire. Finally, he grins a sardonic smile and says, slowly, just above a whisper: "I know that. But she'll sell you out. She'll betray you. She'll lie, she'll eat you for breakfast. One day you'll look at her and say 'Et tu, Jodie.' " (Pollard, 6)

In this strange scenario, Jodie Foster herself is figured as an assassin, once again the castrating femme fatale, deity and demon, a projection of a (psychotic) fan's masochistic fantasies. In this allegory, gay fantasies about Jodie Foster are equated with those of a psychotic, a man who quit the Nazi party because it wasn't militant enough for him. No wonder Jodie Foster's keeping silent. Who can blame her?

Notes

1. De Lauretis most succinctly articulates this notion of an "elsewhere" of female subjectivity in her essay "The Technology of Gender" and applies it to the project of "queer" theory in her introduction to *differences*, "Queer Theory: Lesbian and Gay Sexualities." She describes the essays in the issue as recasting "the terms of the discourses they engage to expand or shift their semantic horizons and to rethink the sexual in new ways, elsewhere and other-wise" (xvi).

2. Typifying the perplexing vagueness with which Jodie Foster's sexuality is treated in the mainstream press, *Time* asks, "How many girls of the '70s wanted to be Jodie Foster? Movie stars are to fall in love with" (Corliss, "A Screen Gem turns Director," 71). What could *Time* magazine be trying to say here? The rhetorical question—"How many girls of the '70s wanted to be Jodie Foster?"—implies the answer, "lots of girls of the 1970s wanted to be Jodie Foster," which isn't accurate at all according to my memory. I was a girl of the seventies, and I do not remember that Jodie Foster had much of a following among the other girls, not the kind of following, for instance, that Tatum O'Neal had. The statement that follows the rhetorical question—"Movie stars are to fall in love with"—is an apparent non sequitur that doesn't really make sense in the context of the previous question. The *Time* question and answer make very good sense, however, if we are talking about the "other" girls—tomboys who wanted to be Jodie Foster in the seventies and grew up to fall in love with her in the eighties and nineties. But *Time*, of course, is not talking about tomboys, at least, not obviously. Instead, it is participating in a remarkable kind of revisionist construction of Jodie Foster's identity, with her cooperation.

3. Compare usage of the term *tomboy* in the seventeenth century ("*Tomboy*, a girle or wench that leaps up and down like a boy" [1656]) to usage in the late nineteenth century ("As a rough tomboy of fourteen, she had shown Catherine, . . . a good many uncouth signs of affection" [1888]).

4. It is important to emphasize that this desexualization is only a strategy, one that inevitably fails. Consider the irony in the fact that while Foster and McGillis avoid eye contact on screen, "rumors of all sorts swirled around the two actresses" (Schruers, "A Kind of Redemption," 56). This raises the issue of the status of gossip in relation to lesbian sexuality, which I wish to address only marginally with respect to rumors about Jodie Foster's sexuality. Eve Kosofsky Sedgwick defends "the precious, devalued arts of gossip," arguing that the "distinctive needs" of gay men and women "are peculiarly disserved by its devaluation" (*Epistemology of the Closet*, 23). But I remain ambivalent about whether to report the rumors I have heard, particularly because I am arguing that verification of *any knowledge* of another's sexuality is impossible.

5. Priscilla Johnson McMillan commented on Hinckley for *The New Republic*:

The picture of this man presented by sorrowing parents and a parade of psychiatrists is the picture of what is becoming an American type: the lone assassin. It is the picture of a man who, lacking a sense of who he is, shops among artifacts of our culture—books, movies, TV programs, song lyrics, newspaper clippings—to fashion a character. This man, who cannot form friendships or hold a steady job, goes on a murderous rampage like that of a character he has seen many times in a film; some of his shots hit the president; he becomes one of the bit players of our history. It is a story that makes us wonder what kind of art we produce, and what kind of life, that the two are so murderously and so frequently intertwined. (16)

6. Since it is very hard to believe a character, or an actress, who does not have

sex, Foster's strategy backfires. For example, one reviewer of *The Silence of the Lambs* ends up weakly speculating that Clarice "might even be a lesbian" because her close friend is a woman and because she doesn't go on dates with men (Klawans, review in *The Nation*, 246).

7. Judith Mayne gave a talk on Arzner's image and feminist film theory, after which B. Ruby Rich asked the question: "Why do you think people are drawn repeatedly to that which they refuse to name?" (Bad Object-Choices, ed., *How Do I Look?*, 143). The same could be asked of Rich's analysis of Foster.

8. Teresa de Lauretis addresses the issues of visibility, cinema, and queer identity with respect to Sheila McLaughlin's film *She Must Be Seeing Things* in her essay "Film and the Visible," in Bad Object-Choices, ed., *How Do I Look?*, 223–64.

Works Cited

"Anything is Possible." *Movieline* (October 1991): 28.

Bad Object-Choices, ed. *How Do I Look? Queer Film and Video*. Seattle: Bay Press, 1991.

Butler, Judith. "Imitation and Gender Insubordination." In Fuss, ed., *Inside/Out*, pp. 13–31.

Caplan, Lincoln. *The Insanity Defense and the Trial of John W. Hinckley, Jr*. Boston: Godine, 1984.

Carroll, Kathleen. "Review of *Alice Doesn't Live Here Anymore*." *New York Daily News* (January 30, 1975).

Case, Sue-Ellen. "Towards a Butch-Femme Aesthetic." *Discourse* 11 (1988–89): 55–73.

Corliss, Richard. "A Screen Gem Turns Director." *Time* (October 14, 1991): 68–72.

de Lauretis, Teresa. "Queer Theory: Lesbian and Gay Sexualities, An Introduction." *differences* 3 (1991): iii–xviii.

Doane, Mary Ann. *Technologies of Gender: Essays on Theory, Film, and Fiction*. Bloomington and Indianapolis: Indiana University Press, 1987.

——. *Femmes Fatales: Feminism, Film Theory, Psychoanalysis*. New York and London: Routledge, 1991.

Foster, Jodie. "Why Me?" *Esquire* (December 1982): 101–8.

Fuss, Diana, ed. *Inside/Out: Lesbian Theories, Gay Theories*. New York and London: Routledge, 1991.

Horton, Robert. "Life Upside Down." *Film Comment* (January–February 1991): 38–39.

"Is He Crazy About Her?" *Time* (October 12, 1981): 30.

Klawans, Stuart. "Review of *The Silence of the Lambs*." *The Nation* (February 25, 1991): 246–47.

Lerner, Michael A. "American Original." *Interview* (September 1987): 69–73.

Mayne, Judith. *The Woman at the Keyhole: Feminism and Women's Cinema*.

Bloomington and Indianapolis: Indiana University Press, 1990.

McMillan, Priscilla Johnson. "An Assassin's Portrait." *The New Republic* (July 12, 1982): 16–18.

Meyer, Richard. "Rock Hudson's Body." In Fuss, ed., *Inside/Out*, pp. 258–88.

Morganthau, Tom. "Jodie Foster: 'Why Me?' " *Newsweek* (November 3, 1982).

Pollard, Eric M. Letter. *Outweek* (April 3, 1991): 6–7.

"Profile of a Gunman." *Newsweek* (April 13, 1981): 41–44.

Rich, B. Ruby. *Jodie Foster: Growing Up On-Screen*. Minneapolis: Walker Art Center, 1991.

——. "Nobody's Handmaid." *Sight and Sound* (December 1991): 7–10.

Schruers, Fred. "A Kind of Redemption." *Premiere* (March 1991): 51.

Sedgwick, Eve Kosofsky. *Epistemology of the Closet*. Berkeley and Los Angeles: University of California Press, 1990.

Segell, Michael. "What's Driving Miss Jodie?" *Redbook* (November 1991): 77.

"Sex, Politics, and *The Silence of the Lambs*." *Village Voice* (March 5, 1991): 49.

14 Sandra Bernhard: Lesbian Postmodern or Modern Postlesbian?

Jean Walton

When formulating the title for this essay, "Sandra Bernhard: Lesbian Postmodern or Modern Postlesbian?" I had intended to register what I perceived to be cynical dissatisfaction about Bernhard's public image among lesbian audiences. This dissatisfaction was best typified by Sarah Pettit in her *Outweek* feature in January of 1991 ("The Lesbian Vanishes: Sandra Bernhard and her Big Joke on the Sisterhood"), where what she called the "Sandra phenomenon" was the story of an adoring and trusting lesbian audience who had been betrayed when Bernhard flirted with but then seemed to refuse to acknowledge a lesbian identity. Pettit recounted, for example, Bernhard's appearance with Madonna on "Late Night with David Letterman" a few years ago, where she seemed to "out" the two of them as lesbian gal pals. As Pettit noted, after the Letterman show, "A wild yet disbelieving cheer escaped from lesbians everywhere, and, for a few days, as the press scrambled to interpret the signs, dykes gloated at being in on the joke. Sadly, it was less a case of being in on the joke than being the butt of it" ("The Lesbian Vanishes," 39).

Bernhard's refusals to confirm the intimations she had made on the show were, according to Pettit, resentful and humorless. Even though the charade was probably just that, a playful—and deliberately provocative—charade, Pettit had hoped that Bernhard would use the media's prurient obsession with her sexuality as an opportunity to speak up for lesbians and to answer the question about her relationship to Madonna with a "No, we're not lovers, but I sleep with women, and I think they rock." Or at least a "No, we're not lovers, and neither one of us identifies as lesbian, but lesbians are fabulous. As a matter of fact, we're planning on donating our time to such-and-such lesbian cause just to show the community that it was all in good faith"(39).

Though Pettit's fantasy was understandable, it disavowed the one consistent element in Bernhard's barbed humor: her (until quite recently) adamant refusal to embrace any "cause" or "community," predicated on her relentlessly deconstructive approach to political, social, and sexual identity. Such a deconstructive approach tended to leave Bernhard open to the charge that it was professionally expedient for her to present her sexuality as "ambiguous" rather than as clearly lesbian, insofar as such a self-presentation might have made it less difficult for her to begin to enter the mainstream. The "cynical" take on her, up until 1992, was that as far as her public identity was concerned, she cultivated for herself a "postlesbian" persona, which transcended simple sexual categories and enabled her to simultaneously pose as superradical in her pansexuality and to be perceived as basically heterosexual by a heterosex*ist* mass audience who prefers to remain blind to same-sex desire in its media icons.[1]

But I am not interested so much in whether Bernhard has been guilty of "selling out," nor do I necessarily want to reclaim her as a heroine for the "lesbian community." What interests me is the challenge she presents to a certain formulation of lesbian (feminist) identity. It is this challenge, I suspect, that is partly what underlies the bitter disillusionment in Pettit's *Outweek* article. For what we find when we look at some of the public remarks Bernhard has made about her sexuality in the past few years is not that she consistently denies her own same-sex desire, nor even her lesbian involvements with other women, but that evidence of this desire and these involvements does not guarantee that we can look to her for a totalizable or unconflicted version of lesbian identity that will serve as a model for "positive" portrayals of lesbians in popular culture. Consider the following characteristically trenchant moments of self-disclosure, for instance.

In her 1988 book, *Confessions of a Pretty Lady*, Bernhard alludes to what seem to be occasional sexual involvements with women. One relationship stands out: an extended affair with a "Suzzane Tint" whom she can only describe in the most unflattering terms: her apartment is "filthy," she serves Bernhard Oscar Mayer wieners for their first dinner date, she has worms, wears chipped Misty Mocha nail polish, and tells endless stories to which Bernhard says she listened "like it was the kind of seminar where you know you won't get your money's worth, but you're stuck"(102). Their relationship ends with "a scene where I cried and went to sleep in the closet"(103).

Asleep in the closet indeed. And when Bernhard emerged from this closet from time to time (up until 1992), her references to her lesbian liaisons were characterized by edginess, ambivalence, or outright bitterness and hatred. In *Truth or Dare*, for instance, Bernhard is shown talking with Madonna about her latest affair: she's been sleeping with a gallery owner in New York and, "like a drug addict," keeps going back for more. When Madonna remarks that she doesn't like the woman, Bernhard assures her "I don't either, believe me. It's sickening." They joke about how they don't like the people they sleep with, Bernhard remarking "that's why you sleep with them; they're hideous."

In an interview with Michael Musto in *Spin*, Bernhard expresses anger toward her "sexually ambiguous" female lover by fantasizing about how she'd like to "get a dildo and knock her over the head with it. . . . Actually, I'd rather just get a black man, take his dick and hit her over the head with it" (50). This scenario leads to another in which she evokes a "cute . . . black man" who wants to sleep with her and imagines following up on it with him at the Royalton wearing her "pais . . . a big fur turban [and] leather cutaway panties." That sleeping with a man (or threatening to) is only something you do as a retaliatory gesture directed at your lesbian lover is implied when she interrupts the hetero fantasy and blurts out, in a fit of bitterness, "Yech, I'm so sick of women. I hate women. Women are bitches. They're horrible. They're great to be friends with, they're horrible to be involved with" (50).

What might have been troubling about all of this to lesbians was not that Bernhard denied a lesbian identity, but that her same-sex relationships were not portrayed as the source of strength or of a sense of well-being in her life: in these cases in particular, her accounts of her own desire for women and of her sexual involvements with them were accompanied apparently by a disturbing note of misogyny. But near the end of 1992 (and roughly coincident with the "coming out" of her character on "Roseanne" as a lesbian whose former marriage to a man was a "phase" she was going through), Bernhard's public persona began to undergo a change. In an interview in December in the *Advocate*, interviewer Lily Burana remarked that Bernhard was "taking pains to disassociate herself from the image of a sexual radical. 'I've had my moments, believe me,' she sighs today. 'But anybody like me, whose Christmas wish is a box of Surf detergent, certainly could not be a dominatrix' " (68). What Burana does not explicitly announce is that Bernhard's dissociation from the "image of a sexual radical" occurred simultaneously with (and was perhaps prerequisite to) her embracing of a certain "image of the lesbian." As it turns out, there are two somewhat conflicting versions of the "radical" that Bernhard began to distance herself from in the interviews of late 1992: one was the "dominatrix" alluded to in the quote above, which I take to mean the persona she adopted when vamping as the kinky, aggressive, sexually voracious devourer of men—that hetero side of her public self, which would help to keep her from being "stuck" in the "genre" of the lesbian but would not seem to acquiesce to a conventional heterosexual model either (in which the woman was supposed to be the passive partner). The other version of the "radical" is to be found in the gay and lesbian rights movement where lesbian activists have gone too far, in Bernhard's opinion. We can only hope she is partly joking when she says things like "Get it fucking together, you know. And stop acting like a bunch of asses. And be women. Have some fucking dignity and self-respect. You don't have to turn yourself into a freak to make a statement" (Hunt, "Sandra Bernhard," 18). In the December 1992 *Advocate* interview, it becomes apparent that the image Bernhard *will* associate herself with is that of a certain kind of committed, monogamous, lesbian homebody who looks forward to having a child with her partner (72). Bernhard seems oblivious to the probability that this constitutes a third version of the "radical" insofar as it undermines the current hegemonic model of the American hetero family.

Significantly, by late 1992 Bernhard was decidedly "out" as a woman whose current sexual life was most intensely focused on other women.[2] And her performances have always evinced a feminist spin on female sexuality: one that affirms women's rights to explore and take active control of their sexual desire and to resist their own objectification in cultural representation and in life. But her lesbianism cannot necessarily be seen as the fountain from which her feminist politics flows. She is by no means what came to be known in the seventies (the decade, incidentally, which Bernhard most frequently "exploits") as the "Woman-identified Woman," i.e., the lesbian whose erotic desire and love for other women is the paradigmatic basis of her feminism.[3]

With this in mind, I'd like to suggest that Pettit's critique of Bernhard is, in part, informed by a definition of lesbianism that relies for its stability on one's all-encompassing solidarity with women, on one's identification with them as a political group, on a demonstration of a supportiveness of them, and indeed, almost an embracing of them in a kind of unconditional love. But it is precisely the lesbian as "woman-identified woman" that is subverted by Bernhard's performance, where we find that neither "woman" in the formulation is stable, nor is the identification of woman with woman an identification with that which is "like" oneself.

This becomes clearest in Bernhard's 1990 film, *Without You I'm Nothing*, where her performance is predicated not on the dichotomization of male and female but on the radical differences among women, indeed, on an undermining of their presumed similarity. It is interesting to note that for Pettit, as perhaps for other disillusioned lesbian Bernhard fans, the film adaptation of *Without You I'm Nothing* seems initially to constitute a shift in emphasis from issues of gender and sexuality to issues of race, and consequently addresses a lesbian audience less overtly. Pettit praises Bernhard's prefilm stage act for what she calls its "shameless series of paeans to female performers" and its "monologues, whose subtexts could only be described as dykey." This Bernhard is "a female artist clearly drawn to other women for inspiration and sustenance," an artist employing an art form that is "deeply indebted to the work of female peers for its own creativity"(39). This is Bernhard as an explicitly "woman-identified woman" performer, in other words. The film comes as a disappointment to Pettit, however, since while it

> still contains Sandra's nods at queer subculture, the appearance of a Black woman as the star's silent doppelgänger, as well as the fixing of the narrative line around a Black supper club, reorient the

central engine of *Without You I'm Nothing*. While I by no means question the validity of highlighting issues of race and racism . . . it is notable that Sandra's tributes to female muses occur with less unabating frequency and with less overarching impact. (41)

It is precisely Bernhard's emphasis on race in the film, however, that challenges Pettit's conception of what constitutes "dykey-ness" in the subtexts of Bernhard's stage monologues. It would be a mistake, I think, to read her "impersonations" informed by camp and drag as unqualified "paeans" to and unconflicted identifications with female artists or to assume that Bernhard's intention is to situate herself in a kind of celebratory "herstory" of female performance. The film suggests that the "woman" Bernhard is on stage is not a consistent, stable, determinable entity, nor are the "women" she "becomes" when she alters her own "identity" to construct a persona. Given that many of Bernhard's personas are coded as black, for instance, her setting of the stage performance in an all black club in the film forces us to confront the appropriative effect of "reproducing" the black female performer in one's own performance; it is difficult, in other words, given the racial history of the U.S., for a white comedian to "pay tribute" to a black performer by impersonating her without also being, in effect, in blackface. If being "drawn to other women for inspiration and sustenance" means impersonating black women who then become the black roots that she draws from as a white woman who wants to be included in a tradition of black rock and pop performers, then this "being drawn" is highly suspect and would conceivably be looked on with deep skepticism and disdain by a black audience.

Thus, to indicate to us her critical distance from the white (Jewish) girl's romanticized and essentialized fantasy of inhabiting a black identity, Bernhard orients the film around a narrative in which "Sandra's" manager (who, with her tough, no-nonsense demeanor and her fat cigar, is the only character in the film styled as a dyke) decides that "Sandra" has gotten "too grand" and therefore must be sent back to her "roots," as she calls them, in Los Angeles. These "roots" turn out to be a black nightclub—the Parisian Room—where "Sandra" must perform before an (almost) all-black audience evincing nothing but contempt for her efforts to impersonate and "speak" for them.[4] She is not even the main attraction, but is given a condescending and perfunctory reception by a master of ceremonies who calls her "Sarah" Bernhard and then shifts into a salacious tone of voice as he introduces the performer the audience has really been waiting for: the club's "very own" Shoshana, a stripper who does a graceless imitation of Madonna and who presumably provides at least some erotic spectacle for the diffident audience. As Marlon Riggs put it,

> At one level [Bernhard] was giving overt tribute to black people. These people were extremely bored by her because they knew what they were getting was an adulterated version of their culture—a version processed and diluted by a white artist, who was achieving success and notoriety on the basis of so-called originality, bravery, courage, and insight. She was, in a word, stealing, as it's been done time and time again, from black people. And yet she constantly acknowledged that fact, as well as the contempt of black people for the very process in which she was complicit. ("Cultural Healing," 10)

As my last few references to Bernhard as "Sandra" indicate, there is a distinct, but not always consistent, distance between Bernhard as filmmaker and "Sandra" as the protagonist of the film here. This already is an indication of the way in which this "woman," Bernhard, who "identifies" with other "women" is not by any means a reliably unitary subject. *Bernhard* is the term I use for the director or filmmaker who, in collaboration with John Boskovitch, has constructed a narrative in which a protagonist, whom I call Sandra, brings her New York off-Broadway show to her "roots" in Los Angeles. It is Sandra who performs her heart out to the unresponsive black audience; it is Bernhard who directs this audience to be unresponsive.

Kobena Mercer, in a rereading of Robert Mapplethorpe's photographs of African-American men, has suggested that "in the light of [the] task of making 'whiteness' visible as a problem for cultural theory . . . the positioning of gay (white) people in the margins of Western culture may serve as a perversely privileged place from which to reexamine the political unconscious of modernity"("Skin Head Sex Thing," 206). I would add that we could extend this hypothesis to include postmodernity as well and to consider the way in which Bernhard can be read as a "gay (white)" person(a) speaking from a "perversely privileged place." To say that Bernhard foregrounds race in her film is not to say that her film is an exploration of any "other" race than her own: it is not. It is, however, an exploration of "whiteness" as part of the subjectivity from which Bernhard performs or of how she performs whiteness as her race. We might consider her film as the occasion for exploring the questions posed by Mercer about the construction of "whiteness":

> The creation of the minstrel mask in cinema, and in popular theatre and the music hall before it, was really the work of white men in blackface. What is taking place in the psychic structures of such historical representations? What is going on when whites assimilate and introject the degraded and devalorized signifiers of racial otherness into the cultural construction of their own identity? If imitation implies identification, in the psychoanalytic sense of the word, then what is it about whiteness that makes the white subject want to be black? ("Skin Head Sex Thing," 207)

What Mercer is interrogating here is a politics of "white" identity that is troubling in its fundamental dependence on the "other" for its definition of "self": a politics that resonates in the title of Bernhard's film, the performer's formulaic tribute to the audience: "Without you, I'm nothing." When Sandra says these words in the film, she slips at first, nearly blurting out what she'd apparently really like to say to the black audience she has been attempting to mirror and (re)construct, "Without me, *you're* nothing."

Mercer's questions are not only pertinent to race, however; we might extend them to interrogate the mechanism of gender and sexual identity in Bernhard's film as well. Through her technique of impersonation and mimicry Bernhard explores the construction of "femaleness," and of "heterosexuality," although in these last two cases, the boundary between the "self" and the "introjected other" is less obviously demarcated. When Bernhard (or Sandra) camps it up in black drag, no one takes her to mean that she is coming out of the closet as an African-American whose identity has been hitherto disguised as white. But there are no clear indicators as to Bernhard's relation to the lesbian personas she adopts (both in the film and in her other public appearances). Indeed, insofar as cross-dressing for Bernhard is always a crossover not into the male but into some version of a socially constructed feminine, it is difficult, if not impossible, to say where her "starting point" is for those impersonations that take gender and sexual orientation as their focal point. This might be to suggest, in fact, that there is no position within the "feminine," nor even within the "lesbian" (and conversely, of course, within the hetero), that is not always already a matter of being in "drag." And although I just suggested that Bernhard could not "come out" as black, the "obviousness" of that suggestion is perhaps called into question by the multiple and simultaneous "crossings" of her performance: might it be possible, in other words, to consider racial identity as much a matter of drag as of skin color?

To lament, as Pettit does, the heightened emphasis on race in *Without You I'm Nothing* is to avoid Bernhard's critique of herself precisely *as* a feminist—indeed, perhaps even as a lesbian feminist. The effect is, of course, to deeply complicate the category of "woman" as a subject position for a (lesbian) feminist politics and not at all to drift away from issues of gender and sexuality.

This will become more clear as we look more specifically at how Bernhard addresses in particular the issue of sexual identity in the film. Only one of the "personas" she adopts is arguably a lesbian persona: a black lounge singer in a polyester jumpsuit and one-inch nails who plugs Remy Martin, then launches into a simultaneously cynical and saccharine version of "Me and Mrs. Jones." The number concludes when Sandra lifts her fist and announces defiantly "The sisters are doin' it for themselves!" Just as the referent for "woman" in "woman-identified woman" can never be stable according to Bernhard's constructions of "woman-" hood, the referent for "sister" here is just as unstable. In other words, it is impossible to ascertain whether this affirmation of sisterhood is meant to point to a solidarity based on women's shared race in the black power struggle, shared gender in the feminist struggle, or shared sexuality in the lesbian rights struggle. Given the multiple levels of mimicry here, it could very well mean all three—but never unproblematically and equally so. The "affirmation" of a black sisterhood is a self-parodied white fantasy of affirmation: while the Sandra of the film is partly an embodiment of Bernhard's own identificatory desire, she is also subjected to Bernhard's derisive satire. Sandra in drag as exaggeratedly feminine "female" nightclub singer crosses a different kind of line: if the race fantasy was a white identification with/appropriation of blackness, then this is a female identification with/appropriation of "femaleness." But if this is so, who or what is appropriated from, except a sort of cultural fantasy of what constitutes the "feminine" (long fingernails, heavy makeup, slinky lingerie, the concept of a "pretty lady, like myself.") This would not seem to be either an impossible nor an exploitative fantasy—one could conceivably "become" the "other" one impersonates. And what about the lesbian drag? This aspect of the persona is indicated by nothing except the lyrics of the song, which identify its singer as someone having an affair with a married woman. But who is the Sandra who has the fantasy in this case then? A hetero performer who impersonates a lesbian? A lesbian performer who impersonates a femme lesbian? A femme lesbian who impersonates a femme lesbian who goes for other straight-seeming, or at least married, women? The ambiguity of the positioning of the "starting point" for the line crossed by the drag in this case emphasizes, perhaps, the ambiguity in the racial and gender crossings.

Bernhard is perhaps most trenchant when she ruthlessly undermines the presumed naturalness of heterosexuality. During her Bachrach medley, for instance, after bewailing the statistics that indicate the unlikelihood that a woman over thirty will be able to "find a husband," Sandra launches into an evocation of what we might take to be a white, middle-class teenage fantasy of the seventies, in which the protagonist moves to San Francisco, gets her dream job as a secretary, and through the agency of all the right products (Herbal Essence shampoo, Clinique cosmetics, Pier 1 Imports) snares a date with the boss. On their perfect date, he takes her to the "crookedest street in the world," and she remarks, campily, "and I never felt straighter." Thus, she is seen to concoct her hetero femininity through commercially advertised products that promise fulfillment and to piece together a phantasmatic identity for herself via a rescue narrative in which the boss/husband allows her to affirm, once and for all, her (white) womanhood. The number ends with Bachrach's "A House is Not a Home," which she sings seated in an armchair and surrounded by male disco dancers in G-strings, clearly coded as gay and thus ironizing the fantasy of straight, married happy bliss in the "house" that is now a "home."

In another number, Bernhard evokes the experience of a young white guy identified as straight in the seventies who is taken to a gay disco by his best buddy. After some initial phobic resistance, he is given poppers, the music is rockin', somebody hands him a tambourine, and Sylvester appears to take him "higher and higher." Then he "comes out" with a vengeance and shouts tributes to all the gay icons of the seventies with whom he had presumably secretly longed to identify. The evocation ends, and Bernhard adds a coda: "Remember, it's 1989, and you can pretend that you're straight." "Straightness," thus, is portrayed as an artificial condition maintained only at the cost of keeping repressed an underlying impulse to become a certain kind of gay man in an (imaginary) hedonistic, pre-AIDS milieu.

Less obvious is the complex play of identification and desire Bernhard sets up with what Pettit has called her "silent doppelgänger," a black woman (whom I will refer to as Roxanne[5]) who appears briefly in different settings outside the diegetic space of the stage performances in the club. Although Pettit sees this woman as merely a sort of alter-ego figure—a black double for Sandra herself—I would suggest that she is both a focus for projective identification and, importantly, an object of Bernhard's unspoken erotic desire. Cross-racial heterosexuality is already explicitly thematized when we discover, through what seems to be a flashback memory to wild lovemaking, that the "boyfriend" named Joe with whom Sandra has just broken up is a black man. Like all the hetero arrangements in the film, this one too is a target of satire, but its fragility rests not on its cross-racial element but on Sandra's penchant for s/m (with a third party) and Joe's infuriating narcissism (evinced by an all-consuming preoccupation with his long hair).

This number, reinforced by pseudointerviews with a "friend" of Sandra who provides gossipy details of her relationship with Joe, would seem to establish Sandra's "sexual identity" in the film as kinky (because of her s/m predilection) but hetero. The intercuts of Roxanne, however, and their culmination in her appearance in the audience at the end of the film, constitute what I would call the "dykey" undertone of that ostensibly hetero narrative.

At this point, I should acknowledge that certain aspects of Bernhard's film call into question whether she is indeed, from that "perversely privileged place" on the margins, really exploring the cultural construction of "whiteness" as a subject position from which one introjects fantasized black otherness. It could be suggested, on the contrary, that she forecloses on a serious exploration by too easily ironizing it through the incorporation of the black audience into the nightclub—as though to create the illusion that there exists in this film a significant distinction between a "real" black perspective (that bored audience) and the white-constructed black perspective (Sandra's personas). Both these "black" perspectives are, after all, Bernhard's inventions. Consider how this contrasts, for instance, with the fantasy Madonna lives in *Truth or Dare*. She would seem to take little or no ironic distance on the role she casts herself in as white housemother to a family of black and Latino gay "children." She unselfconsciously portrays herself as the agency by which voguing, for instance, transcends its roots in a nonwhite gay ghetto and becomes a universal affirmation of how it "makes no difference if you're Black or White." Such apparent obliviousness to the mechanism of appropriation is unthinkable in Bernhard's film, where the white subject's identificatory fantasies are subverted at every turn. Another way of putting this is to say that while Madonna's fancy runs free (and provides much fascinating material about the white psyche in the process), Bernhard's operates guiltily, always in the shadow of a superego that punishes her for her desires. And yet, insofar as the black audience is consciously constructed by Bernhard to play the role of this superego, perhaps the question we ought to be asking is how that audience gets constructed in the first place. This is where I think a focus on the trajectory of Roxanne in the film might be useful.

Roxanne occupies a curious middle ground between the explicitly mimicked blackness in Sandra's personas and the apparently autonomous black audience. Insofar as Roxanne functions as a sort of bridge from the fantasized to the real, her presence in the film indicates, perhaps, the means by which Bernhard "imagines" her black audience into existence. Roxanne's early filmic separation from the diegetic space of the night club renders indeterminate her status as either projected fantasy or real woman in an autonomously existing external space. In the first shot we see of her, as she walks serenely against the backdrop of Watts Towers, she appears to inhabit a completely separate world from Sandra's performance space in the nightclub. At this point, it is impossible to ascertain whether she is Sandra's fantasy (either of an alter-ego, or of an object of desire, or both) or an autonomously existing black woman with a subjectivity of her own, counterpointing the mechanism of projection and desire that marks Sandra's stage performance. The second time we see her, she is positioned in front of a Jewish storefront, reading Harold Bloom's *The Kabbalah and Criticism*. "Jewishness" has already been signaled in the film as one of the positions from which Sandra speaks. It is, for example, the ethnic starting point from which she fantasizes about (in order to critique) the lives of a WASP family in middle America. Although there is still no narrative link between Sandra in the nightclub and Roxanne in her separate setting, the two spaces are associated thematically through these representations of Jewishness. This makes it plausible to wonder if this is Sandra's fantasy that Roxanne—whether she is understood to be autonomous from or an invention of Sandra's—is reciprocating by cathecting across the cultural divide between them.

The next time we see Roxanne is in what would seem to be her own bathroom, leaning toward the mirror; to the beat of rap music that blares from the radio beside her, she painstakingly cuts a minute piece of hair from the end of one of her locks—a striking gesture, since we have seen Bernhard perform exactly the same operation in the opening sequence of the film in her dressing room. But lest we presume we are meant to objectify Roxanne in this intimate moment of her toilet, such a presumption is undermined when she makes her next appearance. A group of white women are shown in a *public* shower this time, striking poses for a voyeuristic audience as the camera pans across their glistening bodies. One woman, crouching to sponge down another, turns to grin knowingly and invitingly at the camera—she may or may not be Robin Byrd (Byrd is among the people who are thanked in the credits of the film)—and a second later, Roxanne is seen walking behind the group, clad modestly in a towel. She glances at them with an expression of neutral detachment, holds herself aloof from what might be an allusion to the sex-affirmative strand of (white) feminism (embodied in pop culture by Madonna) that seeks to explore and re-valorize erotic fantasy and to take control over the public exhibition of the female body.[6] Sandra might like to associate with those Robin Byrd types (indeed, Bernhard *did* take it all off on the "Robin Byrd Show" on New York Cable Television), but Roxanne appears to have different ideas—ideas we (and Sandra) can only guess at.

Later in the film Roxanne's appearances become more causally or logically linked to the diegetic space of the nightclub performance. In a tribute to the seventies clearly inspired by Patti Smith, Sandra remarks, metaphorically, that "history turned a page." The camera cuts to Roxanne at this point, who is wearing protective eyewear and a white lab coat and set in a scientific laboratory where test tubes bubble over Bunsen burners. She is, again, reading—and happens to turn the page as though prompted by Sandra's verbal cue. The coincidence of the page-turning in both instances suggests that Roxanne provides the complementary illustration here, the specifics of what could be meant by history turning a page: its page is turned by a black woman portrayed (albeit somewhat facetiously) in a position of importance within the sciences.

In all of her appearances except the last, Roxanne has inhabited an ambiguous, though evolving, space outside the diegesis of the night-club performance. Her status has been unclear: is she entirely Bern-hard's projective fantasy? Is she partly Bernhard's fantasy, and partly a black woman's implied commentary on the fantasy, a resistance to that fantasy? The question resolves itself into something apparently more concrete by the end of the film, when, during Sandra's finale, Roxanne makes one last appearance, but this time, as a member of the audience in the club where Sandra performs. In other words, she now enters the diegetic space inhabited by Bernhard in the nightclub; she is no longer separated off from the performance as though she belonged to an imagined or fantasized world. Now she takes her place, like oth-ers in the audience, at one of the tables and can be seen looking at San-dra, returning the gaze that Sandra might have, in fantasy, turned on her. The audience has gotten so bored by now that nearly the entire room has emptied out; indeed, it is almost as though the audience has "boiled down" to that one, specifically female entity that has been in the making throughout the entire film. We watch as Sandra drops the American flag in which she has been draped, and gyrates to Prince's "Little Red Corvette," wearing only pasties and a G-string. This would seem to be her enactment of the "sex-affirmative" strand of feminist performance—the taking of control over her body as public spectacle. But by now she is a spectacle for no one but Roxanne, who has been portrayed as abstaining from the sex debates of white femi-nism. What kind of audience will she be then for this Sandra who seems simultaneously to have powerfully declared her right to free-dom of expression and to have vulnerably put her body on display? Will she cease to function as a condemnatory superego and, as a female spectator, be drawn into a lesbian erotics of performance? San-dra finishes her dance and looks expectantly, looks longingly, looks beseechingly over to Roxanne, waiting for the moment of desired con-nection between them, and the music wells up in a crescendo of sus-pense and pathos. We see that Roxanne has written Sandra's name in lipstick on the table—is it a tribute to her performance? A romantic message to her? As Roxanne rises to leave, the camera reveals her full message: "Fuck Sandra Bernhard." On the one hand, this message would seem to suggest that Sandra's fantasy of cross-racial lesbian desire is apparently impossible, sabotaged, it would seem, by the same racist social structure that makes Sandra's "tributes" to female per-formers into acts of appropriation, regardless of how pure her inten-tions might be. On the other hand, the message could function as an expression of lesbian desire and an invitation for other lesbians to respond to Sandra's erotic public display.[7]

For Marlon Riggs, this is the point where the film fails since Bernhard can "read the black woman's contempt within her eyes and then verbalize it with a 'fuck you,' but [she] cannot, in all of her appropriation, articulate the experience of black people"("Cultural Healing," 11). Her film, like all Hollywood films made by whites, "can never articulate black subjectivity, because [it's] so clearly and obviously made through white eyes"(11). Riggs and his interviewer go on to talk about the "need to privilege and explore the black person's sense of ambivalence," as Riggs puts it:

> We buy into myths. Once the myths have been defined for us, that's what we are. What we're talking about is a kind of constant negotiation of multiple and sometimes colliding identities. I think the reason that people have so many conflicts is because of our insistence that things remain stable and simple and essentialistic, when in fact they've never been and never will be. (11)

I would suggest that Riggs' observations vis-à-vis black identities are just as pertinent to the question of (white) lesbian sexual and political identities: there is a need—which Bernhard's work expresses—to "privilege and explore" the lesbian's "sense of ambivalence," precisely as it is played out across the racial and even gender differences that distinguish women from each other. And though Bernhard's film may fail (as it inevitably must) to articulate black subjectivity, it is disturbingly successful in its interrogation of any lesbian, white, or female identity that longs to be "stable and simple and essentialistic."

Notes

1. The tenor of Bernhard's public self-portrayals has always depended, of course, on the forum in which she is interviewed. In a January 1992 *Advocate* interview, intended for an almost exclusively gay and lesbian audience, interviewer Ryan Murphy comments that, in her new stage act, *Giving Till It Hurts*, Bernhard declares herself as "out," interrogates members of her audience on their sexuality, then "goes on to establish herself in the bisexual camp"(82). Later in the same interview, however, she acknowledges "Yeah, I have a preference. But I'm also open to things. I don't put any barriers on my sexuality"(82). In February of 1992, we saw a different Bernhard on "Arsenio Hall," directed at a mainstream late-night television audience. Her sexual "preference" never came up verbally though she did much to convey a flirtatious hetero attraction to Arsenio and

announced her upcoming spread in *Playboy*. In the same year, her HBO special, *Sandra After Dark*, aired, in which she camped it up once again as the sexually demanding hetero counterpart to macho ladykiller Tom Jones (she mimes fellatio on him during his singing performance). At the end of 1992 we find her back in the gay and lesbian forums, much more explicit about her current lesbian love life (*Advocate*, December 1992, and *Christopher Street*, December 1992) as well as about her longstanding queer identification with drag queens (see her interview with RuPaul in *QW*, November 29, 1992).

2. When interviewer Burana remarks that "bisexuals, like me, would yelp for joy if you were to stand up and be counted as bi," Bernhard provisionally agrees to accept the appellation: "I've had long-term sexual relationships with both men and women. If that classifies me as a bisexual, then I'm bisexual" ("Sandra Bernhard," 70). But the involvements with men seem to be things of the past; all other references to her relationships have to do with women.

3. It was Adrienne Rich, of course, in her radically transformational critiques of heterosexism, who most eloquently formulated the concept of the woman-identified woman: consider these lines from "It is the Lesbian in Us" (1976):

> I believe it is the lesbian in every woman who is compelled by female energy, who gravitates toward strong-women, who seeks a literature that will express that energy and strength. It is the lesbian in us who drives us to feel imaginatively, render in language, grasp, the full connection between woman and woman. (200–1)

4. I say an "almost" all-black audience here because we do get brief glimpses of an elderly white couple—parental figures?—whose presence indicates perhaps the other way in which Sandra's act can fail to impress her spectators in the way she intends. The couple, like supportive and proud parents, smile blandly at Sandra, as though they are completely unaware of the irony that is meant to undercut her "dramatic interpretations."

5. I am following C. Carr in her *Artforum* review of *Without You I'm Nothing*. Although she identifies the black woman as Roxanne, played by Cynthia Bailey, the name seems to have a different spelling in the film's barely legible credits.

6. Is it the case that in the realm of "performance art," it has been by and large white women who use their bodies as the medium for feminist and antihomophobic cultural critique? This would seem to be suggested by the collection of interviews with "women performance artists" recently published by Re/search entitled *Angry Women*. Of the fifteen or so women who are represented in the volume, only three—Sapphire, Wanda Coleman, and bell hooks—are black. It is (almost without exception) the interviews with the white women that are accompanied by photos documenting their *bodies* in performance: bodies in costume, in (masculine and feminine) drag, in the buff, adorned with food, paint, tattoos, clay, plucked chickens. The absence of accompanying photos (aside from introductory head and shoulder shots) for Coleman and hooks (and a series of snapshots of Sapphire *not* apparently in performance) would seem to imply that it is in their language, their words, their voices, that the primary force of their critiques is located. It could be,

too, that the contrast I have observed here is more an indication of the way in which the spectrum of female performance artists has been documented than of black women's actual relationship to performance.

7. As Lauren Berlant and Elizabeth Freeman remark in their eloquent reading of the final scene of the film in the context of a queer national politics:

> This syntactically complex statement—a request, a demand, and an expletive—situates the black woman as an object of desire, as an author of feminine discourse, and as an image of the film's hopelessly absent audience. Her proximity to Bernhard's final lesbian-national striptease thus suggests neither a purely sentimental "essentialist" lesbian spectacle, nor a postmodern consumer feminine autoerotics, nor a phallocentrically inspired lust for lesbian "experience," but all of these, and more. ("Queer Nationality," 173)

That some lesbian viewers might have read the phrase as an erotic invitation to them is suggested by the 1992 *Christopher Street* interview, where Hunt tells Bernhard that "A few weeks ago I was at a lesbian bar and I told people I was interviewing Sandra Bernhard, and everyone came up with the same question over and over, 'Ask if I can fuck her' "("Sandra Bernhard," 18).

It occurs neither to Hunt nor to Bernhard that the particular wording of this question might have been prompted by the message on the table at the end of *Without You I'm Nothing*; indeed, it is this aggressive expression of adulation, formulated in Bernhard's own public idiom, that prompts the performer to castigate the lesbian community for "being so crass . . . rude . . . loud and intrusive."

Works Cited

Berlant, Lauren, and Elizabeth Freeman. "Queer Nationality." *boundary 2* 19(1) (Spring 1992): 149–80.

Bernhard, Sandra. *Confessions of a Pretty Lady*. New York: Harper and Row, 1988.

Bernhard, Sandra. "RuPaul Rising. Interview with RuPaul." *QW* 55 (November 29, 1992): 20–23, 62.

Bernhard, Sandra, and John Boskovitch. *Without You I'm Nothing*. Color film in 35 mm., M.C.E.G. Productions, 94 mins., 1990.

Burana, Lily. "Sandra Bernhard: Acting Lesbian. Interview with Bernhard." *Advocate* 618 (December 15, 1992): 66–73.

Carr, C. "C. Carr on Sandra Bernhard." *Artforum* 28 (Summer 1990): 22–23.

Hunt, Scott A. "Sandra Bernhard: Outsider on the Inside Track. Interview with Bernhard." *Christopher Street* 194 (December 21, 1992): 15–18.

Juno, Andrea, and V. Vale, eds. *Angry Women*. San Francisco: Re/Search Publications, 1992.

Mercer, Kobena. "Skin Head Sex Thing: Racial Difference and the Homoerotic Imaginary." In Bad Object-Choices, ed., *How Do I Look: Queer Film and*

Video, pp. 169–210. Seattle: Bay Press, 1991.

Murphy, Ryan. "Why Sandra Bernhard Is Not a Normal Girl: The Comedian on Jeff Stryker's Dildo and What to Tell Jesse Helms." *Advocate* 592 (December 17, 1991): 82–83.

Musto, Michael. "Kiss and Tell. Interview with Sandra Bernhard." *Spin* 5(7) (October 1989): 49–50.

Pettit, Sarah. "The Lesbian Vanishes: Sandra Bernhard and her Big Joke on the Sisterhood." *Outweek* 81 (January 16, 1991): 36–42.

Rich, Adrienne. "It is the Lesbian Within Us. . . ." In *On Lies, Secrets, and Silence: Selected Prose, 1966–78*. New York: Norton, 1979.

Riggs, Marlon. "Cultural Healing: An Interview with Marlon Riggs." *Afterimage* (March 1991): 8–11.

Index